ONE VOTE

BY
J. STEWART WILLIS

Disclaimer

One Vote

Copyrights Reserved © 2020 - *J. Stewart Willis*

Dedication

To Connor and Alex, with love.
May your lives be all you wish them to be.

Other Books by J. Stewart Willis

GESTATION SEVEN,
ONE WAS BLACK AND ONE WAS WHITE

DEADLY HIGHWAY,

THREE DEGREES AND GONE.

Table of Contents

Cast of Characters

THE FAITHLESS ELECTOR – CHANCE FITZBOURNE
HIS WIFE – SHIRLEY FITZBOURNE
HIS SON – CHANCE "JUNIOR" FITZBOURNE
HIS DAUGHTER IN LAW – BEV FITZBOURNE
HIS GRANDDAUGHTER – JENNIFER "JEN" FITZBOURNE
HIS GRANDSON – CHARLES "CHIP" FITZBOURNE

INCUMBENT PRESIDENT – ISAAC AMBLER GOLDIN
PRESIDENT-ELECT – JOHN VICKERS
DNC REPLACEMENT FOR VICKERS – BROCK HENRY
INCUMBENT VICE PRESIDENT – SIDNEY A. STONE
VICE PRESIDENT-ELECT – JANE MEYER GRETE

DEMOCRATIC NATIONAL COMMITTEE:

EDWIN DAMSON, CHAIR
EVERETT GLORE - SENATE MINORITY LEADER
ALLISON GWENTLY - SPEAKER OF THE HOUSE
EMERY ST. JOHN -VICE-CHAIR
LEONORA LEONARD - TREASURER
KRISTI LINDSAY - VICE CHAIRWOMAN
GASTON WEBERLEY - FINANCE CHAIR
GRETCHEN SODERBERG - NATIONAL FINANCE CHAIR
ELWOOD SMETHERS - VICE CHAIR ASDC PRESIDENT
DARLENE MELETTA - VICE CHAIR FOR
CIVICENGAGEMENT AND VOTER PARTICIPATION
JOHN WALTER - SECRETARY

DIRECTOR OF THE SECRET SERVICE – JOHN ROSS
CARNAHAN

VIRGINIA STATE DEMOCRATIC CHAIRMAN – BILL
HASTINGS
PIERCE COUNTY VA DEMOCRATIC CHAIRWOMAN -GWEN
ELLEN DUNBARDY,
NEW YORK STATE DEMOCRATIC CHAIRWOMAN –HILDI
VAN HAYDEN
EDITOR OF THE PIERCE COUNTY OBSERVER –JASON
"JACE" PHELPS,
OTHERS AS THEY APPEAR.

Chapter One

"Make America a Democracy Again – Vote – Vickers for President – Grete for Vice President."

The sign was blue with a white border. The printing was white, except for the V's in 'Vote' and 'Vickers'. They were red and looked a little like checkmarks.

It was a large sign with two posts. Marvin set to hammering it into the ground.

Chance was working on a smaller, "John Vickers for President", sign.

The signpost immediately split when Chance hit it with the hammer held by his tired arm. The hammer continued down through the split and hit his thumb. "Damn, damn, damn," Chance shouted as he flinched and shook his hand as if that would do any good.

Marvin looked up from his work with a small sledge on the large sign and commented, "You hit it too hard, Chance. Those little signs have cheap posts, the kind of wood they use to make pallets – that kind of stuff. Splits easy."

Chance squeezed his thumb with his right hand and fumed, "Hell, I didn't think it was mahogany – just didn't know it was that cheap. I must have pounded a hundred of them today. Should have had one split earlier so I could have gone home and spent the day recovering. If I'd done that, my arm wouldn't feel feeble and my shoulder wouldn't hurt."

Marvin shook his head and chortled. "Quit the griping, Chance. You know you're dedicated to this work. Nothing's too much for the Party to ask."

"Yeah, they've been asking it for forty years. I'm too old to be swinging a hammer all day."

Marvin hit the posts on his sign two more times. "If you can't hammer anymore, at least help me out. Is this sign level?"

Chance sighed and climbed down the road-corner hill, being careful, as they were working in the headlights of Marvin's truck and visibility wasn't great. Halfway down the hill he turned, looked back, and instructed, "Hit the left post one more time."

"Left is your left?"

"Yeah."

Marvin hit it and looked at Chance who squinted at the sign. "You hit it too hard. Tap the right one."

Marvin made a face. "Damn, Chance, this could go on all day."

"Just a tap."

Marvin turned toward the sign, tapped the right post, and walked away."

Chance watched him go. "How do you know it's level?"

Marvin snarled, "It'll do."

"If it's not level, it could cost Vickers the election. Voters want to know the candidate's on the level."

"Ha, ha, very funny."

Marvin started putting his tools in the back of his pickup as he watched Chance rub his right shoulder and then wince as he realized he was using his sore thumb. "Chance, quit the act."

"It's no act. I'm too old for this."

"Hey, every time we knock on a door and ask permission to install a sign, you talk for fifteen minutes and rest. You spend more time talking than you do hammering. How old are you, anyway?"

"Sixty-seven. Two years on social security. Still working and making money. Just giving the social security back to the government."

"Didn't think you did much work. Thought your kids and grandkids did it all."

"All? You've got no idea. Junior and Bev have their own lives, their own families, their own jobs. They help, but it's on me and a couple of part-times I hire. Cattle are a full-time job."

"There you go. You've got hired help."

"Part-time. Emphasis on the 'part'. The price I get for a heifer, I can't pay much."

"Yeah, sad story I hear from all the farmers."

Chance popped the rear door of his Explorer. "Sadly, the story's true – and sad. We doing this tomorrow? Do I need to wrap my thumb?"

Marvin sifted through the signs in the bed of his pickup. "Yeah. Got about thirty to go. Hope the Party doesn't ship out more."

"Better tell the chairwoman not to ask for more."

"You think Gwen Ellen will listen?"

Chance took off his blue "Restore America's Democratic Republic – Read the Constitution" cap and threw it into the front seat of his car. "Probably not."

Chapter Two

As Chance drove home, he squinted at the two-lane. As cars passed him coming the other way, he had to concentrate extra hard to keep the car straight on the road, hoping the road was still there after the cars passed.

He thought to himself, as he had many times before, *I need to go see my eye doctor. Either I need new glasses or those cataracts she told me about are getting worse. Maybe I'll go next week if Gwen Ellen doesn't come up with more signs.*

Damn signs. Forty years of signs. Legislature one year, governor the next, then the legislature and now the president. Over and over. Seems like the younger guys could take over – as if there were younger guys. Never see any at party meetings. Hear about them marching in protests, maybe volunteering for campaigns, doing the exciting stuff. At least that's what the kids who went to college do. If they didn't go to college, they don't have time for politics. They must earn a living. Then in middle age, they start getting interested. Seems like some of them could take over. Trouble is, Gwen Ellen Dunbardy, the chair, knows who she can depend on. God, I wish I could tell her "no". Damn it, I'll do it the next time I see her!

Finally, up ahead, Chance saw the sign hanging by the entrance to his farm, "Wood Fern Farm".

He half-smiled at being home as he turned into the drive and rumbled over the cattle gate.

Then a light caught his eye from out in the field.

"Oh, shit!"

He turned off the drive and drove across the field, the car shuddering on the rough turf.

He stopped about fifty feet from three figures outlined by a lamp, two standing, and one behind a dark hulk on the ground. He walked quickly toward the men. "Who is it?"

A man with a scruffy black beard answered. "Woodfern 582."

"Gertie."

The man kneeling on the ground muttered to himself as he worked. "Damn, Dad. I wish you wouldn't name them."

Chance looked down. "Can't remember the numbers. You know that." He bent down to look. "You got the chains right – around the pasterns?"

Junior FitzBourne didn't look up as he carefully pulled the chains, alternating the two. "Of course, Dad. Doc attached them."

Chance looked up and nodded at the veterinarian, Jeff Forjambi. "Doc."

Forjambi nodded back. "Chance. Don't worry. Junior's doing fine. The calf was in a normal position. Just big. Got it turned just fine."

"Did we need you?" Chance was thinking about the money.

"Playing it safe, Chance. They couldn't get the heifer into the barn area and she was lying in the field. No one could get hold of you." He flipped his thumb toward the man with the beard. "While Pete was adding hay to the feeders, he sensed the heifer was dilating and went to the house to tell Shirley and she called Junior."

Chance sighed. "Yeah, I was in the valley. No cell service."

"Yeah, way it goes. Complain to the supervisors. Truth is we need to triple the population Make us significant to the cell phone providers."

"Ha, we can dream."

"Anyway, Junior's more comfortable with me here."

"Yeah, here and watching."

"Hey, I turned the calf. I'll turn it again when the head and shoulders are out."

Chance frowned. "I can do that."

"Hell, I'm gloved up, Chance, and I'm here."

Chance continued to grimace and felt his thumb throbbing. "Yeah, the head came out okay so I guess you can handle it."

Junior stood and backed off while Forjambi got down and worked to turn the calf. He looked up at Junior. "Okay, go back to work. Pull it out one hip at a time."

After the calf was on its feet and the placenta discharged, Forjambi bid them farewell and started across the field.

Chance shouted after him, "Don't turn your ankle. I don't want to pay for that too."

Forjambi looked back over his shoulder. "Is that a thank you?"

"Are you doing it for free?"

"Nope."

"Then, maybe it's half a thank you."

"Anytime, Chance."

Chance turned to his son. "Will you help me get them to the barn? I don't want the calf chilled. Might not be healthy anyway. It needs care."

Junior shook his head. "Sorry, Dad, Pete can help you. I'm already late for Chip's football game and I've got to change before I go there."

Chance shook his head. "Farming's twenty-four-seven."

"Yeah, well I don't know who invented that term but if it were so, you wouldn't be playing a politician. Besides, I'm no farmer. I've got a job."

"Yeah, depending on the state to pay you – working for VDOT."

"Working for the Department is better than driving to Northern, Virginia to drive nails into boards." He looked down and back up. "Or worrying about the price of heifers and what

the big packers do to you. You need to think of letting up, Dad.
Keep a couple of pets for grazing and put your feet up.”

Chance took in a deep breath and sighed. “My life, son.”

“Yeah, and you’ll drop dead from it someday.”

“Well, if I don’t raise cows, how’ll I pay the taxes? How’ll
I pay for life? Social Security won’t do it. I’ll lose the farm.”

“You always say that.”

“It’s true.”

“Dad, maybe that’s what needs to happen.”

Chance sighed and ignored what Junior had said. “At
least carry a couple of buckets while you’re headed for your car.”
He turned to his hired help. “How many extra hours, Pete?”

“Three.”

Chance groaned. “Okay, let’s add to that. Get Gertie up
and bring her to the barn. The calf will follow. I’ll drive my car
back and clean up tomorrow.”

Chapter Three

It was nearly ten o'clock when Chance arrived at his house. Shirley was waiting in the kitchen. He always entered the house through the kitchen. They didn't have a mudroom. The inside of the kitchen entrance to the house was the mudroom. The house was built in the 1930s. Chance guessed that mudrooms weren't fashionable then. As he bent down to unlace his work shoes, he said, "Don't think I've got any cow crap on them, but it was dark."

His wife, Shirley, was sitting at the kitchen table nursing a cup of coffee. The little television on the counter was on. She'd been watching it and waiting. "Heck of a way to greet me."

Chance sighed deeply. "Sorry. Just tired."

"Hang your coat and sit down. The calf all right?"

"Yeah, got him and Gertie in the barn, out of the wind, but can't do much about the chill. Hope he survives."

"Hope so too. Every dollar we get from a sale counts. What about the momma?"

"Okay, but we'll have to cull her. She's a bad statistic. Can't afford it again. Bad for the bull too, but that's my fault. He was too big for her."

"Can't sell the calf for breeding either?"

"No, not after the rough birth. He's a bad statistic - bad EPD."

"Sorry about the heifer. We'll have to replace her. That will cost."

"Yeah. Fortunately, she's still young. Won't have to sell her for a hamburger."

"No way to save her?"

"No. You know we can't afford to have a cow that may not produce. Can't afford pets."

Bev sighed. "Bet you haven't eaten."

"No, but I'll just eat a sandwich."

Bev laughed. "You know better. I put the soup on the stove after Pete came up. I knew you'd need to eat. All I need to do is heat it. You want crackers or a biscuit with it?"

"Biscuit – butter – a little jelly. Whatever is in the refrigerator door?"

"Grape or apricot?"

"Grape's for Chip and Jen."

"Even they're too old for it. Think I'll throw it out."

Shirley turned on the stove under the soup, then buttered a biscuit and put it in the toaster oven. "Junior help you?"

Chance grunted. "Helped a little. Got Forjambi in to do most of the work. The vet left right after the birth. Chip's got a game tonight. Junior doesn't want to be a farmer and says so."

"How come you didn't go to the game? You like them."

"Had to work with Pete to get the heifer and the calf put away."

"Had you planned to go?"

"Thought about it. I was tired after putting up the signs. Not sure I would have gone."

"But you like watching Chip?"

"Love it, but there's only so much a man can do."

Shirley frowned. "Don't sound so down. Why are you keeping your hand in your lap?"

Chance sighed again. "Hit my thumb with the hammer."

Bev turned off the stove and turned back to Chance. "Let me see."

Chance held up the hand and peered at it. "First time I've seen it in the light. At least I hit it up from the fingernail. The nail would have been worse. Just tore a little skin."

Bev held it up to the light. "Don't think it needs stitches. You wash it while I get your food up. Then I'll go get a bandage and Neosporin."

Chance went to the sink and looked at the wound while he squirted on dish detergent, turned on the water, scrubbed and flushed the wound, and thought, *stupid, you should have washed this earlier. What were you thinking? Stupid pride. Hiding it from Shirley.*

He returned to his seat as Shirley set the dinner before him. "Shirl don't bother about a bandage. I'll get it when I finish dinner."

"Don't be silly. I'll be back in a minute."

While she was gone, Chance sipped his soup and nibbled his biscuit.

When Shirley returned, she glanced at the soup. "What, you're not hungry?"

Chance slid back his chair afoot. "Guess it's too late. Too near bedtime. Guess I've been going too hard."

"Maybe so. Hold up your hand."

While she bandaged the finger, she inquired, "So, what are you doing tomorrow?"

"I'll check on the calf and then Marvin will pick me up and we'll do more signs."

Shirley moaned, "Oh, Lord. At least don't hit them hard."

"Got to. It hasn't rained in two weeks and the ground is hard as a rock."

Shirley picked up Chance's dishes and went to the sink. "Let Marvin Gerry do it then. He's fifteen years younger than you."

Chance groaned. "Are you telling me I'm old too?"

"What do you mean, 'too'?

Chance took a deep breath. "Junior was after me out in the field."

As Shirley threw out the leftover food, she acknowledged what she had heard. "Well, that's nothing new. You should be used to it by now."

Chance grimaced. "He's just afraid of being stuck with this place."

"No, he's not. He's worried about you. No way he can be 'stuck' with it. If you go first, I'll sell the farm. You know I can't run it."

"But you'd try to."

Shirley looked at her husband. She didn't want to hurt him. "I couldn't Chance. I can't."

Chance looked down at his bandaged finger and studied it for a moment. Then he looked up at Shirley in resignation. "I guess you can't. I think you could, but you'd have to want to. So, I guess you can't."

Shirley sat down opposite her husband and folded her hands on the table. "You know, running this place is hard, Chance, and you're not the only one who is old. I know the thought of this place going out of the family is hard for you to think about, but you know that running a small farm has almost become a hobby. Labor costs a lot and I can't do the work you do. I'm just not capable of it. And there's little money in it. You do it because there's a joy in it, a source of pride, a love of the animals and the land. It takes a certain kind of person to feel that. That's you. Some of it has rubbed off, but for me, it depends on living with you. Without you, it will be too much for me. You may not want to know that, but in your heart you do. I'll have to sell this place. Financially and physically, I'll have to. I could pretend to you, but you know better."

Chance lowered his hands into his lap and leaned back, sitting quietly. "Yeah, I know. I had hopes that Junior would take over, but he won't. There's too much unknown with farming. Like with most things, the big guys have taken over. They have lobbies, money, and government support. The big guys rule the world."

Shirley studied her husband. "Chance, you know I'll stick with you as long as you want, but it's getting hard – financially hard now, but the physical strain on you is coming. You know it."

"Yeah....I do."

Chapter Four

It was almost ten-thirty when Junior and Chip arrived home. Junior parked his Silverado next to his wife's Kia. He sat in the truck for a moment and considered his house, a one-story-vinyl-sided frame house in line along his road with a hodge-podge of houses, most one story, some two, all lined up at random setbacks. The two-story houses were mostly leftover from a time before Junior's was built. His house was bigger than most in that, somewhere in time, the house had been extended at one end to add a third bedroom. The addition's siding didn't match because it was larger in width with a beige-coloring that didn't quite blend. Still, he was proud that he could provide it for his family.

Chip was sitting beside his father still wearing his pads. His hip hurt from a tackle he received in the third quarter and was quickly tightening up when he shifted in the seat. He wasn't anxious to get out of the truck. He knew he would be hobbled but also knew a hot shower would help. Still, he just sat, waiting for his father to move, wondering what the man was thinking.

Finally, Junior spoke. "I'm sorry I missed your touchdown."

Chip sighed. "Yeah, for a minute there I thought we might win."

He opened the truck's door and gingerly slid out and onto his feet.

Junior watched him. "You going to make it?"

"Yeah, just taking it easy. The hip hurts."

"Yeah, I didn't see the touchdown, but I saw the tackle. Maybe you need to take a hot bath."

"Haven't taken a bath in years."

"Believe me, there are times when it beats a shower."

"Yeah, when's the last time you took one?"

"Ha, I don't remember. Probably after the first time, I went skiing and fell a dozen times."

"You fell a dozen times?"

"As best I can remember. I should have started when I was six years old as you did."

"Okay, maybe I'll try. Always thought it was dumb to have to take showers in a bathtub."

Junior got out of the truck and followed Chip as he slowly made his way to the front door. Inside they were met by Junior's wife, Bev. "Gosh, Chip. You don't look like you're in good shape. Do we need to get you to the doctor?"

"Nah," Junior replied. "Just football. Needs a hot bath and a couple of days. He'll be all right."

Bev looked dubious.

Chip averted his eyes and headed for the bathroom.

Bev shouted, "You can't go in there. Jen's taking a shower."

Chip threw up his hands toward the ceiling and closed his eyes. "Sisters!"

Bev corrected him. "You only have one."

"Thank God. Can you get her out of there before she uses all the hot water?"

Bev hurried to the bathroom door and knocked. "Jen, you need to get out of there. Chip got hurt playing football and needs to get a hot bath."

The shower turned off. "What'd you say?"

"Chip needs to get in there."

"Tell him to use the half bath off the kitchen."

"He hurt himself playing football and needs a hot bath."

"Stupid game – not my doing. I've got my hair all shampooed up. He'll have to wait." With that, the shower turned back on.

Bev shouted. "Don't use all the hot water."

There was no reply.

15

Bev hurried back to the living room where Chip had collapsed into a wing chair. "She'll hurry."

Chip shook his head. "Not what I heard."

"Yeah, but I'm sure she'll try."
Chip struggled back onto his feet and headed for his bedroom. "At least I can get out of this uniform and get on my pajamas and robe."

Junior and Bev watched as he struggled. Bev turned to Junior and whispered. "He looks bad."

Junior chuckled. "Worse now than when he came in from the truck. Part real – part drama."

"Yeah, well I hope the bath helps."

"What you need to hope for is that Jen doesn't use all the hot water."

Bev headed for the kitchen. "Maybe he'd drink some hot tea? Did the team win?"

"No, and no. He'll never drink hot tea. Maybe a Mountain Dew. And they lost 21 to 7, but Chip scored the touchdown."

"Hey, that's good. How'd he do it?"

"Two-yard run, but I didn't see it. Had to help deliver a calf at Dad's."

"Your Dad couldn't do it without you?"

"He wasn't there. He was in the valley putting up signs for the Party."

"He won't give that up, will he?"

"No, he's been at it a long time. Besides, he thinks Goldin is despicable. As close as I've ever seen him disliking someone."

"Well, I don't like the man either, but I can't get worked up about it. You really think Chip is all right?"

"Right now, that depends on his sister. How come she's taking a shower so late?"

"She just came home."

"Oh, where was she?"

"Went to a movie with that Ransome boy."

"Yeah, he anything like his parents?"

"I don't know. Is that good or bad?"

"Not good. The father works part-time, doing a little yard work, but doesn't seem to have anything steady. They live with his mother in a little rental house going up the mountain west of Dansville."

"Nothing wrong with a little house."

"Not if you keep it up."

"I'll talk to her."

"You think she'll listen?"

Bev sighed. "I didn't at her age."

"Yeah, I remember."

Bev threatened to hit him, and he ducked.

Chapter Five

Chance hadn't slept well. There had been too much to think about. Getting up was almost a relief. He was out of the house early to check on Gertie and the calf and then go to check the streams across the farm. They were running low from a two-week drought. He pulled out his cell phone and called Pete to come to fill the galvanized water tubs in the fields. He had to phone then because he and Marvin were going to put signs in the yards of Dansville and there was no cell service in that part of the Pierce County.

Marvin picked Chance up at eight. They would have liked to have started earlier, but people weren't happy with the idea of men hammering signs in their front yards at seven in the morning. Out on the highways where farm lanes met the road, early starts caused no problems.

Normally, Chance would have driven his own SUV so he could get back to his farm if necessary. However, since no one could phone him in Dansville, it made no difference. He wished he were working in the north part of the county where there was cell service.

Marvin parked his pickup in the Methodist Church parking lot. They picked up handfuls of signs and hammers from the bed of the pickup and headed for the last house on the main road through town. All the signs in the town yards were to be small except the one for Gordon Raney's yard. Gordon was an ardent Democrat and wanted the largest sign possible. They decided to do the rest of the signs first and then drive to Gordon's house which was at the corner where the highway turned from the road they were starting on, bending to the left.

Chance claimed he was tired and a little out of sorts. He asked Marvin to interface with the homeowners to get permission to emplace the signs. Marvin looked quizzically at him. "What's wrong, Chance? You love to talk to these people. Gives you a chance to rest. What's going on?"

"Just got things on my mind, Marvin. I'm weary and my thumb hurts. Just want to get this done and get back to the newborn calf. Have to get it tagged and get on with life."

"Okay, whatever you want."

Chance waited for Marvin to give him a thumbs up from the door of the first house. When it came, he started hammering. They worked from house to house down the road that way. They knew most of the Republicans and avoided them. Occasionally, they didn't get approval and mentally added that house to the list of the enemy.

Many vehicles went by. The eighteen-wheelers, the dump trucks, flatbeds hauling equipment and the logging trucks all shook the ground. The yards were only fifteen to twenty feet deep and Chance thought about the noise the residents had to endure. Pickups and some cars honked at him. Some drivers gave thumbs up while others gave thumbs down. A few stopped to talk. Chance let Marvin handle it. His mind was elsewhere. He was hammering by rote.

He thought about the farm. It was not his creation. It was his inheritance, not just a land inheritance, but a responsibility inheritance. There had never been any other thoughts in the family while he was growing up. It was the natural order of things. In the early and middle Twentieth Century, Pierce County was rural. Not many people had money. You were important if you had land.

Chance's family had not always been important. Chance's great grandfather, "Bricks" Borne, had been displaced from the Blue Ridge when the government bought up land for the Skyline Drive. The displacement had been physical. He and his wife, Maise, and three children had been packed up and put in a wagon early one morning and their house set afire. Years later they went back to the site and found that only part of the brick chimney remained. It had been the only brick chimney in the mountains, the one from which old man Bricks took his nickname.

"Bricks" Borne's family had been put in a house, a small house, on Settlement Road. There were many "settlement" roads in the foothills of the Blue Ridge, all much alike. Bricks learned how to live in the new environment, without his garden, his hogs, his horse, and his chestnuts. He worked on farms, he picked apples, he cut trees, he hauled trees and he set aside money. He quickly saw that if he was going to be anyone, he needed to own land. In those days, the land was cheap, but not if you had no money at all and money was hard to earn. Even the large landowners had no money. They were living through the Depression. Bricks finally bought a few acres. When he died in 1937, he owned almost ten acres.

The land passed to Chance's grandfather, Aubrey, who for his thirty years had worked the land. He had felt it was as much his as it had been his father's. There was no question that he was going to expand it, become a property owner, and play with the big landowners. He worked the farm, sold real estate, and worked in the post office. His real estate experience and a small inheritance from an uncle led to his selling his father's farm and buying forty acres along with its Nineteenth-Century house. He named it Wood Fern Farm after the ferns in the woods on its western edge where it backed up to the Shenandoah National Park. With the status the land gave him, he became a horseman and joined the hunt. During the Second World War, he and his wife, Elizabeth, partied with the wealthy horsemen who served their country by training horses at the remount in an adjoining county, horses for a war that didn't use horses.

In keeping with what Aubrey felt was his new status, he decided to resurrect his family's ancient name, and Borne returned to being FitzBourne, and all documentation, bank accounts, cattle, and horse registrations, etc. were changed accordingly.

Aubrey passed in 1981. By that time, he had expanded the land beyond his forty acres by buying seven acres of adjacent woodland and still lived in his Nineteenth Century house. At the time, his son Charles (Chaz) was forty-six years old. He lived along Gibson River in Borne Hollow three miles downriver from where his grandfather had lived in the mountains. The house was on the opposite side of the river from the Borne Hollow Road. Fortunately, at that point, going up into the hollow, the river was normally only nine or ten feet wide, but you had to allow for heavy rain. Thus, Chaz's house was reached by a bridge made of concrete poured over three four-foot diameter corrugated-metal culverts.

When Aubrey died, Chaz and his wife, Jenn, were somewhat reluctant to leave their home. They could have moved in with their mother in the big house. That was the custom years before, but they prized their independence and privacy. Chaz had taken over his father's real estate business and was doing well-selling land to a new population of people seeking country and retirement homes, some weekenders, and some permanent.

However, the pressure and responsibility were there. Chaz had always helped his father and understood the mandate that he takes over the farm. Initially, he worked the farm from his home in the hollow, seeking to modernize. He replaced all the brown cattle on the farm with the then-popular Angus breed, initially selling his calves to the feeders, and later raising some breeder stock. When his mother died, Chaz felt he had no choice and moved to Wood Fern Farm.

Chaz was only fifty-nine-years-old when he and Jenn were caught on a flooded road in Gibbs Hollow outside the county seat of Wainright after a party on a Saturday night in 1992. A dam of logs and brush had broken on the Gibbs Run in the mountains above them during a heavy rainstorm and had suddenly loosed a torrent of water that spread across the road. Panicking, the couple tried to abandon their car and reach a hillside beside the road. They never made it. At the age of thirty-five, Chance FitzBourne inherited Wood Fern Farm.

It had never dawned on Chance that he would inherit it so soon. He had become deeply involved in the breeding and raising of Angus cattle from an early age. It seemed a natural life for him. He loved every minute.

As Chance hammered the candidate signs, he pondered his lineage, the passing of the gauntlet, how he had failed to involve his son. He couldn't blame Junior. He himself complained about the problems of the small farmer, the prices that were controlled by the big packers, the trade agreements the government signed, the tax laws that helped the large corporations all that took the life out of the small farm. Junior couldn't have helped listening. He wanted a stable life for his family. Chance couldn't blame him. Why should his struggle be passed on to his son? To continue, a man had to love the farm, the cattle, the auctions, the breeding, the births - everything that was involved, and the dream that the money would come - that things would change – and get better.

Chance lay his hammer down, walked to the edge of the road, and looked back. The yard, fifteen feet deep and sixty feet wide, now contained the entrance to a driveway in which a pickup and an SUV were parked, a sidewalk, and a patch of grass containing four signs, one for the president and vice-president, one for a state senator, one for the local congressman, and one for the delegate to the statehouse. He wondered if he could get away with one more for only the president. He also wondered if the house's owner would get mad and pull out half the signs before the week was out. He wouldn't blame them.

He picked up the hammer and signs and headed for the next house where Marvin was standing at the front door talking.

The door closed and Marvin stepped out into the house's front yard waving Chance on to the next house. "Seth and I had a nice conversation, but he said 'no way' to the signs. Says he's always voted Republican. Says his father did and his grandfather did. Says he's got nothing against a woman Vice-

President unless she's a Democrat. Tried to talk to him about the issues, but he wasn't interested."

"You think if the Republicans nominated a woman for President, he'd vote for her?"

"Hell, I don't know. It would be hard not to. He'd have to defy a tradition."

Chance nodded and sighed. "Okay, knock on the next door. Don't tell them it's four signs."

Chance walked to Marvin's pickup, pulled a bottle of water out of a cooler, and drank half the bottle while Marvin was talking. As he walked back, Marvin was looking hesitant. Looking somewhere over Chance's head, he said, "One sign – the presidential one. Says he doesn't even know the guy running for the statehouse."

"Must be Gwen Ellen's fault – not getting the word out."

"She put two editorials in the paper this week."

"Yeah, you think someone reads them. The writers are mostly people thanking someone in the community or someone bitching about something. If someone you know writes one, you might read what he wrote so you can pat him on the back and agree or stay away from him the next time you see him."

"Or her."

"Or her. Life used to be easy. Didn't have to worry about gender."

"Anyway, pull out a sign. I'll do the hammering – give you a break."

Chance bent down and pulled out a sign from the pile he had left on the ground. Handing it and the hammer to Marvin, he said, "Watch your thumb."

"Ha, ha, we're not all accident-prone."

"Yeah, well I'd ask for employee compensation, but I'm not an employee. Just slave labor."

"Volunteer', Chance."

"Yeah, well that means I have a choice."

"Right, let's see what you do about it."

Chapter Six

Sunday morning Junior and Bev sat at the dining room table, savoring their coffee. The house was old and the adjacent kitchen small. Their to-do list included knocking down the wall between the two and making it into a more modern kitchen. That was in the future. It was a bearing wall and would cost a lot. As the years passed, they seldom talked about it.

Jen came from her bedroom and went straight into the kitchen.

Bev called through the kitchen door. "Good morning. Do you want some eggs and toast?"

A weak replay came. "Morning."

A cabinet door opened and closed.

"Nah – No thank you. I got a protein bar."

"That's not much."

"I'm in a hurry."

"Oh, why's that?"

"Denny's coming to pick me up."

"Yeah, who's Denny and where are you going? You've got your room to clean and homework to do."

Jen seemed to ignore the question. "Haven't got much homework. I'll get it all done tomorrow."

Junior was listening to the exchange and became impatient. "How about coming in here so we can see you."

"I'm getting coffee."

"Yeah, well bring it in here."

Jen entered the dining room with her coffee and protein bar, looking wary.

She set her coffee on the table and began unwrapping her protein bar. "So?"

Junior sighed. "So, we'd like to see you. Why don't you sit?"

"He'll be here anytime now."

"Well, you can get back up. Your mother asked where you were going."

"Hiking up in the park."

"Hiking? You don't have any shoes that are safe to hike in."

"I've got my Converse runners."

"Yeah, but you can feel every rock in them."

"I'll be careful. We're just going someplace we can have a picnic."

"Like on a blanket?"

Jen's eyes looked down. "Yeah, sandwiches and soda."

"With Denny?"

"Yes."

"Denny Ransome?"

"Yeah."

"Do you go to school with Denny?"

"Yes."

"What year is he in school?"

"What is this, an inquisition?"

Bev rejoined the conversation. "As a matter of fact, it is. Your father knows Denny Ransome's father, knows where he lives. Denny's a little questionable. A picnic blanket in the woods is a little questionable."

"Christ, mother, who said anything about a blanket?"

"You're going to sit on the ground?"

Jen looked at her father for help. "I don't know. I'm sixteen-years-old, for goodness sake. I'm not a child."

Junior didn't help. "We know you're sixteen and we know you're not a child. We also know this kid Ransome's eighteen."

"He's nineteen."

"Well, that helps a lot. Was he held back in school?"

"I don't know. He's a cool guy."

25

Bev groaned. "Cool, huh. Does that mean nice, or trustworthy?"

"For goodness sake, Mom. It means he's good looking and fun. What am I supposed to do – go out with nerds?"

Junior shook his head. "It's hard for us, seeing you dating someone we worry is questionable, and going with him by yourself."

Jen gave a cynical smile. "And into the woods."

Junior nodded. "And into the woods."

"For goodness sake, Dad, I'm not naïve. I know you were teenagers once, and all that. I guarantee I'll be all right. Cross my heart."

"Jen, have you met his parents? Have you seen the little house he lives in?"

"Lord, Dad. We live in a little house."

"Not the same, Jen. Stand back and look at the houses."

Bev sighed. "Protecting you is our job, Jen. That's what parents do. We can't tell you everything to do. All we can say is use your head."

Jen nodded and became serious. "I will."

A car honked, and Jen was quickly up.

Bev pleaded, "Invite him in."

"No way."

They watched her go and looked at each other powerlessly.

Bev sighed. "You think we'll make it?"

"Do the best we can. Play it by ear."

"We can ban him."

"Got to be worth the fight."

Junior got up and warmed his coffee. "Babe, you want some more?"

"Huh? You haven't called me 'babe' in a while."

"Reminding myself how lucky I am."

He topped up Bev's coffee and then sat back at the table with his own."

They passed some minutes in silence.

Finally, Bev looked at her husband. "You look pensive."

Junior made a slight nod. "What do you think about what Jen said about the house?"

"She was trying to be nasty."

"Yeah, but it came from somewhere."

"Look, honey, I haven't seen the Ransome house, but I can't believe it compares. Ours is a nice house, well cared for. I'm happy. Isn't that what counts?"

"Yeah, but if I farmed, we might inherit the farmhouse someday."

"Hey, there's no guarantee. Your father may live forever. Our kids are getting old. It may not matter."

Junior looked down. "What you're saying is that we need a big house now. Years from now is too late."

"No, I didn't mean that. I said I'm happy. And you're moving up in VDOT. You got your MBA online. It's just a matter of time before you're promoted some more. We'll think about another house then."

"After the kids are gone."

"They'll come home."

Just then Chip came into the kitchen.

Bev got up from the table. "Good morning. How many eggs?"

"Morning. Three I guess."

"Bacon and toast, too."

"Please."

While Bev cracked the eggs into a frying pan, Chip went to the refrigerator, took out the orange juice, and poured himself a glass.

Junior followed the boy with his eyes. "What do you have planned for this weekend?"

"Studying."

"Oh, have you got a test?"

"No. For the SATs. Juniors start taking them this year kind of as practice."

"SATs for college. You know, I didn't go to college."

“I know. You decided not to.”

“Yeah, I did.”

There was silence for a moment. Finally, Chip looked at his father. “Dad, I’d like to. Maybe be a vet.”

“A veterinarian?”

“Yes.”

“Big animals or little ones?”

“Big.”

Bev interrupted by placing the breakfast plate in front of Chip.

While the boy ate, Junior sat quietly.

After the boy finished eating and went back to his bedroom, Junior observed, “Sounds like cows skipped a generation.”

“It’s a solid occupation.”

“How many years of school will it take?”

“I don’t know. I’m sure he’ll work.”

“Well, we’ll pay what we can.”

“Of course.”

Bev topped up Junior’s coffee again and sat down. “You know, sweetheart, I love this house. It’s just fine.”

Chapter Seven

Friday morning, Chance and Pete tagged Gertie's calf and one other that had been born two days earlier. He then passed all the information to Shirley to use to fill out the registration applications she would mail off to the American Angus Association.

After lunch, he drove into Wainright to buy stamps at the post office. He only bought one sheet of stamps at a time because he enjoyed going by the post office and hopefully seeing someone he knew. He pulled into the parking lot next to a Jeep Cherokee he recognized as belonging to Roxanne Yarrow. Roxie was coming out of the post office as he approached the door. "Hey, Roxie, how did your meeting of the Town BZA go last night?" Chance knew that the board had heard the application of Jane and Eddie Borden to build a carport in their side yard.

Roxie frowned and shook her head. "The meeting went all right. There was no one in the audience and we turned down the application because of the backset required by the ordinance. Didn't really have any choice, but by the time I got home, Millie Davis was on the phone, giving me hell for not taking care of the old-timers in town. Said such a thing would never have happened when she was younger. People used to take care of each other."

"Well, there was a time the Town didn't have ordinances – back before the State got involved. The Town just did what they thought people wanted. Now it's down in black and white."

"Yeah, but it doesn't always make people happy. Saw you down in the valley early in the week setting up signs. You about done?"

"Yeah. I'm getting old for it. Time to turn it over to the younger guys."

"Uh-huh, I'll believe that when I see it. See you around Chance."

She got into the Cherokee and started the engine while Chance opened the post office door and went in. He immediately noticed Gary Winters checking his mailbox and thought, *Boy, am I glad I get home delivery. Poor people in Town must come here every day.* "Hey, Gary. How are you? Saw your letter to the editor in the paper yesterday."

"Hey, Chance, you read it?"

"I did. Don't read many but had to see what you had to say."

"Spitting in the wind, but I've got to try. Traffic through Town is getting awfully late in the day with all those people going up to the Lodge, especially on weekends."

"Yeah, who would have thought? Build it, put in some tennis courts and riding trails, serve dinners, and manage well, and the world comes."

"Yeah, I think they built the bypass on the wrong side of Town."

"Gary, the mountains are on the other side of Town."

"Yeah, you just wouldn't want the bypass going through your farm."

"No way would that happen. I'm in a different hollow with a mountain between us. You be careful. If you're too noisy, VDOT will put a stoplight in the middle of Town."

"Yeah, we had a blinker once."

"That was before the bypass. No stoplights in the County, now. Let's keep it that way."

"Heck, you can talk, Chance. You don't live in Town."

"You're right, Gary, and my sympathies go out to you."

"You don't sound heartfelt to me."

"Hey, what can I say? See you around. Keep writing."

"At least you read it. You going to be at the Democrats' Meeting tomorrow."

"Yeah, I've got some things to discuss with Gwen Ellen."

"Yeah, I'll see you there."

The door opened and Gary was gone.

Chance turned to the counter.

Betty Cosgrove was behind the counter waiting for him. "Chance, I never thought you'd stop talking. Been standing here twiddling my thumbs. Could have been putting mail in the boxes. One book of stamps as usual?"

"Sorry, Betty. No, I'd like to try a sheet of something pretty. The stamps in the books are getting old."

"Baseball players, flowers, or panda bears?"

"Panda bears."

"Going for the cute, huh?"

Chance counted out the money. "The price goes up this week?"

Betty took the money and lay the stamps and receipt on the top of the scales. "No, that was last month. You should stock up. These are good forever."

"Then I'd have no reason to come see your sunny face."

"Yeah, you're a lucky man. I'll even smile for you."

When she did, Chance laughed. "Hey, take it easy on me. See you in a week or so."

Betty turned from the counter. "Make my day."

Chance laughed and headed back to his car. He drove to the next street and went into the Treasurer's office. Jean Wild got up from her desk. "Chance, what can I do for you?"

Chance lay a twenty-dollar bill and two rabies certificates on the counter. "Two dog tags, please."

Jean gave the certificates a quick perusal and put the bill carefully in a cash drawer. As she took two tags out of another drawer, noted the numbers next to the dogs' names in a register, and passed them to Chance, she observed, "You're a month early – losing interest on your twenty dollars."

31

Chance guffawed, "One percent annual on twenty. Think I'll survive and I'll save the interest I'd have to pay if I forget to get the tags. Besides, I don't want to have to list a few cents on my taxes. You have a wonderful day."

"Always.

Chance turned and headed home; his weekly errands run.

Chapter Eight

Saturday morning, Chance pulled to a stop on the road's shoulder across from the Wainright Town Hall. He was twenty-five minutes early for the Meeting of the Pierce County Democratic Committee which used the town hall. He hoped he could corner Gwen Ellen and talk to her about letting upon him – to not continue asking him to put up the signs and do other labor.

Last night, while he attached the dog tags to his yellow labs, Griffin and Brune (for Brunhilda), he had practiced on Shirley – forty years he had worked for the committee and was proud of having done it, but it was time for the younger guys to do the work.

Shirley had pointed out that there weren't many younger guys.

He had argued that ten years was younger.

She had sighed and accepted that.

Chance entered the meeting room and saw Gwen Ellen talking to the Committee Treasurer, Gene Banks. He sighed. He'd have to wait. A couple of other attendees greeted him. He responded perfunctorily and walked to the coffee table in the corner of the room. He poured himself a cup and ignored the sweet buns. He stood by himself, vague in the room, and suddenly found Gwen Ellen approaching him. He set down his coffee and reached out his hand to greet her. She spoke before he could say anything. "Chance, I'm so glad you're here early. I think you're in for a big surprise that will please you. I'm making an announcement early in the meeting. You're going to be the elector for the district."

Chance stammered, "The elector, as in presidential elector, a member of the Electoral College?"

Gwen Ellen beamed. "That's it."

"You're kidding. I thought the big guys kept that for themselves. I didn't even make it to the convention this year.

Thought the electors were all appointed, seventy-some odd days before the election."

"They were, but Gabby Davis, the elector we appointed from our district, just had an aortic valve replaced and backed out of the job. I put in a request for you to replace him – said you deserve it after forty years with this committee, serving two years as chairman, four as vice chairman, many years on the raffle committee and I don't know how many years working the tables at the polls."

"And hammering in thousands of signs."

"That too. You deserve it. Everyone's going to be excited. Are you thrilled?"

"More like dismayed – flabbergasted."

"You know it just involves taking the election results, filling out a form, and going to a meeting in December to file the form. But it's a heck of an honor."

"Yeah, I know. It really is an honor. Thank you."

✳✳✳

After the meeting, everyone tried to shake his hand before they left except for two people he knew were jealous. They had served years with him, but not forty years.

At home, Shirley greeted him, "Well, did you tell Gwen Ellen? Are you still in good standing, or did she tell you to find another past time?

"Didn't get to talk to her?"

"After all your preparation?"

"She ambushed me."

"Gave you more work."

"Had I appointed an elector?"

"A what?"

"A Presidential elector – our district's representative on the Electoral College."

"Yeah, what does that mean?"

"I go to Richmond in December, fill out a form on the elected president and vice-president and turn it in."

"Does someone pay for the trip – you stay in a hotel – what's involved?"

"I've got no idea, but it's a heck of an honor. Are you proud of me?"

"I guess."

Chapter Nine

The next morning when Chance and Shirley returned from church, the telephone was blinking with a message. Shirley dialed in the code and listened. Then she looked at Chance. "Jason Phelps wants to come by tomorrow and do an interview."

"Interview? What's that about?"

Shirley headed toward the coffee pot, poured two cups, and stuck them in the microwave to reheat. "Probably about your being an elector. I suspect it's a big deal."

"Gee, I hope that this is not a precursor – which the thing is going to be more trouble than it's worth."

Shirley looked at Chance in mild disgust. "Chance, you've been honored. I was talking to Sally Jennings yesterday about it. She made a big deal over it. Said it was special – a real honor. She doesn't know anyone who has been an elector. She was really impressed."

"What did you say?"

"I said it was about time you were recognized – that you had earned it. It reflected a good part of forty years of your life."

"Did she agree?"

"Well, kind of. I don't think she has any idea of what you've done. It's not as if all the Democrats in the county go to the meetings. What do you have there, thirty or forty people in attendance?"

Chance felt chagrined. "Yeah, forty at a good meeting."

"So, thirty or forty know about what you've done to become an elector. Play it up to Jace Phelps. Let the world know you're important."

Chance took the coffee from the microwave and set the mugs on the kitchen table. "So, you think I should call Jace back?"

"What kind of question is that? Of course, you should call him back. You need to be polite if nothing else. But it's important. Jace doesn't come to do interviews very often. Most people have to take articles to him."

***

Jason "Jace" Phelps arrived seven minutes later than the agreed time often on Monday morning.

He mumbled as he shook Chance's hand, "You live further out in this hollow than I remember."

He lay his camera and a copy of the Pierce County Observer on the kitchen table. He looked at Chance with a wry smile, gave a thumbs up, turned back to the table, and pointed at the center of the front page. "This is where you're going to be next week. You're a big story. No one has ever been an elector from this county. It's exciting as hell."

Shirley had poured coffee from a fresh pot and brought the mugs to the table. "Sugar, cream, what do you take Jace?"

"A little sugar, Shirl. How's it going, living with the big man."

As Shirley brought the sugar bowl and a spoon to the table, she smiled reservedly. "You really think it's a big deal, Jace?"

"Biggest news since Jim Farley broke his leg hiking in the mountains and we had to get a helicopter in."

Shirl made a face. "That was bad news. I hope this doesn't equate."

Jace was suddenly sheepish. "Just meant it's front-page news – big headline."

"Okay, I'll let you two have at it. I'll go watch *Rachael* or *The View* or something." She pointed at the counter. "If you need more coffee, help yourself."

"What do I do with the spoon?"

"Get a napkin out of the holder and set it on it."

"Thanks, Shirl."

Jace pulled a notebook and pen from his pockets and turned to Chance. "Sounds like Shirl's not certain about this whole deal."

Chance suddenly felt he had to be defensive. "Oh, she's been excited ever since I told her Saturday."

"Well, that's good. You need to tell me why you earned the honor."

Unexpectedly, Chance wondered if what he had done in his years with the Democratic Committee were really a big deal. "Well, I've been a member of the Democratic Committee for forty years."

"How does that compare with the other members?"

"Oh, it's at least ten years longer than anyone else."

"Umm. Are you older than the others?"

Suddenly Chance felt that the forty years wasn't so much. "I guess, older than most. I think Benji Ward is seventy."

"How old are you?"

"Sixty-seven."

Jace smiled. "You've ten years on me. Been working on newspapers since I was seventeen."

"Guess that's forty years too?"

"Hey, you're quick with your math."

"For a farmer?"

Jace was suddenly reticent. "Hell, good for anyone, Chance. Farmers couldn't make a living if they couldn't do the math. Don't take me for a smart-ass."

Chance felt a little chagrined and confessed, "Sorry, Jace, I'm a little perplexed. I don't know whether being an elector is really a big deal. Doesn't seem like a big deal. Go to Richmond and fill out a form. Just need to be able to spell the names correctly."

Jace smiled. "And if the Republicans win, you don't do anything."

Chance chuckled. "Hadn't thought about that."

"Live in your glory while you can." Jace flipped a page in his

38

Chapter Ten

Junior arrived home late after work on Thursday. Everyone was already at the dining room table.

Bev asked, "How come you're working late?"

"We had to patch the road up through Cheney Hollow. Orders came down from Richmond as if it were a crisis."

"Was the road that bad?"

"Nah. Some politicians must have gotten involved."

"Why would they do that?"

"You know why."

"The Wainright Lodge and Retreat?"

"Has to be. Someone must have hit a bump driving out there and complained."

"You really think someone would do that?"

"It's only hollow in the County that has cell service. Do you think that was because the cell company thought there was a major market? Important people want their comforts."

Jen entered the conversation. "The school bus hits potholes and ruts all the time out here in our hollow. Who do I call in Richmond to get the road fixed?"

Junior chuckled. "You could call your state rep, maybe even your congressman. Get yourself added to the queue."

"How long's the queue?"

"Depends on your importance."

Jen frowned. "Are you sending me into a black hole?"

"Well, you could ask me about your importance."

"Yeah, I've got influence with you?"

"A little - depends on my mood."

"The pothole's in front of the Darby's"

"I'll have a look at it."

After the discussion, Junior took off his coat, put it in the closet, and then joined his family at the table.

Chip looked as if he'd been waiting. "What's this in the paper about Granddad being an elector?"

Junior folded his napkin in his lap. "Yeah, he replaced some guy who got sick."

"Is it important?

"I suspect it's more like an honor. Your Granddad's put in a lot of work over the years for the Democratic Party."

"Don't electors select the President?"

"No, not exactly. They vote for whoever gets the most votes in the state."

"But I've heard that Presidents have been elected by electors even though they didn't get the most votes."

"That's the most votes in the Country. People who get a lot of votes in one state can still lose if their opponent squeaks out small majorities in other states."

"That's stupid," interjected Jen.

Junior chuckled again. "Yeah, some people think so. It was some-kind-of-compromise way back when the Country was figuring out how to elect a President."

"Dumb compromise."

"I guess the folks writing the Constitution didn't think so."

Chip chortled. "So, Granddad will elect the President."

"He'll vote for whoever wins the popular vote in Virginia."

"So, he really doesn't have any power."

"I'm afraid not."

Jen sat back. "Geez, talk about not really being important."

Chip took a forkful of his dinner. "I'll see what Old Man Bennett has to say about that."

Bev was suddenly alerted. "Who's Old Man Bennett?"

"Mr. Bennett, my history teacher."

"Can't you address him with more dignity?"

"Heck, he knows he's called that. Our defender of the Constitution. He'll set me straight." He looked across at Jen. "Then I'll set my little sister straight."

Jen stuck out her tongue.

Chapter Eleven

A few weeks later, Chance winced internally as he pulled into the parking lot in front of the Wainright Volunteer Fire Department. Gwen Ellen's Volvo was already there, whispers of exhaust emanating from behind it. It was five after six in the morning, five minutes after the polls in the firehouse had opened. The Republican poll tent was already up, a large sign hanging from the front. Chance knew Gwen Ellen would be fuming.

Chance got out of his Explorer and shivered as the wind hit him. He hunched over and wrapped his arms across his body as he approached Gwen Ellen's car. Her window rolled down, but she didn't turn to look at him. "Where the hell have you been? The Republicans are running circles around his. Barry Stackhouse has been over giving me a hard time. Says we Democrats can't get our act together. Says it's been downhill for us ever since Iowa. I hate the son-of-a-bitch."

"Ah, Gwen Ellen, it's still early. We won't miss voters."

"Like hell. We've missed two already. Tradesmen headed for Northern Virginia – machine operators, carpenters, masons. Where do you think county-people work?" She started to get out of her car. "Get the tent and let's get it up."

Chance jumped back from the car door. "Marvin's got the tent on his truck."

Gwen Ellen looked appalled and then defeated. "You're kidding me?"

"He'll be here in a minute. You can depend on him."

"Yeah, like I depended on you. Half the county's going to vote before we're set up!"

Just then Marvin's F-150 rounded the corner into the parking lot. He swung the truck around so that the rear pointed to the area the Democrats had selected for their tent, slammed the truck into reverse, and began backing as Gwen Ellen and

Chance moved quickly out of the way, Gwen Ellen exclaiming, "The madman is going to kill us all!"

Stackhouse shouted from the Republican tent, "He missed you, Gwen Ellen. Probably be the high point of your day."

Gwen Ellen tried to give Stackhouse her best glare. She would have loved to give him the bird but was afraid someone would see her. She looked around to see if Jace was there with his camera. *A free press,* she fumed to herself.

She turned back to the truck where Marvin and Chance were scrambling to get the tent out. "Where do you want it?" Chance shouted.

"Line the damned thing up with the Republicans. At least we can look neat."

While Chance and Marvin worked to get the tent up, Gwen Ellen started pulling signs and a hammer out of Chance's SUV. She set up a sign and started hammering. Marvin turned and proffered, "Damn, Gwen Ellen, the ground's frozen. The other guys attached their signatures to the tent. You can do the same when we get the tent up."

"You mean all these signs are wasted."

"Hope not. I brought a steel bar and a sled. We'll try to make holes and get the signs up at the entrance after we get the tent up."

"Darn, Marvin, maybe you're not so bad after all."

"Getting that stuff and the coffee was what made me late."

"Coffee?!"

"Yeah. It's in an urn in the front seat, along with some breakfast Danish."

"An urn. Hell, I'm going to fire Chance as the elector and turn it over to you."

"Really?"

"No. Sorry, it's too late.

With the tent up, Chance and Marvin grabbed tables and chairs, unfolded them, and set them up.

Gwen Ellen brought sample ballots and brochures from her Volvo and tried to set them on the table, but the wind caught the papers and she barely got her hand on them before they were gone. "Oh, damn."

She looked at the Republicans. They were tying white cloths around the sides and back of their tent. "What the hell?"

She turned to Chance. "Have we got sides to our tent?"

Chance scratched his head. "They don't come with sides - just four polls and a top."

Marvin knew the answer immediately. "Smallwood's a painter. Those are drop cloths from his truck."

Gwen Ellen looked perplexed. "I thought drop cloths were plastic,"

"Not for real painters."

"Hell, what do we do? We're going to sit here holding our papers in our gloves and freezing our butts off. I didn't think winter started until December."

Chance volunteered, "The Coop opens at seven. I'll get some drop cloths then."

"Like the Republicans?"

"No, plastic, held up with duct tape.

"We'll look like the Beverly Hillbillies."

"Better than green plastic bags," Marvin observed.

Gwen Ellen looked around. "Hell, we'll be frozen before the Coop opens. I think I'll put the sample ballots and the rest of the crap back in my car. We don't even have a rock to hold them down in this wind."

Marvin grinned. "You want to rock? I'll get you one." He took a step toward the nearby woods.

Gwen Ellen shook her head. "Forget it. I'm freezing anyway. She glared at her two volunteers. "You guys go pound in some signs down by the entrance. That is if the Republicans haven't filled all the space. See how many you can get up before one of you goes to the Coop."

"No, why the Republicans are going to beat us," Marvin grinned, as he picked up his iron bar and sled. "Chance grabs the signs. I'll do the hammering. We'll save your thumb, that way."

Chance sighed deeply. "Damn, Marvin that was a cheap signpost – not my fault. Stop the crap."

Gwen Ellen watched them go and then looked at the Republican tent. Stackhouse and Smallwood had tacked down the drop cloths and moved their table back from the front of the tent. They were standing behind the table wrapping themselves in blankets before they sat down. *Damn it, why didn't I think of blankets?* She started back toward her car. *Hope the heater hasn't cooled off.*

Before she got to her car, a pickup truck turned into the parking lot. It parked up against the fire hall building, too close for Gwen Ellen to approach the occupants. *Damned boundaries. How am I supposed to solicit – give people brochures and such?* Two men in jeans got out of the truck. Gwen Ellen hurried to her tent, backing, and staring at the men. *Hey, you guys. Look this way. Give me a thumbs up or something.*

The two men entered the building without looking back at the tents.

Gwen Ellen turned toward the Republicans and threw up her hands. Stackhouse threw up his hands, as well, and shouted, "Must be Democrats. No charm."

Gwen Ellen waved Stackhouse off, turned, and walked to her car.

✳✳✳

Marvin was gone a long time getting the plastic drop cloths. When he returned, Gwen Ellen stalked up to his truck. "God, where've you been? Chance and I are frozen."

Marvin ignored her and looked around. "Yeah, where is he?"

"In his SUV, warming up."

"He left you out in the cold?"

"His turn. We're switching off."

Marvin nodded and gave her a warm smile. "You're a leader to be admired."

Gwen Ellen looked at Marvin with disgust. "We had to adapt while you were running around in your warm truck."

"Hey, I had to pick up some bricks to weigh down the skirt of the drop cloth."

"Yeah, where is it?"

"The drop cloth?"

"Isn't that what you went for?"

Marvin vacillated between being annoyed or simply accepting the sarcasm. He pointed through the truck window. "That package in the front seat."

"That little thing?"

"Ten yards by three. All crammed in that package. Going to be fun opening it up in this wind. Let's get Chance out here to join in the fun."

Gwen Ellen was still looking through the truck's window. "Gosh, Marvin. What are all those masks and gloves on the floor?"

Marvin picked up the package of drop cloths. "Oh, they're leftover from the pandemic."

"Why don't you throw them out?"

"I have them stockpiled for the next pandemic."

"Fifteen or twenty used masks?"

"Better stockpile than the Nation had at the start of the last pandemic."

✳✳✳

As the day dragged on, the wind let up and the earth warmed. Voters came and went. Most ignored the tents, but some friends came over. Chance thought some people he knew didn't want to commit to being on one side or another. Some wore red baseball caps, and he knew who they were for – Isaac Ambler Goldin – Glossy Goldin, the lie machine. The red hats made Chance seethe inside. *Stupid people believe everything he says, even though eighty percent is crap and falsehoods. Goldin could lose a hundred-yard dash by thirty yards and make these people believe he had won. They hear what they want to hear. They love the carnival. They love the clowns and the bearded lady. They hate immigrants and love their guns. They don't want the government telling them what to do.*

Greg Malloy left the Republican tent and came over to visit Chance. "Funny looking tent, Chance. I've seen fancier ones in the underpasses in D.C. You buy out all the masking tape at the Coop?"

Chance grinned. He was damned if he was going to be bated. "Gosh, Greg. You should have seen it earlier when the duct tape was all crisscrossed and we were freezing to death while you were sitting at home with your bacon and eggs and your mug of coffee."

"Poor Chance. Sacrificing for the Party."

"Yeah, bless me for that. Tomorrow, that red hat you're wearing is going to be relegated to the back of your closet."

"Don't make me laugh, Chance. I'll be waving it next to my American flag."

"Under your Ku-Klux hood."

The smile left Greg's face. "That's a bunch of shit, Chance. I don't know anything about any Klan."

"So, do you support immigration?"

"Immigration's got nothing to do with the word 'Klan'."

"Maybe not, but the immigrants aren't white."

"That's got nothing to do with it. They take our jobs, diminish our neighborhoods, and use our services. They bring gangs and crime. They rape our women."

"So, Goldin says."

"Fact, Chance. Read the papers. Read about the gang murders."

"You think that reflects on all the immigrants. Most are good. They do the work you won't do. America couldn't run without them."

"Damn, Chance, you and I pay for all their needs. Be real."

"I am real. They are human beings."

"I don't want to hurt them, Chance. I just want them to stay where they belong."

"Is that what the Statue of Liberty means?"

"The Statue of Liberty is an anachronism, Chance. This Country's full up. We can't save all 'the wretched masses of your teeming shores'. We've got enough 'wretched masses' of our own."

"You mean we should ditch the Country's principles?"

"Hell, yes. Time's change."

"Damn, Greg, somewhere in the past you were an immigrant."

"Yeah. Came over in the seventeen-hundreds. My ancestors indentured themselves to get on the boat. Sold on the docks an Alexandria like damn slaves. George Washington was probably bidding. They earned their way – not like these people looking for handouts. Bet your ancestors came over on a silver platter."

"Catholics to Maryland, escaping Cromwell."

"You're Catholic?"

"Guess we were at some time."

"Like the gangs coming from Central America."

"I think it's the people escaping the gangs in Central America, Greg."

"The whole package comes, Chance. The worst of the lot. We need to arm against them. Shouldn't have to, but they keep coming."

"That why you've got the '2 A' on the back of your red hat?"

"Second Amendment, Chance, Second Amendment."

Chance gave a frustrated sigh. "Damn, Greg, I bet you believe in AK-47s too."

"Hell of a lot of fun, Chance. Really tear up the targets. You ought to get one, fella. You'd have fun."

"A torn-up deer's not good for much, Greg, and I sure as hell don't need an AK-47 to kill a groundhog."

"Having an AK-47 is a Constitutional Right, Chance. That's what counts. You don't mess with rights. You give an inch and your rights are gone."

"The Second Amendment was written over two hundred-years-ago. To quote Greg Malloy, 'times change'."

"Only if you're weak, Chance. Only if you're weak."

***

As the day progressed, the three Democrats became bored. They sat, leaning back with their arms crossed, speaking only when a voter caught their attention and required a comment. Most voters went straight about their business as if they needed to hurry off and do something or meet someone. Few even looked at the political tents as if they were afraid of being caught and given an inquisitional thrashing about their vote and sent to the rack for the foolishness of what they had done. Still, now and then, a friend would walk over, announce what they had done and wait for a compatriot's praise.

Late in the morning, Lizbeth Harlowe replaced Gwen Ellen. Chance had gone to school with Lizbeth who had then been called Bessie, Bessie Darnell, at the time. Her name changed before she married Johnson Harlowe, one of the attorneys in the county. Chance guessed 'Bessie' was too bovine – that sophistication was needed. When she arrived, Chance only glanced at her full figure. He felt bad about it, but she would always be Bessie to him.

About one in the afternoon, Jimmy Settle replaced Marvin. He brought soft drinks, hamburgers, and soggy French fries from the Fast Stop. Chance was grateful. Marvin's breakfast buns seemed like something from ancient history and the coffee had long since gone from cool to almost frozen. He had wanted to dump the urn. He had pictured it splashing about in his SUV as he went home in the evening, but he didn't have the nerve to dump it out into the drainage ditch by the parking lot in front of gaping members of the electorate exiting the fire hall. As he bit into his hamburger, he thought to himself, *dumping the coffee might cost the election.*

As the thought of losing the election drifted through Chance's mind, he noticed Jason Phelps just outside the fire hall talking to a couple who were sporting their new red, white, and blue 'I Voted' stickers. After the couple left, Jace stood casually to the side of the door and nodded pleasantly to new voters as they arrived. A few minutes later, as the same innocent citizens exited the door, he sprang upon them with a fox's smile.

After Jace released the voters, he again stood to the side of the door. Time passed and, after ten minutes, no voters had come. At last, Jace wandered over to the Democratic tent. He stood by Chance who had strolled out into the parking lot in front of the tent. He nodded to Lizbeth and Jimmy. "Hi, how's the Democratic world?"

Jimmy responded to Lisbeth. "You playing sides, Jace? You're going to be in trouble."
Jace waved his hand to dismiss Jimmy's thought. "No worries.

I'll go to see them next. Might even spend more time there. Pull your string a little."

Lizbeth decided to do some pulling off her own. "Hell, Jace, are you even legal? Are you supposed to be that close to the fire hall bugging the voters?"

"Hell, if I know. I'm not proselytizing. Just asking friendly questions."

Chance nodded and grinned. "Jace is doing what they call 'exit polling'. At seven o'clock this evening he'll phone into CNN so they can make their predictions and project the winners."

Jace sighed and shook his head. "Just want to have some quotes to put in Thursday's paper – give out more than numbers. Unfortunately, lots of people don't want to say who they voted for, except some of the Goldin people who want to shove it in your face."

Lizbeth was still shaking her head. "Still don't know if standing outside the door is legal. I'll have to check with Johnson and see."

Jimmy looked at Lizbeth as if impressed. "Johnson's an expert on Constitutional law?"

Chance interjected. "Bet he can be in five or ten minutes."

Lizbeth frowned. "Hey, no sarcasm. He knows how to read the law. It's what he does."

Chance tried to look chagrined but couldn't shake his smile. "Didn't mean to offend you, Lizbeth. We all use Johnson, but lawyers attract jokes and sarcasm. Responding to it is part of the law exam. Comes with the job. Is Johnson sensitive?"

Lizbeth glared down at the table. "He takes his job seriously."

Chance played it safe. "As he should."

He turned back to Jace. "And you take your job seriously, too?"

"Do you take cattle seriously, Chance?"

"Of course."

"There you go."

"Jeez, people, what's all the blackness. The sun's shining. A joke's meant to be nothing more than a joke. We're here to win an election. Let's be happy."

Jace drew in a deep breath of air. "I think I'll go see the Republicans."

Chance stared after him as he left. "Jeez!"

***

Seven P. M. was close. Chance couldn't wait for the polls to close. He had spent the day and had pretty much decided it was stupid. He was feeling importance and responsibility as a member of the Electoral College, but no one seemed to know that. *It was in the paper over a month ago. Someone should think it's important.*

Gwen Ellen returned ten minutes before the polls closed. As she approached the tent, she frowned at Chance. "Did you really stay here all day? Do you think you had an impact? Did you get to the conscience of some of your friends?"

"Damn, Gwen Ellen, you make me feel like I wasted my time."

Gwen Ellen looked away. "No, Chance, I'm sorry. I'm sure you helped. Just that I've been listening to the radio. Thought we'd have a landslide, but the talking heads are sounding like it's closer than expected."

"You're kidding? People are still supporting Goldin?"

"Supporting their party, supporting guns-rights, supporting anti-abortion, not supporting programs to support the poor, supporting not spending on social programs, etc. Hell, I don't know. Maybe some are even supporting Goldin – think he's entertaining – puts on a good show."

"Gosh, you sound depressing. How do you think we did here in the county?"

"Be real, Chance. How do we ever do? We're just country enough not to be Democratic."

"Jeez, Gwen Ellen, where did all the encouragement and rah, rah from the last couple of months go?"

"Still planning to win the state, Chance. The celebratory party will be in Richmond. I'll watch it on TV and the spirit will come back. The County just frustrates me."

"Hope you're right. I'd hate to be an elector for nothing."

"You won't be. We'll win the state."

"There you go. Your chin's coming up."

She turned toward the fire hall. "You coming in before they close the door, Chance? Want to hear the results first-hand?"

"No, it's been a long day. Phone me with the results."

"Don't take your shirt off. I'll have you over for a drink when we win the County."

"I can change out of my pajamas pretty quickly."

Chapter Twelve

The Republicans won the County and the Democrats won the State and Country, the latter with 272 Electoral Votes, two more than needed for the required majority. Democrats partied in Richmond and Northern Virginia. They partied in Washington and across the Country. Two votes were as good as a million. Goldin was defeated. What could be better than that?!

Jace interviewed Gwen Ellen, but no one else did. She was from the wrong part of the state. He tried to talk to her about the County, but she was all about the triumph over Goldin, not the Republican Party, but the man. "That's what the election was all about. Now," She extolled, "the nation can return to its fundamental principles, to a nation of values and virtues – to honesty – to trust in our elected leaders. The rose garden will bloom again! The nation will fold its umbrellas and walk in the sun again!"

Jace wondered if Gwen Ellen's memory went back more than four years, but thought, Oh well. A winner's a winner. Let her enjoy her moment. The real world will return soon enough. January the Twentieth will sneak up on everyone.

At Chance's house, they wondered what it meant. Chance wondered if he had a real role or if he was just a rubber stamp. The Secretary of the Commonwealth would announce the winner when she was satisfied with the vote. Then, Chance would go to Richmond and put the names on a form and sign it. After that, it would all be done. A couple of weeks of his Republican friends not talking to him, and then everyone would move on.

Shirley wondered if Chance would have to spend the night in Richmond. Driving down was fine – two hours each way – a little gas burned. That wouldn't be bad. But would he have to spend the night and was the place he stayed specified? A night at the Jefferson would cost. Two nights would cost a lot.

Junior came over the day after the election. "You're important, Dad."

"How come? You always say there's no future for me."

"Yeah, that's true – no future in farming. But now you're a big deal – at least the kids think so. The Electoral College is a topic in school right now and they've got bragging rights."

"No kidding? The kids are talking about it?"

"Bragging to all their classmates. You need to live it up while you can. After December, it's all over."

"Well, Chip and Jen will have to come over before I go and cast the vote. Hopefully, I'll know more about being an elector in a couple of weeks. No one from around here has ever been an elector before. It's a job the big wheels usually get - an honor and all that. Hopefully, Gwen Ellen has some knowledge about what I need to do."

"You mean you haven't learned about it yet?"

"No, I'm a working man. No sense letting the bull out in the pasture until the heifers have been picked."

"You mean electing a President is like selecting heifers to breed."

"Yeah," Chance laughed. "They're unknown but you hope they're going to produce."

Junior shook his head, "Well, I expect Vickers will have more input to what's produced than the heifers do."

Chance sobered. "Yeah, we'll all see. Elections are about promises. Once elected, it's about reality. Remember Trump's border wall – the symbol of promises gone wrong."

"Well, there are still people around who believe a wall would solve our problems.   Symbol of different things to different people. But, back to the original subject – when do you think you can talk to the kids about your role as an elector?"

"Heck, I don't know, Junior. You know I've got an auction in ten days. The kids can go along if they'd like to. They've always liked auctions in the past."

"Yeah, but don't let their interest in your role as an elector get old. They're interested and proud now, but it won't last forever. In a high school class, a hundred years of history can pass in ten days.”

“Yeah, okay. I’ll try to see Gwen Ellen this weekend. She’s flying high right now - been interviewed by Jace – be in the paper tomorrow. Hopefully, she’ll be normal by Saturday.”

“The auction’s not a big deal, anyway, is it?”

“Seven head. Four steers I need to get rid of, a couple of young cows that haven’t bred well, and that Strother bull.”

“Hey, I remember you taking a heifer over to Jim Strother’s to breed to his bull. I thought you really liked that bull you got – liked his confirmation and all.”

“Yeah, I do, and he’s still has a few years of breeding in him. I need to sell him before he gets too old. I’m keeping a young bull the Strother bull sired here.”

“You think he’s a good replacement.”

“I think he’ll be okay – that he’ll produce animals I can sell to the feeders.”

“Still, you liked the Strother bull.”

“And still do, but I hope he’ll bring a good price.”

“And you need the money.”

Chance frowned. “Don’t know about ‘need’, but, yes, we can use the money.”

“’ We’? Mom’s involved.”

“Mom’s always involved.”

Chapter Thirteen

Chance sat in his club chair to watch the news on television. It was a routine he liked to keep, although his cattle often interfered. He contentedly leaned back and sipped his glass of Claret.

He held out his glass and swished the red wine around, allowing the light from the television to glisten through it. He couldn't find the wine in the grocery store, at least not the one Shirley went to. He had to order it. His friends told him he was living in the Nineteenth Century. Some friends had never heard of Claret. Junior claimed Chance thought he was lord of the manor drinking such an ancient brew. He told his father he should drink beer as he and his friends did. Chance remonstrated that he was not a red neck, but a man of sophistication who lived a style of life that pleased him. Besides, at $28 a bottle, Claret was a wine he could afford.

He had drunk beer until he was about thirty, but it was going to his waist and made him feel bloated. He had decided that there had to be a better way to live.

He set down his glass on the coffee table. Dinner would be at seven - part of the routine – in fifteen minutes. The evening news was going into its routine of two minutes of commercials after every two minutes of news. His mind turned it off. He sipped his wine and thought about Jace's interview with Gwen Ellen. She had been riding high, bragging about all the work the county Democrats had done, about their part in the broad state Democratic Party that had carried the election, a state that had overwhelmingly voted for Vickers, resulting in the networks projecting the winner early and leading to the onslaught that swept across the county and led to a major victory. You'd have thought Gwen Ellen had done it herself and that it was a major victory. She emphasized the triumph by two million votes and didn't mention the Electoral College.

Just then the telephone rang. Chance squeezed his eyes closed as if the ring had caused sudden pain. *I'll be damned if I'm going to answer that. This is my time.*

After two rings, the ringing stopped. Chance leaned back and kept his eyes closed. *Darn, Shirl's picked up.*

Sure enough, Shirley called from the dining room, "Chance, pick up the phone. It's Gwen Ellen. Don't talk long. Dinner's about ready."

Oh, goodness, Chance thought. She's going to want me to start picking up the signs tomorrow. No rest for the weary.

He slid forward in the chair and then rose to his feet. He walked across the room to the telephone, setting his glass beside it on the table. He put the phone to his ear. "Hey, Gwen Ellen. What's up?"

"Vickers is in trouble."

"Huh, what? He didn't win the election?"

"No, damnit. He's collapsed."

"Yeah, so, something happened to him?"

"Yes, damn it. Collapsed in the middle of a news conference announcing his chief of staff."

"So, who did he announce?"

"Chance, it doesn't matter. Our President's on the way to the hospital. Aren't you watching the news?"

"I turned it off five minutes ago in the middle of a commercial."

"Well, turn it back on."

"Shirley's got dinner ready."

"So, eat on your lap. What the hell's with you, Chance? You drunk on your evening wine? This is the most important thing that's happened since the election – may be the most important thing that's happened in years."

"So, if it's serious, who do I vote for in the Electoral Cottage?"

"Chance, I don't know. Turn on the damned television!"

She hung up.

Chance stared at the phone and then hung it up. He picked up his glass of wine, walked back to his chair, stood for a moment contemplating what had happened, drained his glass, and thought *What the hell does she expect me to do?*

He sat down and turned on the television. The news was over, and the quiz show that followed it was on. *Well, what's important is important.* The news about Vickers began streaming across the bottom of the picture. Chance sighed. *At least someone thinks it's important.*

Chapter Fourteen

Shirley entered the living room where Chance was watching television. "Goodness, Chance, are you watching a quiz show? Dinner's ready. What's with you?"

"Quiz show?" Chance suddenly noted the screen. "Oh, heck no. I'm watching the banner across the bottom. Vickers collapsed. He's being taken to the hospital - to George Washington University Hospital."

"Isn't that where they took Reagan?"

"Yeah. I guess it's nearby."

"Well, you can't help and dinner's going to get cold."

"Hey, can't I eat in here?"

"You know you hate eating on your lap. We don't even have any trays."

"Can't we use a cookie sheet or something?"

"You're serious, aren't you?"

"Yes. This is going to affect my life."

"Oh, come on Chance. Whether the man's all right or not, it's not going to affect your life. I don't know how many degrees of separation there is between you and Vickers, but I suspect it's the maximum."

"Yeah, but if the man dies, who do I vote for as an elector?"

"Chance, you vote for whomever the powers tell you to. The same degrees of separation say that's not you."

"Yes, I guess you're right. I'd still like to know that the man's okay."

"Alright, let me get a cookie sheet. Just don't let your plate slide. I'll come to eat with you. Isn't there something else we can watch while the news is streaming across the screen?"

***

"We interrupt the scheduled programming to bring you a special announcement!"

It was 8:17 and dinner was over.

Shirley had brought cake and coffee into the living room.

Chance held his fork in the air, a piece of cake still stuck in the prongs.

"We regret to inform you that President-elect, John Hornsby Vickers, passed away at George Washington University Hospital this evening following his collapse during a press conference two hours earlier. As seen here, his collapse was documented by the networks who were filming the press conference for later use on news programs. Although no formal announcement has been made at this time, personnel at the hospital have indicated to our reporters that it was a heart attack. As far as is known, the President-elect had no history of heart problems and his death was completely unexpected. At the time of his death, his wife, Elizabeth, had just arrived at the hospital. As you can see here, she is seen arriving at the hospital in what is believed to be her personal car. The driver is unknown. She was met at the door by a man in a suit, perhaps one on the newly assigned secret service agents. As more is learned, we will interrupt the scheduled programming to provide updated information."

Chance finally set down his fork. "I guess the fat lady hasn't sung."

Shirley looked at Chance incredulously. "What's a 'fat lady' got to do with this?"

"Just something Yogi Berra once said."

"Yogi who? What are you talking about?"

"Oh, Goodness. Never mind Shirl. Just means nothing's ever over. You never know what will happen next."

"So, what does that have to do to you? Are you still an elector?"

"Heck, I don't know. I guess I'll find out. Maybe *The Washington Post* will tell me in the morning."

Chapter Fifteen

Chance knocked on Gwen Ellen's door at seven-thirty the next morning. Her husband, Charley, answered the door. "Jesus, Chance, it's just after seven in the morning."

"Seven-thirty."

"Okay, seven-thirty. It's still early."

"I need to talk to Gwen Ellen."

"Chance, she hasn't had breakfast. She's still in her robe."

Chance didn't even look guilty. "Okay, I'll go to the Fast Stop and get a cup of coffee. Be back in twenty minutes or so."

"Chance, can you stretch that to half-an-hour?"

"That will be at eight o'clock."

"Right."

"Okay, see you then."

Charley closed the door and headed to the kitchen where Gwen Ellen was drinking her coffee. "Who the heck was that?"

"Chance."

"FitzBourne?"

"Yeah. Said he'd be back at eight."

"Damn, I haven't had my coffee. I told him last night I didn't know anything. He's just going to have to see me in this bathrobe."

Charley Dunbardy stood back and appraised his wife. "I don't know. You're pretty sexy looking."

"Chrissy Teigen wouldn't look sexy in this bathrobe."

"Hey, it's in the eye of the beholder and I remember."

"In your dreams, sweetheart."

"Ah, but they're good dreams. The Democratic Sweetheart."

"Yeah, of 1981."

"You haven't aged a day."

"Christ, what woke you up this morning?"

"You, in your bathrobe, darling."

"Lord, you'd think you were Irish."

"Maybe, somewhere in the family tree."

"What family tree. You know you don't know where 'Dunbardy' comes from."

"No one else does either. Anyway, you have fifteen minutes left."

"Shit."

"Ah, ah, language?"

"Shit."

***

Chance parked in front of the Dunbardy house at two-minutes-to-eight and took a sip from his paper coffee cup.

He thought he heard a voice and rolled down his window. Charley was standing with the front door of the house open. "Chance, you might as well come in and get a decent cup of coffee. We have real mugs."

Chance got out of the car and started toward the door.

Charley looked disgusted. "Dump that poison, Chance."

Chance held the cup up. "Might kill the grass."

"Don't think so."

Chance dumped the cup. "I'll check in the spring."

Charley closed the door behind them. "She's in the kitchen. I'm going to turn on *Morning Joe*."

"Maybe he knows what's going on."

"He and his pals will at least have an opinion."

"No doubt."

Chance knew the way to the kitchen. He found Gwen Ellen sitting at the table with her cup of coffee. She didn't get up.

Chance looked at the bathrobe. "You're looking pretty sexy, lady."

"Chance cut the crap. I've had enough of that this morning."

Chance drew his chin back. "Oh, Okay."

"You know I don't know anything. Told you that last night. And no one calls me in the middle of the night to tell me things. That's for big wheels. I imagine the Democratic National Committee members are still at their respective homes having breakfast. They'll decide something in due time, then tell the states and the state committees will pass it down. I'll officially learn a couple of hours after CNN makes its announcement."

"You don't think they'll just move up Jane Meyer Grete from the VP slot. That's what would have happened if Vickers had already been sworn in."

"Yeah, but he wasn't. So, you know as much as I do."

"So, what do I do?"

"You go home, check your cows, kiss Shirley and watch CNN."

"Charley said I could have a cup of coffee."

"Geez," she said as she got up and poured Chance a cup of coffee. "Here, take this and go watch *Morning Joe* with Charley."

Chapter Sixteen

Chance came through the kitchen door and closed it harder than usual. Shirley knew from the slouch of his shoulders that she should wait a minute.

He sat on the bench they maintained immediately inside the door and slipped off his shoes. Then he rose, opened the door again, and set the shoes outside. "Clean you later."

He went to the kitchen sink, tore off a paper towel, wet it, returned to the bench, and washed the floor. After throwing the towel out, he looked at Shirley. "Judy 2 rubbed herself against the fence, tore off a long splinter, and left it stuck inside her."

"Woodfern 162?"

"Yeah, aka Woodfern 162. How do you remember?"

"The Woodfern numbers are easy. I register them, you know? It's correlating them with your names for them that's hard."

"Yeah. I had to get Forjambi in to extract it, clean the wound, and give me antibiotic ointment. Damn, puncture wound. I need to keep it open and squeeze in the ointment twice a day. Pain in the neck." He looked at her. "What?"

"Just waiting to tell you Gwen Ellen called. I know you're a little down on her now."

"Hell, the woman treated me like I was her whiney child this morning. Didn't take me seriously. Sent me off to sit with Charley as if she needed me out of her hair."

"Well, Chance, in all fairness, she had no way of knowing what was going on. This County and its people are little wheels in the great scheme of things."

"Hey, don't defend her. I'm a smaller wheel in that scheme. I just want to know what's going on. As an elector, I have a responsibility."

"Don't you have till sometime in December before you really have to do anything?"

"First Monday after the second Wednesday in December."

"Gosh, sweetheart, that's five or six weeks from now. The Party will let you know what to do long before that."

"What if I don't like the candidate?"

"So, what if you don't? You're one vote out of over five hundred."

"538."

"Okay, 538. You're less than one percent of the Electoral College."

"Less than two-tenths of a percent."

"Right, almost nothing."

"I still count."

"Honey, of course, you do."

"Are you patronizing me?"

"Are you patronizing yourself, Chance? Come on. Be real. You vote for whom the party tells you to and that's it. You're a Democratic and you do the Party thing.

"Yeah, I guess. Anyway, what did Gwen Ellen want?"

"She said you probably already knew from watching television that the Democratic National Committee is meeting today to review the situation."

"The 'situation' – that's what they called it – the 'situation'?"

"I guess. Seems as good a name as anything."

"It's not their 'situation'. It's my 'situation'. I'm the one who votes."

"538 of you vote. The Party decides how you vote – they make the decision."

"Is that what Gwen Ellen said – the Party decides? It's not that the Vice President-elect automatically moves up. The Party decides?"

"No, she said to watch television tonight at six o'clock. The Democratic National Committee is having a news conference."

"The National Committee?"

"Yeah, I guess so."

"272."

"272 what?"

"The Democratic National Committee, or whoever, will only decide how 272 electors vote. We Democrats only won 272 Electoral Votes. The Republicans already know who they're voting for."

"You think?"

"You being funny?"

"What do you think?"

Chapter Seventeen

Edison Damson settled with relief into the backseat of his chauffeured gray Cadillac ST5. He savored the comfort and silence. Outside, he could see some reporters and cameramen. He knew they were disappointed, but it was too early to talk. He'd had Bennie Hernandez pull the car close to the curb in front of his Georgetown home. He was grateful the reporters didn't press him as he exited the house and climbed into the car. They could take pictures of him leaving the house. He had even walked to the far side of the car so they could get good pictures - no harm in that.

As the car pulled away from the curb, he opened the copy of *The Washington Post* he held in his hand next to his briefcase. He glanced down at the picture of Vickers in the black frame that dominated the front page. He shook his head. *The man worked all his life to be President and will never serve a day.*

Damson folded the newspaper and leaned back against the headrest; his eyes closed.

He couldn't read a newspaper in a moving car. He couldn't read anything as Bennie drove them into DC. It would make him sick. It had been that way since he threw up in the family car when he was six years old. *Fifteen minutes wasted every morning and every night, sometimes half an hour. I sure could use the time.*

As the car followed Ohio Drive under the Arlington Memorial Bridge, left the Lincoln Memorial behind, and straightened onto Lexington Avenue, Damson stroked his fingers over the soft, leather seat. He liked the luxury. He liked being driven. He thought the car was so much better than an Escalade. That was too much ostentation. Black Suburbans were too "Washington". Still, the car made him feel important. He knew most Americans didn't know his name. Maybe none of them did. He was Chairman of the Democratic National

Committee. He administered things. He ran things. He wasn't a politician, but he dealt with them, all the time.

As Bennie turned the car into the short drive to the parking lot under his building, Damson frowned. Is the damned building brown or beige? *Seems like it can't decide. Boxy. Windows with no trim. Dark rectangles with no life. I hate the damned building. Home of the Democratic National Committee. My building. God, I wish it had more life.*

As he exited the car, he leaned back in and said to Bennie, "I expect to be in meetings all day. Check with Skylar now and then to see if anything changes."

"She has my cell number, boss. I'll be around anyway. Have my own coffee pot and coffee. The DNC's is awful."

Damson hurried up the stairs and entered his office suite. His personal administrative assistant was Skylar Rose. He always thought a surname should follow that, but it was "Rose". He always thought that a woman named Skylar should be young and svelte. Skylar wasn't. She was fifty-three years old with a body as solid as a tree trunk – not fat - solid. She knew her job. She was good at it.

"Morning, Skylar."

"Morning, Boss."

As Damson passed her desk, he stopped, and she handed him a piece of typed paper. "This morning's tweets. He's been up early."

"Not unusual. What's it say?"

"That the Democratic Party's in chaos. They were stupid for nominating a seventy-six-year-old man with a bad heart."

"No one knew he had a heart problem."

"What's it matter? Goldin says he did. Now it's common knowledge."

"Skylar, you're giving me a hard time."

"No, I'm not. You know his supporters will believe him. Maybe others will wonder."

"Bastard. Goldin's seventy-three."

"Humm, he doesn't mention that."

“Of course not.”

“And there’s another tweet.”

“Oh, shit.”

“It says, and I quote, ‘Democrats cheat – shameful – Pennsylvania election put in question.’”

“What the hell is that about?”

“Some state legislative candidate faked signatures on his petition to run.”

“Yeah, how does that affect us?”

“Goldin says it brings into question the entire Pennsylvania election.”

“Bunch of crap.”

“Yeah, well, I bet you hear more about it. We won Pennsylvania, but not by much. I’m sure Goldin will say that it affects the validity of the whole election.”

“I’ll deal with it later.”

“Your choice.”

He headed for his office, fuming.

Skylar called after him. “The meeting’s in the conference room in twenty minutes.”

“Buzz me when it’s time.”

He set his briefcase on his desk and stood a moment without acting. *Why the hell do I let Goldin bother me? We won the damned election.*

He took his notebook out of the briefcase and sat down to review what he had written the night before. He sighed, and thought, *God, I’m tired. How many phone calls did I get last night? Must have been half the state chairmen -the Speaker of the House at nine o’clock and again at one in the morning - Glore from the Senate at six this morning. The phone was ringing when I went out the door this morning, for Christ’s sake.*

Suddenly his thoughts came together, and he phoned his chief of staff, Dominic Rossi, to come to his office and bring Skylar in with him. When they arrived, he waved them to sit. “Guys, I don’t know what’s going to happen today, but I’m sure we'll need to hold a press conference.   Between the two of you, set it up. Get a room in a hotel, tables with white cloths and a gap in the middle for our lectern, chairs for everyone on the committee plus one more in case we need it, full sound system - you know the deal. Set it up for six o'clock prime time so we can hopefully finish before the national news. Make plenty of room for the press, reporters, and cameramen. Get the word out so we have a full house."

Damson's chief of staff raised his hand.

Damson looked at him in resignation, "Damn, Dom, you think this is a classroom or something? Speak up."

Rossi leaned forward to make a point. "If we announce it too early, Goldin is going to schedule something at the same time."

Damson sighed. "So, how early do you think we can announce the meeting?"

"I don't know. It's Monday. It's not like Goldin is thinking about flying to Florida and who he's going to play golf with. He's probably going to be alert."

"Okay, about three o'clock, announce that we'll be having a news conference this evening. Don't say when. We'll announce the place and time about five."

"He still may react. All he has to do is walk down the hall."

"Yeah, hopefully, the press will be scrambling for our meeting before he reacts. Anything else?"

"No, I'm on it, boss."

As Skylar exited the office, Damson asked. "What's happening with my telephone calls, Skylar?"

"You've been in a meeting all morning."

"You're a doll."

"Too old for that, boss, and it's not gendered appropriate."

"Between you and me, Skylar – just the two of us."

Chapter Eighteen

Damson entered the conference room exactly at nine-thirty He liked to be prompt.

He sat at the head of the table, Bill Glore, the Senate Democratic Leader to his right, and Speaker of the House, Allison Gwently to his left.

He looked around the table. "Where's Elwood?" Elwood Smethers was the Vice-Chair and ASDC President; that is, he was the president of the association of all the state chairmen and vice-chairmen.

Vice-Chair Emery St. John offered, "He was on the phone when I passed his office. In fact, he's been on the phone every time I've passed his office this morning."

Damson shook his head. "I thought I'd talked to all the state people last night. Guess I didn't give the right answers. The simple fact is we need him. If he isn't here in two minutes, will you go get him, Emery?"

"Sure."

Damson crossed his hands on the table in front of himself and waited.

Glore chuckled his seemingly permanently tanned face crinkling, bringing his white mustache and blue eyes to the fore. "You nervous, Ed?"

"Yeah. Everyone's waiting for guidance, to be told what to do."

"You think that's our job?"

"Yes."

"Just yes?"

"Who else is going to do it?"

"I don't think it's in the by-laws."

"Presidents-elect are not supposed to die."

"I guess that's why election law doesn't address it. It says we can replace a nominee up until when the ballots are printed. It doesn't say anything about what happens after the election."

Damson was growing impatient. "He looked down the table. Emery, please go get Elwood. Tell him the whole committee is waiting for him."

Emery left the room.

Glore placed his hand on Damson's arm and spoke under his breath, "You shouldn't have picked the black guy to run your errand."

Damson made a face. "It's not an errand. He's got the office next to Elwood's."

"It's called sensitivity, Ed. Sensitivity."

"We're a team, Bill. We're alike."

"You're dreaming, Ed."

Just then, Elwood Smethers rushed into the room, followed by Emery St John, who looked more bothered than Smethers who was repeating over and over, "Sorry, sorry, sorry."

Damson looked at him. "The state chairs giving you a fit, Elwood?"

"Yeah, they want to know what their role is in selecting a replacement for Vickers."

"Yes. That's one of our questions. Gentleman, Ladies, the President says we're in chaos today – that the Democratic Party is a mess. Our job today is to persuade the nation that that is not true – that we're under control – which we know what we're doing and are dealing effectively with the Nation's loss of its President-elect. A death like this hasn't happened since Horace Greeley died in 1872. He was the loser, so it really didn't matter. Grant won, but Greeley's loss provides us a lesson. His electors ended up going to four different individuals. We can't afford for that to happen. If it did, the Republicans could win this election without a majority of Electoral Votes. We must provide one candidate and do everything in our power to ensure that he or she receives all the 272 Electoral Votes won by Vickers. To do otherwise would be the tragedy of our lifetimes."

Glore interjected. "Listen to what Ed is saying. Pay attention. If we end up divided, Goldin wins. He's already begun to sew dissension. He'll try his best to split us. We could become the first Party in history to win an election, both in votes and Electoral Votes, and still lose the Presidency. This is serious as hell."

Ed looked down the table. "Elwood, I waited for you because you're our interface with the state chairs. I heard from many of them last night, but I'd like to hear your beliefs about what they want before I convey what I've been hearing. Give us your thoughts."

Elwood looked down with a degree of uncertainty as if the weight of the world had suddenly been dumped on his shoulders, but then looked back up and around the table. "They want guidance. They want leadership. They also want to know their roles. They don't want to be left out, but they want direction. Some are more forceful. They want an active role. They want to participate in the selection of an individual to replace Vickers. I'd say a quarter to a third of the chairs fall into that category. The others are less specific. They'll do what we want. I expect they would be thrilled to participate."

"Okay," Damson responded. "So, we know there's an interest, to varying degrees, in participating in a selection process. Do we let them vote, one vote to a chair, multiple votes based on their electors – do we do it by mail or email – do we hold a convention?" He looked down the table at his National Finance Chair, Gretchen Soderberg. "Do we have money for a convention, Gretchen.

"Yes, there's money left over from the election. How much are we talking about?"

Damson turned to his Vice Chairman of Finance, Gaston Weberley. "What would it cost, Gas?"

"Uh, are we talking about state chairs, vice-chairs, spouses, staff, what? Five-hundred people, two nights and meals, airline tickets, say 500 people at a thousand dollars each, plus a facility, interactions with the press? Could approach a million."

"So, what do you think?"

"Drop in the bucket compared to the election."

"So, we could do it?"

"Sure."

"How about a campaign? Do we give people a couple of weeks to campaign for the job – go back to all the candidates we had this time last year?"

Gwently pounded her fists on the table. "That would be awful. We were accused of speaking with many conflicting voices at the time. There's no way we want to go back to that."

Ed patted her on the arm. "Maybe we can narrow it down. How many people got votes the first round at the convention?"

"Hey, that included some favorite sons."

"And daughters."

"I think, one daughter. Anyway, we don't want them mucking things up."

Ed removed his hand. "So, what do we do? If there's a campaign, how do we limit the candidates?"

Vice-Chair Kristin Lindsey joined in. "There ought to be a woman candidate."

Emery St. John was immediately alert. "And a minority."

Weberley said, "We already have a black woman as the Vice President-elect."

St. John scoffed, "You know what I mean."

Lindsey came back. "So, you're saying we already have a woman and a black?"

St. John protested, "Can't we have a President with those credentials too? What's wrong with that?"

Damson replied, "Nothing that a Hispanic might not complain about."

"There weren't any Hispanics in the primaries."

Damson agreed, "True enough. How about this? Let everyone who won delegates in the primaries run. Would that do it, Emery?"

"I don't know. How many people won delegates?"

Glore shook his head. "Six or seven. I can see it now. We get mail-in votes after a campaign of a couple of weeks, get votes for seven different people and then spend the two weeks before the electors meet in their respective states trying to get them voting for the same person. It isn't going to work."

Leonora Leonard pictured herself writing checks. "So, we hold a convention. We don't let them out of the room until everyone agrees – just like an old-fashioned convention."

Gwently groaned. "This day and age it would have to be televised. Arguing over candidates would just expose our warts. It could really show divisions."

Kristin Lindsey suggested, "So, we don't televise. It's not a government meeting. We'll just have a big, closed session."

Gwently groaned again. "Have you been living under a rock? This is the real world. We'd never get away with it."

"Well," Damson offered. "Maybe we should try to limit it to just a couple of candidates."

Glore shook his head. "How are we going to do that? What are the criteria for selection? Vickers had sixty percent of the delegates going into the convention, Brock Henry over thirty. The next closest person had less than two percent. How do you pick two candidates out of that?"

Suddenly Darlene Meletta, the Vice Chair for Civic Engagement and Voter Participation, spoke up, "Seems to me you're all talking in circles. Practically everything you've been talking about is just going to divide the Party and we won't have time to fix it. We need to make a decision. Henry was the runner-up. We need to say he's the Party's choice, bring the state chairs in line and get on with it."

St John recoiled. "But he's an ass hole."

Darlene sighed. "I agree, he's an ass."

"An ass hole!"

Darlene shrugged. "Whatever. The question is this: What's better, a Democratic ass or a Republican ass? We must work with what we've got. Lots of people voted for Henry in the primaries and they'll still support him. Asses like asses. Maybe he'll even get some support from Goldin's minions. What do you think, Elwood? Can you bring the state chairs together?"

Smethers considered it. "A lot of them will grouse, but I think they're pragmatic. Maybe we should give them a benefit. Have our pseudo convention and make it a rally in support of Brock Henry – a giant peer-pressure thing. One for all and all for one. A big party – dancing girls – the whole thing."

Gwently shook her head. "Dancing girls?"

Damson patted her on the arm again. "Entertainment, Allison, entertainment – dinner – free drinks – a real party – on the DNC."

Gwently leaned back in her chair. "As Darlene says, 'whatever'."

Damson looked around the table. "What do you think? Anybody against it?" He waited for a minute. "Anybody for it?"

There was a lot of sighing around the room. Finally, Kristine Lindsey said a small, "Yes."

There was murmuring and nodding.

Glore looked at Damson. "I think that's a yes."

Damson glared at the table. "I need more than that. Everyone who's for making Henry the DNC choice and working to ensure that choice is supported by state chairs and electors, raise your hand."

All hands were raised, although some reluctantly.

Damson bit his lip in thought. "Okay, let's get it done. Darlene, set up the convention, work with Elwood to get everyone invited. Elwood, I'll announce Henry as our choice at the press conference tonight. You and your staff start working with the state people immediately. Bring them on – make them commit. Use the convention as a come on. Free flights, free hotel rooms, free meals. Press the party unity aspect to get our candidate across. Emphasize the unity. It's essential to get Goldin out of the White House. If we're not together, this could be a disaster. We must be together.

We'll adjourn now, but all of you play your parts. Keep each other informed. Keep an eye out for anything that might go wrong. We can't be complacent. Some think we won the election and it's all settled, but we only won by two Electoral Votes. We can still screw this thing up.

Unity, unity, unity – dream it, embrace it, and preach it.

See you tonight at the press conference. Be seated about ten minutes before six – smiles and comradery."

Damson watched everyone file out. Who'd have thought? It's just a little after eleven. Maybe I can get hold of Dill before lunch.

He hurried back to his office. On the way, he passed Skylar. "Get me Jimmy Dill of the phone."

"Henry's campaign manager?"

"Right."

"Thought his campaign was closed."

"Officially, yes, but he phoned me twice last night."

"I'll have to find his phone number."

"I bet he's on the list of calls you've blocked today. You can probably find the number there."

Damson sat at his desk, picked up a pen, and started tapping it on his desk.

The phone buzzed. He picked it up and heard Skylar say, "Mr. Dill is on line 2."

Damson punched the button, leaned back, and put his feet on the desk. "Jimmy, how you doing? Ed Damson here. Have you missed me? Have you been off cooling your heels? Well, it's time to wake up. Is Brock in town?...Yeah, is there any other Brock?...... You think you can get him in a suit and tie by six o'clock?.......What for?........ Hell, ask him if he wants to be President."

Chapter Nineteen

amson had convinced Jimmy Dill that Brock Henry should be at the press conference so that he could be introduced, but had further convinced Dill that Henry should not speak, just smile and wave after he was announced as the Democrat's choice. He emphasized to Dill that time was not available. It was essential that the press conference be short and to the point so that it would make the national evening news, hopefully as the lede. In truth, Damson didn't want Henry speaking off-the-cuff and putting his foot in his mouth. He had made an appointment with Dill for the next morning to discuss Henry's approach to the next few weeks.

After finishing with Dill, Damson had turned to the Goldin tweets. Normally, his philosophy was to ignore them and let the press and the pundits deal with them. They were good at calling lies as they saw them. Unfortunately, the press and the pundits were almost as partisan as the politicians and the American public listened to those with whom they agreed.

He had decided not to deal with the age issue, that Henry was fifteen years younger than Goldin. That he would deal with over the next few weeks.

In the meantime, he had decided to post a press release:

It is with regret that the Democratic Party has learned that one of its candidates for the state legislature in Pennsylvania violated the rules of the election process in falsifying signatures on his petition to run for office. Such behavior clearly violates the principals and spirit of our Party and is not to be tolerated. The National Party would note, however, that the behavior in question had no effect on the national election, affecting only one district in Pennsylvania and that its handling is entirely within the province of the State of Pennsylvania. Further, the candidate lost the election, so it cannot even be said that the man's actions affected his district in any significant way. The man lost as he should have.

With that done, Damson spent the remainder of the day preparing for the press conference. He had to compartmentalize. With one thing done, he forgot about it and moved on to the next.

***

The Shorham Hotel (Omni Shorham) was a bit of an old lady, a little off the beaten path, but Damson loved the ride out through Rock Creek Park. They had called the conference late in the game, trying to keep it from the White House, and even though it was Monday night, many of the hotels hadn't been able, or wished, to set the conference up, especially when they were told to keep it under wraps. The Shorham had come through.

Damson didn't know how the secrecy and the late announcement to the press had worked. The announcement of Henry's selection was certainly no longer a surprise. Elwood Smethers and his staff had been on the phones all afternoon with the state chairs, trying to ensure that they would not be caught off guard and working to obtain their buy-in. The loyal troops couldn't be in the dark at a moment such as this. Damson didn't expect them to remain quiet. Information brought notoriety. Most of the state chairs liked that. They were suddenly nationally important. Damson didn't normally listen to the radio in his car, but he had Bennie tune into WTOP on the way to the hotel. The word was out.

Dominic Rossi met Damson at the hotel entrance and led him quickly to the ballroom which had been cut in half by movable partitions. Rossi brought him around to a side door. He stood and watched the tables fill with members of the DNC leadership. Place holders ensured that everyone sat at the right places.

Damson felt a tap on the shoulder and wheeled around. Rossi followed his motion. Jimmy Dill stood in the doorway with a grinning Brock Henry behind him. Skylar had brought them. She had a look on her face – they're all yours now.

Damson reached past Dill, who tactfully moved to the side, and shook Henry's hand. "Welcome, Brock, it's a good night. Congratulations."

"Damn, Ed, it's about time. I should have won this at the convention – Vickers mealy-mouthed the middle ground, unwilling to commit to what he knew was right. You sure that there's not time for me to speak?"

"No, Brock. We've got to fit the news cycle. Come on, let's get you seated. You're on one side of the podium and I'm on the other."

"Ha, so, you still are splitting off from me."

"Just making sure we're both in the middle of the room. Nothing personal intended."

"Yeah, but you still don't like me?"

"We're putting you at the head of the ticket, aren't we?"

"Your choice or the DNC's choice."

"I'm announcing that you've been chosen, aren't I?"

"As you damn well should."

"Come on."

They headed for the tables, but Henry didn't sit. He went along behind the tables, shaking the hands of all the members of the DNC, some of whom tried not to appear reluctant. Finally, he pulled out his chair, but before he sat, he grinned and waved to the crowd.

All the while, Damson stood at the podium and waited.

Finally, after Henry was seated, the Chair of the DNC spoke, with a fleeting smile. "I guess there's no surprise here."

There was some chuckling from the crowd.

"I'd like to welcome you to this news conference. We're all here with heavy hearts tonight. The sudden death of President-elect Vickers was a shock and a great loss to this Country. As a Nation, we have lost a great leader. President-elect Vickers had received a complete physical check-up only two weeks before the election. He had passed with flying colors.

81

Thus, his death came completely out of the blue. This was a man who had just won the election by over two million votes. He had been given a mandate to restore our nation to its world leadership in supporting democratic institutions and in fighting global warming, Nationally, we all looked forward to his rolling back changes the current government has made, not only with respect to the climate, but also with respect to support for our middle-class citizens, not only in terms of spreading out financial wealth, but also with respect to their health, their jobs, their housing and their education.

As we all know, time is short. The electors who have just been selected in our national election will meet in their respective states on December the 19th to select the President. With the loss of the chosen President-elect, there is suddenly a vacuum in who that will be. The Democratic Party has an obvious choice to fill that void. Brock Henry, one of the nation's foremost Senators, was the close runner-up to John Vickers in the process of selecting the Democratic candidate for the Presidency and is the obvious choice to fill the role. That choice has been communicated to the state party chairmen this afternoon and is receiving their hearty endorsement."

He turned to Henry. "Senator, I would like to congratulate you. You have the support of your Party and the Nation."

Henry stood and waved to the crowd and took a step toward the podium.

Damson quickly turned toward Glore. "Senator Glore would like to make some comments and lend his endorsement of Senator Henry."

Henry stopped after less than two steps, as Glore strode to the podium.

Glore looked at Henry as he sat back down. "Brock, it's your time."

Henry looked a little uncertain.

"Brock Henry for years has supported programs that support the middle class of this country. He has won the respect and support of millions of United States citizens, as clearly demonstrated by the votes he received in the primaries of the past year. His supporters were the most demonstrative during the Democratic National Convention. I have served in the Senate with Brock for many years and have learned to respect him as a great legislator and patriot. I know he will serve this Nation well. I ask the Nation to back him as they would have John Vickers. We have important work to do. Our Democracy must be restored. Brock Henry is the man for the job. Let's get to work."

Damson quickly replaced Glore at the podium. "Thank you for coming today. That's all we have for you. There will be opportunities for questions in the next few days."

All the members of the DNC quickly rose and exited the room, leaving Henry standing by his chair.

Reporters quickly crowded around him.

"Comments, Senator?"

"Where's Governor Grete?"

"Does the Vice President-elect know about this?"

"Does Grete endorse you?"

"Why isn't Governor Grete here?"

Henry felt naked with no members of the DNC behind him.

Suddenly, Dill was whispering in his ear.

He nodded and came to life. He held up his hands for quiet. "We'll be holding a press conference in the next day or two."

Chapter Twenty

Chance poured himself his glass of claret and settle in front of the television.

He had just come in from working with Pete preparing for the auction.

The six o'clock local news had just come on. There was no sign of a press conference. After a commercial, the newscaster announced, "The Democratic National Committee is now holding a news conference. It is being broadcast live on Channel 8. It is announcing...."

Chance cut her off as he switched to news channels. Men and women were standing around or sitting behind two tables. Obviously, the conference hadn't started. He recognized Senator Glore and Speaker Gwently. The people all began taking their seats. The camera panned to a door. Two men were coming in. Chance thought he recognized one but couldn't remember his name. He was followed by Brock Henry. Chance's mouth gaped. *What the hell is he doing there?*

The man Chance couldn't remember stood behind a lectern while Henry went down the line behind the tables shaking hands. Then he stood by his chair, smiled, and waved to the crowd, before he took his seat. Chance winced. *The man's acting like the conquering hero.*

Once Henry was seated, the man at the lectern turned toward the audience of reporters and began speaking. He didn't introduce himself. Chance guessed he thought everyone knew him. It soon became obvious he was some Democratic big wheel.

Brock Henry's name was mentioned. God, my worst fears are coming true.

As it sank in, Chance leaned back, groaned, and shouted. "No...no, no, no!"

Shirley hurried into the room. "Chance, what's wrong. Are you all right?"

"No, I'm not all right. I'll never be all right again."

"What are you talking about? Are you sick?"

"Yeah. The Democratic Party has made Brock Henry its replacement for John Vickers. It's horrible. I want to throw up."

"Chance, it can't be that bad. The Party's got to know what it's doing."

"They're replacing one narcistic loud-mouth with another."

"Vickers was narcistic?"

"No, not Goldin. We won the election. We're replacing Goldin."

"But Henry must believe in Democratic Party principles."

"He's a socialist, Party principles in the extreme."

"Socialist. You mean he's going to take over the railroads, the airlines, the gasoline industry, and have the government run them?"

"No, nothing like that – just medicine, education and the like – free things for the people."

"Is that all bad?"

"Someone has to pay for it."

"Yes, who?"

"You and me."

'Don't we already pay for it?"

"The medical stuff."

"Yes, not everyone has insurance. Who paid for the Covid 19 when it was running wild?"

"We did."

"So, what's changing?"

85

“I think the government just printed money during the virus. They’ll want to balance things now.”

“Well, if there’s no money, will Congress approve what Henry wants to do?”

“I hope not.”

“Yeah, well, what are you going to do? Don’t you have to do what the state party tells you to do? Didn’t you sign a paper saying you would support the party’s candidate?”

“Yeah, but that was Vickers.”

“Really, does his death allow you to ignore your pledge?”

“Let them stop me. I’m phoning Gwen Ellen right now. She doesn’t like Brock Henry either.”

“I thought she was Party-loyal.”

“Jesus, I don’t know. I’ll tell her my thoughts just the same. No way I can vote for Henry.”

Chapter Twenty-One

Damson arrived at his office just before 8:30. Skylar looked up, a little surprised. "Governor Grete just called."

"Lord, isn't it just as early in Annapolis?"

"I don't know. Maybe. Also, Mr. Dill phoned."

"Everyone's up early. What did the Goldin have to say this morning?"

Skylar read from the typed sheet before handing it to Damson:

"Vicker's not even buried – Blockhead Brock to stomp on the grave - sad."

"You see it? Anti-American Dill whispering in Henry's ear - criminal."

"Anti-American?"

"He advised Canada on the American grain industry ten or twelve years ago."

"Yeah, but he was registered, paid his taxes, everything. The Country's already been through this with Dill."

"Goldin has an elephant's memory."

"Wasn't that a *Washington Post* cartoon?"

"Several times. Goldin doesn't care. If he says 'anti-American' ten times, people believe."

"Yeah, well, get Grete on the phone. I thought I'd calmed her down yesterday."

Damson sat at his desk and waited for the phone to ring. There was a knock at the door. "Come in."

Skylar entered carrying a cup of coffee. "Grete's got another call – will phone you back in a moment. Thought you could use this before you took her on."

Damson usually got his own coffee. He didn't believe in being waited on. It wasn't what his staff was for, but he was grateful. "You're a doll, Skylar."

"I keep telling you I'm too old to be a 'doll'. It's not appropriate anyway."

"I keep forgetting."

"Too much on your mind?"

"Yeah, that's my excuse."

Skylar left. He waited. *What can I do while I wait?* His mind wouldn't shift.

The phone buzzed. The usual song and dance. "Governor Grete is on the phone."

"Put her on."

"Ed?"

"Good morning, Jane Meyer. Is that with a hyphen or not?"

"You trying to distract me, Ed?"

"Never. What can I do for you?"

"You went and did it."

"I told you I was going to."

"So, what am I supposed to do? Say I like the man?"

"Just play it cool. Say you'll work with him. Say you know he's a good man."

"He's not."

"Maybe, but don't say it."

"You know you should have picked me. I've got the executive experience."

"Yeah, but you don't know anything about foreign policy."

"Does, Henry? He's not even on a committee that has anything to do with that."

"He's a Senator. All Senators are experts on foreign policy. Hell, they approve treaties. They must know something."

"You're hassling me, Ed."

"No, damn it, Jane Meyer. It's decided, and you're for it. You're a Democrat, and you're going to support the Party. You'll be a good soldier and stand behind Henry when he speaks in the Rose Garden, looking solemn and listening intently."

"Fuck you, Ed."

“You’ll do it, Jane Meyer, because it’s your path to the Presidency.”

“You think I’m that ambitious.”

“Yes, I do.”

“Damn it. You know what’s going to happen. He’ll make me the lead of a committee on every messy problem.”

“And you’ll excel.”

“Again, fuck you, Ed.”

“Say it as many times as you like. Hopefully, it makes you feel better. You’re doing your duty. You’re getting rid of Goldin. Smooth transition, Jane Meyer. Everything’s going to be sunny.”

“I don’t like using this language, but it’s appropriate. Screw you, Ed.”

“Well, there’s some variety in that. Have a good day.”

He hung up. Dill’s next. I’d dial him myself, but the formality gives me some control.

He buzzed Skylar.

“Yes, boss?”

“Please get me, Jimmy Dill, on the phone, Doll?”

“Ed?”

“Boss.”

“Boss?”

“Yes, Skylar.”

“Oh, forget it.”

“Forget what?”

“Anybody said ‘fuck you’ today?”

“Matter of fact, yes. Part of my routine.”

“Okay, Jimmy Dill. Willy, Nilly, Dilly.”

“Skylar, don’t let Goldin hear you.”

“You think he’d like that?”

“Yes, and he’d quote you. Get me, Dill.”

“Yes, sir.”

Damson hung up the phone and waited for the buzz. *My life is spent waiting for the buzz.*

The phone buzzed.

"You got him, Skylar?"

"Line two."

Damson pressed two.

"You there, Jimmy."

"Called you twenty minutes ago."

"Patience, lad. You're not the only one in the queue."

"How come you screwed Brock last night?"

"What do you mean, Jimmy? I gave Henry a grand introduction. The Democratic Leader of the United States Senate did too."

"But you didn't let him speak."

"Time was of the essence, Jimmy. We wanted it on the national news."

"Hell, it was on the national news anyway. Everyone knew about it by three yesterday afternoon."

"True."

"That's all you've got to say."

"Well, it's true."

"So, why the press conference?"

"To give it clout. It was only rumor from the state chairs up till then."

"So, you had a television forum. Brock could have spoken. You talk about clout. You needed to get his image up there – get his agenda up there."

"Jimmy, let's be honest. Brock can tick off people. And his agenda needs to be toned down. We want to get away from the 'Democratic socialist'. You need to make him less radical. You've got to realize that your man is going to be President. He just needs to control himself for a while. Don't let him screw things up. Do you think you can do that, Jimmy? Do you want to be chief of staff? Make your boy behave. Think of the stakes, Jimmy. Think of the stakes."

"You don't have to repeat yourself, Ed."

"You sure, Jimmy? A lot's riding on you, Tonto. My ass. Your ass. The Democratic ass."

"It's a donkey, Ed."

"Not if we screw this thing up."

Chapter Twenty-Two

Chance waited overnight, sleeping little.

The first thing in the morning he phoned Gwen Ellen.

"Damn Chance, this is two days in a row I've had to talk to you before I finished my coffee."

"You're lucky it wasn't last night."

"You don't sound like you're in a good mood, Chance."

"It's not a day to be flippant, Gwen Ellen."

"Jesus, Chance, you'd think the world had ended."

"It damned near has. The stupid DNC has anointed Brock Henry as Vickers's replacement. They're making him the President. Brock Henry, for God's sake! They're replacing one self-centered loudmouth with another. Is this what the Virginia party is supporting? Have we no standards?"

"Stay cool, Chance. I haven't talked to any of the state officers. I'm sure they'll get out the word. Did you listen to the news conference last night?"

"Yeah."

"Well, you heard Damson and Glore. It's announced now. There's no going back. That would be suicide. I'm sure that Richmond is supporting the decision. There's no way for them not to."

"Are you supporting it, Gwen Ellen?"

"Chance, you're asking ridiculous questions. I support the Party. Getting Goldin out of there is what counts."

"Your moral sense is not more important?"

"For goodness sake, Chance, you're blowing this out of proportion. Henry's a Democrat. He believes the same things we do."

"In extremes. In socialistic extremes."

"Health care for everyone, college education for everyone, yes. Government taking over industries, no. Don't use the word socialist. It's not appropriate. It will hurt us. Do you understand that, Chance? It's a dirty word. Not using it starts with us."

"Yeah, well Goldin uses it regularly to describe the Democratic Party. He believes that if you say things enough, people will believe him, and they will believe it's a dirty word."

"Chance, for Lord's sake, Brock Henry's not a socialist. He's liberal."

"Goldin uses that as a dirty word too."

"Yes, I know. The whole Republican Party does."

"Goldin and the Republican Party are synonymous. When I'm talking about one, I'm talking about the other."

"So, you feel strongly – Goldin has to go. We need to get the job done – finish him off. We must be united as a Party to do that. Henry has a lot of supporters. He had a lot of delegates at the convention. He's a natural choice."

"He's a bigoted ass, Gwen Ellen."

"He's the Party's choice, Chance."

"Do you agree that he's a bigoted, loud-mouthed ass?"

"Of course not. He's the Party's choice."

"Are you the same Gwen Ellen I talked to after Henry dropped out at the convention?"

"I'm a Democrat, Chance. I've been loyal for a long, long time. Getting Goldin out of the White House is my primary goal in life. We have to be united to ensure that."

"You've got no conscience?"

Chance heard Gwen Ellen sigh deeply. "What I've got, Chance is purpose."

"It's a sad world, Gwen Ellen."

"It is what it is, Chance. Be seeing you."

She hung up, while Chance still held the phone.

Shirley had been sitting in a chair watching him. "I don't know what you're going to do, sweetheart, but think hard about it."

"Life's short, Shirl."

93

"That's why you need to think about it. Are you going to be tilting with windmills? Is the whole damn thing going to fall on you?"

"More like tilting with Jell-O."

"If there's enough Jell-O, it can hurt you too."

Chapter Twenty-Three

Damson left Reagan National Airport on the same plane as Glore and Gwently. They and others on the plane made him feel conspicuous. Most people in the Country didn't recognize him, although the news conference the night before had increased his prominence. At O'Hare, as he killed time waiting to transfer to a plane for Des Moines, he avoided the airline clubs and decided to settle at a table in one of the fast-food restaurants with a sandwich and soda. There were no tables that weren't occupied. A young couple swept away their wrappings and motioned for him to sit in one of the two vacant chairs at their table. As he unwrapped his sandwich, he felt the woman staring at him. Oh, damn. He brushed some imaginary crumbs off his suit jacket and tried not to look at her.

Finally, she spoke. "Don't I know you from somewhere?"

Damson unwrapped his straw and stuck it in his drink. As he raised the drink to his lips, he spoke under his breath, "I try to be inconspicuous."

The young woman looked incredulous. "By eating in an airport fast food restaurant?"

Her partner put his hand on her arm. "Honey, the man wants to be left alone."

"Hey, I'm just talking to him. Maybe he'll sign an autograph."

Damson smiled. "Do you know who I am?

"No."

"Just a politician from Washington."

"Oh, I thought you were on television."

"Well, occasionally on MSNBC."

"Oh, one of those pundit guys."

"Kind of."

"Oh, well, all I have is a napkin."

"Well, they don't hold up well for autographs."

"No, I guess not."

Damson quickly stuffed the last of his sandwich in his mouth, picked up his drink, looked at the couple as he turned to leave, and said, "You know, some artists draw little pictures on napkins. Software developers write down lines of code. People do all kinds of things. If you get one of those, save it."

He walked off, leaving the couple looking baffled.

***

By the time, Damson was settled in at his hotel in Des Moines; it was nine-thirty. He was tired. Unfortunately, before they left Washington, Glore had suggested that they meet in the hotel bar.

As he entered the bar, he saw Glore sitting in a booth with another gentleman. Damson stopped at the bar and ordered a Scotch while he scanned his mind for the name to Glore's partner. *Oh no, I'm supposed to be good at this. Who the hell is he? Iowa. Goddamn, it's Iowa. Alex? Alex, who? Jones, Johns, Johnson? Johnson, but with a 't'. Johnston, I think. Governor? Call him 'Governor,' with a capital. It's safe.*

He picked up his drink, paid the bartender, fished change from his pocket, threw it in the tip bowl and headed for Glore's table.

Glore and Johns(t?)on tried to stand as they shook Damson's hand but were blocked by the table and awkwardly reseated themselves.

Johns(t)on emoted. "Edison Damson, we finally meet. You do a hell of a job in Washington. About time you got out into the hinterlands. The real US of A."

"I'm pleased to meet you, Governor. I would have been here sooner or later. I'm trying to get around the country to meet everyone. It's just unfortunate there had to be a funeral to get us together."

"Yeah, a hell of a sad day. Vickers was a great man. A great son of the State of Iowa. Would have been a great President. Hell of a loss."

“Indeed, it is.” He looked at Glore. “Anything special I should know about tomorrow?”

“You’re not going to believe this.”

“Oh, what?”

“Goldin is flying in for the funeral. Flying on Air Force one - photoshoot when leaving DC - photoshoot when arriving here. He flew in the cars yesterday. He’ll arrive at the cemetery with a motorcycle escort. If you want to be there, you’ll need to be a half-hour early. The Secret Service is going to arrange the graveside chairs, sit Goldin next to Liz.”

“Christ, does Brock know this? Are you sitting him on the other side of Mrs. Vickers?”

“No, her kids and their wives will be there. Brock wants to sit next to Goldin so he can poke him in the ribs.”

“The Secret Service okay with that?”

“They don’t know about it yet. Brock is just going to walk in and do it. Dare them to make a scene.”

“Doesn’t Brock have Secret Service agents too?”

“Since last night.”

“You think there’ll be a Secret Service war?”

“If there is, it will be on national television.”

“What’s Mrs. Vickers saying about that?”

“Liz is not happy. She thought she had arranged a quiet ceremony.”

“The press coming?”

“Would Goldin have it any other way?”

“He hates the press.”

“Not the photographers.”

“What’s Brock driving?”

“We upgraded him to a Cadillac.”

“Buy America.”

“Always”

“How about you?”

“The Governor and his wife are in another Caddy. Allison and I in a third.”

“Chauffeurs?”

"You bet."

"I'll have to hide my Sentra."

"You're riding with Brock. After last night, you're his face."

"You're kidding? Where's Dill?"

"On his own."

"Does he want a Sentra?"

Chapter Twenty-Four

Damson was amazed at the crowd. Brock Henry's car passed parked cars long before the gravesite came into view. They were waved through. He guessed that three black Cadillacs in a row received special consideration. He wondered about the men waving them through – dark suits, short hair - funeral staff or Secret Service. He suspected the crowd was too big for the funeral staff.

The cars pulled up a couple of hundred feet from the tent-covering that marked the location of the grave. The tent was bigger than any he'd ever seen at a funeral. Men in dark suits opened a path through the crowd. The cars disgorged their dignitaries who proceeded down the lane of dark suits. Damson trailed behind. Suddenly, he was cut off by one of the dark suits. "I'm sorry, this path is just for the Governor and his entourage."

"Hey, that's the newly nominated President of the United States and the Democratic leaders of the Senate and House."

"Yes, I know. And who are you?"

"I'm the Chair of the Democratic National Committee."

"Do you have some ID that says that?"

"I have a driver's license."

"No Press Pass or anything?"

"Uh, no."

"Your name?"

"Edison Damson."

The man shook his head. "I'll have to check."

He folded up his lapel and began to talk.

Damson paid no attention. He was stretching up on his toes, trying to see what was going on. Uh-oh, Jane Meyer Grete is sitting in the front row. Where did she come from? She's sitting in one of two chairs marked with the Presidential Seals! Two of them. She must be sitting in Vice President Stone's seat!

As Damson watched, Brock Henry approached Grete. She rose partway to shake his hand, and the two had some words. Then he motioned with his hands as if telling her to get up. She looked away from him and continued to sit. Henry motioned to one of the men in the dark suits who came over and listened to him. The man then leaned over and talked to Grete. She smiled and shook her head, and the man turned back and spoke to Henry, who threw up his hands and took the seat next to Grete. The other dignitaries took seats further down.

Oh, Lord. It's all on national television, the future President and Vice President butting heads - white against black - shit, shit, shit.

The man who had stopped Damson continued listening to his earbud, holding the palm of his hand toward Damson, telling him to wait. Damson waved him off. "I'll go stand behind the tent."

The man signaled that he understood. He looked relieved.

Just then there was some commotion at the other end of the row of seats. Elizabeth Vickers appeared with her two sons and their wives. Damson had met them at the convention and had spoken to the woman several times during the campaign. She looked uncertain. A black suit, older than the dark suits, with longish, greying hair, led her and pointed to her seat. *Funeral director*. She pointed to the President's seat and said something. The man replied and left to go back down the line. Before Mrs. Vickers could sit, Henry was in front of her offering his hand and saying some words, after which he returned to his seat. Grete leaned across the Presidential chair and spoke to Mrs. Vickers and extended her hand as well. Grete did not leave her seat. Damson shook his head. *The territory is marked.*

Several minutes passed. The burial was scheduled for eleven o'clock. By quarter after, people were getting restless. The hundreds of people standing were shifting their feet. At twenty minutes after, motorcycles could be heard in the distance. Dark suits were hustling everywhere.

The motorcycles roared up to where Damson had been discharged earlier. Damson thought, *Why the hell didn't they stay at the gate, maintain a little solemnity.*

Five black Suburbans pulled up and stopped behind the motorcycles. Dark suits poured out of the last three. Damson rolled his eyes. *Maybe they're afraid someone will steal the body.*

One of the dark suits rushed to the rear door of the second Suburban and opened it. President Goldin eased himself out of the back seat, stood straight, smiled, and raised both hands to the crowd as if in triumph. It almost looked as if he were going to say some words. While Vice President Sidney Stone exited the other side of the car, Goldin's chief of staff, David Osborne, rushed from the first Suburban to join the President just as the funeral director and a Secret Service agent arrived to greet him. After a few words, the funeral director led the group to the chairs. They stood in front of the two chairs with Presidential Seals and looked around at the other chairs, while the seals were being removed. Grete leaned forward to accommodate the removal. After some discussion, the funeral director approached Jane Meyer Grete, who shook her head and pointed to seats down the line. The President did not look happy. He motioned for the Vice President to talk to Grete. Stone didn't understand because he moved past Henry to the next seat where Governor Johnston's wife was sitting. After a moment, she rose and moved to the other side of her husband. Stone sat down in the seat next to Henry. The two didn't greet each other. They didn't even look at each other. Goldin stood for a moment looking at Stone and then disgustedly waved Osborne to a seat at the end of the line.

Damson thought, the now and future leaders of the free world playing ring around the mulberry bush.

All the while, the Vickers family sat and watched the show. The funeral director whispered something to Goldin, who glanced at Mrs. Vickers. He then approached her and stood there for a minute as if expecting her to stand and greet him.

She didn't.

He finally leaned over and took her hand in his two hands and said some words. Finally, she motioned to his chair, and he sat down.

A minister approached the head of the coffin. He was a grey-haired man, late fifties, or early sixties. He said a prayer, welcomed the President and all those who had come to mourn and celebrate the life of John Vickers and admitted he was a little overwhelmed as to how to greet so many dignitaries. He had grown up in Des Moines and had known John and Elizabeth Vickers most of his life. He described them warmly and told several stories. He read from the Bible and gave a final benediction.

As the minister stepped aside, the funeral director stepped forward as if to lead the guests to recognize and give their condolences to the family. Still, before anyone moved, President Goldin was on his feet, followed by the Vice President and headed for the spot where the minister had stood. As soon as the two had stood, Brock Henry was on his feet following them.

As Goldin reached the spot where he planned to stand, the Vice President passed him and moved to a position where he would be to the right rear of the President. He took an erect stance, standing as if providing his firm support for the leader of the free world. He was serious, sad, and stone-faced.

Goldin turned to face the grave and was startled when Henry passed him and turned to stand behind his left shoulder. Goldin momentarily looked uncertain, but then began to speak. "My fellow citizens...."

Damn, thought Damson in a flash, what's wrong with 'Ladies and Gentlemen". Save "my fellow citizens" for White House briefings. You're not the boss here.

"We are here today to honor John Vickers, my opponent in this year's recent Presidential Election. John was certainly a strong opponent and an honorable man. During the Presidential campaign, I listened to what he said and even agreed with some of it, although he was clearly off base in some of his beliefs. He needed to learn. Unfortunately, the Democratic Party, in selecting him as their candidate, didn't understand the stress that a campaign puts on a man, especially one as senior as John Vickers. So sad. There are some of us who can take it and others who can't. His death is a real tragedy, from which we all should learn. Despite his heart problems, he nonetheless ran a strong campaign, a campaign we all still wish to see concluded. Time will tell."

Twice, during the time Goldin spoke, he rolled his eyes and glanced back at Henry who at one time approached within inches of the President's left shoulder. Interestingly enough, the Vice President had looked straight forward the whole time, as if refusing to give Henry any credence.

When Goldin finished, he headed back down the line of chairs with Stone on his tail. He passed the Vickers family and the gang of Democrats, finally coming to his chief of staff, who pointed at Mrs. Vickers. Goldin looked back, hunched his shoulders as if to dismiss the comment, and proceeded toward his Suburban, a trail of dark suits following him.

Henry shouted after him, "Whoa, Mr. President. I've got some words to say."

Goldin acted like he didn't hear Henry. Maybe he didn't. He was moving with firm steps. He didn't look happy. A dark suit opened his car door, and he climbed in while the motorcycles roared to life. The Vice President ran to the other side of the vehicle as if he were afraid of being left behind. Then Osborne and a contingent of dark suits moved just as quickly to the other black Suburbans. The vehicles' doors were barely closed as the convoy drove off.

Two white Suburbans, which had arrived during the ceremony, were left behind. The remaining dark suits climbed in the vehicles, and they drove off.

Brock Henry announced, "There goes the leader of the free world."

All the heads that had been turned to watch the spectacle of the President's departure, turned back to Brock Henry who looked them over. "The dark suits are gone. Your security is gone. The public is free to come. But have no fear. As of last night, I have Secret Service agents assigned. They caught up with me an hour ago. Chris DeJohn and Juan Hernandez are standing behind the last row of seats. Wave to the crowd guys." Henry extended his hand to the agents. "Glad to have you with us."

He turned back to the crowd. "Did you hear the man? John Vickers whipped him badly. John Vickers did the job. Still, it appears that Goldin doesn't know it – refuses to see it. Maybe his staff is afraid to tell him. They shouldn't be afraid. What does matter if they're fired today? They only have a couple of months left anyway.

Still, it sounds like he's got something up his sleeve. You think so? I do. Maybe he's going to use the courts. He owns them. He doesn't mind making them laughing stocks. Wait and see. Are we waiting with bated breath? Does anyone know what 'bated' mean? All I know is that I'm not 'bated'. Oh, hum, let's wait and see.

Ladies and gentlemen, have we forgotten that we're at a funeral today? We're here to remember a great man, President-elect John Vickers, a man who has made history but sadly will never reap the reward he deserves. It was a quiet, dignified ceremony, a ceremony to be celebrated by family and friends. His family chose not to have John rest in the state in the National Capitol or to be taken to his resting place with horse-drawn caissons. They brought him home. He deserves the dignity they sought."

He looked down at the coffin. "Rest in peace, John. You did well."

Henry walked back toward the seats, stopping before each member of the Vickers family, shaking their hands, and saying a few words. The other Democrats rose from their chairs and joined the line, Jane Meyer leading the way.

Henry stopped before Elizabeth Vickers and took her hand. "I'm sorry, Elizabeth. I tend to be a bit daring. I can't match Goldin, but I get carried away sometimes. As I said, I'm sorry – sorry that I took so long to get this service back on track. John was a fine man. I'm so sorry for your loss – for the nation's loss." He patted her hand. "God bless you."

He released her hand.

She looked him in the eye. "Thank you, Brock. Do the job he would have."

"God, woman, you ask a lot."

He walked off, looking over the crowd. Chris DeJohn, his Secret Service agent, was suddenly beside him. The agent leaned towards Henry's ear to be heard above the crowd. "Agent Hernandez is pulling up your car, Senator."

"What happened to the chauffeur?"

"He's riding in one of the other cars, sir."

"Okay."

This all made Henry a little uncertain. He wasn't accustomed to his life feeling quite this controlled.

He kept looking around.

DeJohn asked, "Are you looking for someone, Senator?"

"I'm looking for Damson. He's riding with me."

"Damson? Who's Damson?"

Henry chuckled. "Chairman of the DNC."

"DNC? Democratic something?"

"...National Committee. There he is."

Henry and DeJohn stood still while Damson approached.

Henry introduced him to the agent. "How'd I do Ed?"

"Uh, maybe a little strong."

"Over the top.?"

"A little."

"Yeah, I do that."

DeJohn rolled his eyes and looked nervous.

As they walked toward the car, Henry burst out laughing. "Did you see me intimidate Goldin?"

"When you stood behind him?"

"Yeah, the same as he did to Vickers during the debates. Poor John was only five-nine. I'm six-three. Hopefully, Goldin learned the difference."

"Don't know about the intimidation, but you certainly ticked him off."

"Made him angry, huh? Good."

As they approached the Cadillac, a Hispanic man in a suit held the door open for Henry, who turned to Damson, "Agent Juan Hernandez."

Damson reached out to shake the hand of the agent, who was momentarily flustered trying to shake hands and hold the door at the same time.

Damson asked, "Where's the chauffeur?"
Henry replied as he settled himself in the back seat, "He didn't carry a gun."

Damson thought, *Oh,* as the car door was closed. He hurried around the back of the car while Hernandez went around the front and DeJohn settled himself in the front passenger seat.
Damson shook his head. We look like a bunch of circus clowns. Wonder if we were on television. I forgot to track the cameras.

Henry fastened his seat belt and settled himself into his seat. "What's with this Jane Meyer Grete?"

"You have words with her."

"Nah, she was fairly pleasant. Smiled and said the right words but wasn't about to move her black ass out of that chair."
Damson motioned to catch Henry's attention and pointed at the Secret Service agents.

Henry looked at the agents and back at Damson. "Ah, don't worry."

He tapped DeJohn on the shoulder. "You guys don't talk, do you?"

"No, sir."

"Well, if you do, I'll know about it."

He turned back to Damson, "So, what's with her?   I wanted to sit there and give Goldin a hard time.   Ended up sitting between Grete and Stone."

"I hate to tell you Brock, but it looked like you were in pain the whole time. It looked like you were ignoring them both."

"Hell, I just wanted to ignore Stoney-face Stone.

"Well, it didn't look good. Grete's going to be your Vice President. You needed to be friendly."

"She took my damn seat."

"Nonetheless, you need to be friends. You've met her before, haven't you?"

"No. I haven't met many Governors. Today was the first time I met Johnston."

With a "t", thought Damson. "Well, you're going to get to know Grete well. You've got four years of her coming up."

"Yeah, I'll just have to make sure she knows who's President."

Damson decided to change the subject. "Do you think Goldin is in the air yet?"

"If he were, he would have buzzed the cemetery. Nah, he's sleeping or playing golf."

Damson was surprised. "He's still in town?"

"Yeah, he's got one of his rallies at the Wells Fargo Arena late this afternoon."

"You mean the burial wasn't enough? Doesn't he know the election is over?"

"No, you heard him today. Something's in the works, and there are never too many photo ops."

"I guess you do them where you find them."

"No, Ed, you do them where you make them."

Chapter Twenty-Five

Chance watched the funeral on the television in his living room. Shirley had said it was too sad and hadn't joined him.

Halfway through the ceremony, he decided that the television coverage was having a field day. Where the hell is dignity? Where is respect? Where is simple decency? Goldin is being his usual asinine self, putting on a show. What else could we expect? I can picture Goldin supporters sitting at bars across the nation, laughing and guffawing, their hopes for the future being reignited.

And Henry is not far behind. I'm glad to see he seemed to show some reserve toward the end.

And Jane Meyer Grete? – no spectacle there. Smiled and acted friendly. Didn't kowtow to Henry. Held her ground. As Vice President, she won't be like Stone - her own woman.

The cameras followed Henry's Cadillac drive away and then a commercial came on, four commercials as it turned out.

Chance shook his head. What happened to the family? Did someone throw some soil onto the casket? What happened to Senator Glore and all the dignitaries? Maybe they'll show us after the commercials.

The commercials ended, and a newscaster came on. He introduced four contributors, pundits, or whatever they were. They began discussing the funeral.

Chance flicked off the television, stood up and walked through the kitchen on his way to the back door where his coat and hat were hanging on hooks.

Shirley asked if the funeral was over.

"Elizabeth Vickers may still be sitting there, for all I know."

"What does that mean?"

"They cut to commercials."

"Before it was over?"

"The show was over. Goldin and Henry had left."

"Henry was as bad as Goldin?"

Chance was putting on his coat. "Nobody's as bad as Goldin, but Henry tries."

"Where are you going?"

"To the newspaper office, to see Jason."

"To talk about voting for Henry?"

"To talk about voting for Grete."

"Oh, Lord, Chance. Are you sure?"

***

Chance pulled into the narrow, gravel parking lot in front of the small newspaper building, the front of his car almost touching the building. He avoided parking in front of the entrance door. The paper's secretary, administrator or whatever, Belle Wilson, had given him hell about that once and he liked to say he was a fast learner.

He sat for a moment, gripping the steering wheel, and staring at its center. He shook himself, turned off the ignition, put on the parking brake, and stepped out. He zipped up his jacket to the neck, shivered, and entered the newspaper office. Wilson looked up. "Chance."

"Hey, Belle Weather. You have any hot news today?"

"You mean news to come. You are going to give me some, Chance."

"Maybe Jason will give you something after I leave."

"By then, it will be in print. You know as well as I that you're going to sitting eight feet from me with the door opened. Stories change when they're repeated, and we don't want that."

"Is Jason in?"

"You can see him through the door."

"So, I can."

Jason's voice came from the office, "Chance, come on in. Haven't heard from you since Gwen Ellen picked you to be an elector."

"The District picked me."

"Because Gwen Ellen recommended you."

"Whatever."

"You're talking like your kids do. Are you about to do something foolish?"

"I can't vote for Brock Henry."

"Can't? That means you've broken your arm and can't raise a pencil?"

"It means I won't."

"As in you're not voting at all or you're voting for someone else. I need the whole story."

"I'm going to vote for Jane Meyer Grete."

"Christ, Chance. Did you see her at the funeral? She told Henry to bug off – wouldn't give up that seat to Jesus if he'd been there. Don't the Democrats need a team?"

"I don't like Brock Henry, and she doesn't either. She held her ground against him."

"And the fool let her."

"Yeah, maybe he's smarter than I give him credit for."

"So, why do you think Grete is better?"

"Fundamentally, she's not a clown."

"The Country likes a clown. They want to be entertained."

"They want to be governed."

"Says who? Goldin is constantly in the papers, on television. He's always saying something, some of which his true. Isn't that governing?"

"No, but Henry's going to do the same damn thing – at least kind of."

"And Grete's not?"

"No. She's stable, middle of the road. She doesn't make promises she can't fulfill."

"Yeah, well, I don't remember her making any promises. She followed Vickers's lead. Mainly, they both attacked Goldin."

"As they should have. Plenty of fodder there."

"Not if you're a true believer."

"Goldin is not a religion, Jace."

"Yeah, since when? You probably believe that his backers are all 'deplorable'."

"Aren't they?"

"No. Lots of them just wouldn't vote for a Republican under any circumstances – no liberals, thank you. No one is giving away their tax dollars."

"Didn't come here to argue politics, Jace. Just want the county to know what I'm going to do."

"Yeah, well I'll put it in the paper. Do you think our citizens will hold a parade for you? Not going to happen, Chance. People don't know how to handle renegades. Don't know if they can trust them. Do you want to think about that before I put it out? I've got till four o'clock this afternoon.

"No. I've thought about it. Maybe don't use Grete's name. Just say someone else."

"Does Gwen Ellen know?"

"No."

"Better tell her. The shit's going to land on her."

✱✱✱

Chance returned to his Explorer and sat in the driver's seat. He picked up his cell phone and looked at it and thought, If I were at the farm, this phone wouldn't work, and I'd have an excuse, but it works in Town thanks to the Lodge and its important guests. Hell, I kind of hinted to Gwen Ellen the other day that I don't like Brock Henry. It shouldn't be a surprise.

111

He continued to sit, looking at the phone. *If I don't have her phone number, I can't call.* He opened his list of phone numbers. There they were, her home number and her cell number. *Maybe she's not home.* He took a deep breath, let it out, and tapped Gwen Ellen's home phone number.

"Gwen Ellen speaking."

Damn, she's home.

"Chance here, Gwen Ellen."

"Oh, hi Chance, have you gotten down the election signs yet. In all the commotion, I forgot to remind you."

"Uh, no. I took down a few."

"A few? What does that mean?"

"I took down the ones on the road out toward my farm."

"That's only a couple of dozen."

"Fourteen."

"Oh, damn, Chance. Everyone's going to be hounding me."

"Maybe you could take down the ones on the road out to your place?"

"Yeah, okay, but that's a drop in the bucket. Do you think you and Marvin can get the rest?

"Yeah. I'll talk to Marvin. Maybe we can do it this weekend. Gwen Ellen, I'm not going to vote for Brock Henry."

There was silence for a moment. "We were talking about signs."

"Yeah, but I changed the subject. I didn't call about signs."

"What are you talking about, Chance? I know you don't like Henry. You told me that. But you have to vote for him."

"I don't like him."

"You signed a paper that as an elector, you would support the Party's candidate."

"That was a slate of John Vickers and Jane Meyer Grete. I'll vote for Grete."

"No, you pledged that you would vote for the Party's candidate. Any candidate. For whomever the Democratic Party of Virginia says is the candidate."

"The Constitution doesn't say that."

"The Constitution leaves it up to the states."

So, the State is going to sue me?"

"Maybe."

"But the Party's not the state. The Constitution says the state is responsible. Besides, I haven't violated what I signed."

"You said you were going to."

"But I haven't done it."

"But you're going to?"

"I'll think about it."

"Who else knows?"

"The Pierce County Observer."

"Jason?"

"I'm parked outside his office now."

"Oh, damn. Hang up. I'll phone Jace now."

Chapter Twenty-Six

Damson took an Uber home from Dulles. He threw his coat on the back of his sofa and glanced at the telephone. It had messages. *Tomorrow and tomorrow. They can wait.*

He pulled his cell phone from his pocket. He had turned it off while flying. He turned It on. It also had messages.

No rest for the weary.

As he held the cell phone, it rang. He jerked as if he had been bitten. He held it for a moment, hesitating. He wasn't in the air anymore. He didn't have an excuse.

His thumb responded almost by reflex, and he held the phone to his ear.

"Damson, where the hell have you been?"

"I'm sorry. Who is this?"

"James Cosgrove, U. S. Senator from New York."

"Yes, Senator, I know who you are."

"Damn it, I've phoned you half a dozen times. Your phones are full up. You need to be available."

"Yes sir, I'm sorry. I was flying back from the funeral."

"The funeral is a goddamn problem."

"The problem?"

"You lost control of it."

"I lost control?"

"Yes, that damned Vice President of yours."

"Stone?"

"No, damn it. Stone's not yours. He's a damn Republican."

"Yes sir, I know. Are you talking about Jane Meyer Grete?"

"Of course. Have you got any other Vice President?"

"No, Sir."

"Well, she's the news. Haven't you been watching television?"

"No, sir. I've been on an airplane."

"Don't they have news on airplanes?"

"I'm sorry. I read the book."

"Damn it, Damson, stuff the books. I've been calling Glore. I've been calling Gwently. Nobody answers. The whole Party's without leadership."

"Sir, they were flying too. What's happened? What did Jane Meyer do?"

"Weren't you at the funeral?"

"Yes, sir."

"Didn't you see her stiff-arm, Brock Henry?"

"Uh, stiff-arm?"

"Not give him her seat."

"Yeah, I saw that."

"And you didn't do anything about it?"

"Sir, I wasn't among the people in the front row."

"You didn't see her half rise and shake Brock's hand and then plop her ass back down?"

"Yes, sir. Henry took the next seat."

"The Vice-President-elect wouldn't give her seat to the next President of the United States. It's news, Damson – lousy news, bad news."

"Because Henry took the next seat."

"No, because she demeaned him."

"Sir, it just seemed like a momentary thing."

"Not to the newscasters, not to the pundits. It's all they're talking about."

"Not Goldin grandstanding? Not Henry's speech?"

"Nah, Goldin is an old hat. He got twenty seconds, rally, and all. Bet he's angry. No, the news was all about Grete. About her sitting in a Presidential seat. About her blowing off Henry when they are supposed to be the new team in town - supposed to be working together."

"How do you know she blew him off?"

"The networks found themselves some lip readers. Seems Henry was asking her to move. Henry couldn't believe she wouldn't move. He called her a bitch."

"God, what did she say?"

"Her back was to the camera."

"So, we don't know?"

"No, but the conjectures are running wild. What we know is that she plopped her ass back down."

"So, what do you expect me to do, Senator?"

"Straighten out your goddamn Vice President. Get her on board. Change the scenario. Get the Party on track. That's your damn job."

Cosgrove hung up.

Damson slowly withdrew his cell phone from his ear and sighed deeply.

He lay it on the kitchen counter, went to a cabinet, and took out a bottle of Cutty Sark. Damn, I'll have to stay up and watch the eleven o'clock news. Thank Goodness, Henry didn't call her a 'black' bitch.

Chapter Twenty-Seven

The next morning Damson was late getting into his car. "Sorry to keep you waiting, Bennie. I needed to watch the morning shows."

"Bad news, boss?"

"You watch the news?"

"Yeah, enough said."

"Right, you should hear Fox. It's not pretty."

"I can imagine."

Damson plopped his newspapers on the seat. He had scanned them, but, as always, he couldn't read them in the car. *Maybe just as well. I'll close my eyes for a moment.*

As he passed Skylar's desk, she handed him his usual sheet of paper.

"So, what does Goldin say today?"

"Multiple tweets:

"Received a warm welcome at the funeral – felt the love;"

"Rally at Wells Fargo Arena great success – my support continues – invigorating;"

"Dems in chaos – leaders not talking to each other – tragic spectacle – more to come;"

"He called her a B... - she earned it – appropriate? -you betcha."

"Get her on the phone."

"Grete?"

"Subject of the day."

He closed the door of his office, plopped his briefcase on the floor, loosened his necktie, sat at his desk, and waited for the buzz.

It came and he connected to Grete. Her voice was warm and friendly. "Good morning, Ed. I hope things are well with you."

"Jane Meyer, you know they're not. I know you've seen the papers, heard the news. You don't live in a gopher hole."

"No, and it's not a black pit either, and I emphasize the 'black'. As a matter of fact, it's a rather nice house in Annapolis. Government House, the Governor's Mansion. I really enjoy it. And Ed, please call me Meyer. Jane Meyer is my public persona."

"' Meyer", huh? I'm sure the Governor's Mansion is nice, but you'll be moving into Number One Observatory Circle in two months. It's rather nice too."

"I'm looking forward to it. The White House would have been nicer."

"Meyer, you didn't win the primaries. You weren't selected by the delegates at the convention."

"I know, but John Vickers picked me. If he died on 21 January next year, I'd be President. The DNC should have picked me, not a buffoon like Brock Henry."

"We've already talked about this, Meyer. What is, is."

"I heard you before, Ed. But when someone is an arrogant bastard, you have to respond."

"Not if you have a role to play."

"Is that what it is – a role? I have to be an obsequious stoney-face?"

"No, you have to be Jane Meyer Grete, the woman Vickers picked."

"I can't just be Meyer? I can't be smart, but smiley at the same time?"

"Of course, you can be smiley and pleasant."

"Pleasant, huh? Doesn't sound like fun."

"You can't be Vice President to be fun. It doesn't work that way. It's a serious business. You're a leader of the nation."

"But not THE LEADER. Just a shadow in the background."

"It's what you make it, Meyer. It's what you make it. But you can't make it if you're butting heads with the President."

"So, I'm his bitch and I've got to be a pleasant bitch."

"That was unfortunate."

"More than unfortunate, Ed. If he does it again, I'll sit again."

"Okay, I understand."

"You'll talk to him?"

"Part of the job."

"Good, be clear. Make sure you get through his thick skull."

"Then you'll play the part?"

"My role, yeah. The heroine of the Party."

Chapter Twenty-Eight

The alarms by the gate set off the buzzer in the house.

After a couple of minutes, there was a loud pounding on the kitchen door. Chance almost spilled his coffee. Shirley opened the door as quickly as she could. "Lord, I thought the Sheriff was raiding us."

Gwen Ellen burst into the room. "Damn Sheriff only has four bulletproof vests. Works from her car with a megaphone. I charge in. Where is he?"

"The Sheriff?"

"No, Chance."

Shirley knew what was coming. "Dining room."

Gwen Ellen whirled and barreled into the dining room and leaned across the table to be in Chance's space.

Chance tried to look innocent. "Morning, Gwen Ellen. Coffee?"

She threw a copy of the morning's Pierce County Observer on the table. "Have you seen this?"

"Today's paper. Comes in the mail around noon. How'd you get a copy?"

"Got it at the Fast Stop."

"Gosh, you must have been there when the papers came in."

"Had to. I knew I was going to get all kinds of crap. Wanted to be prepared."

"Heck. Only the locals know you're the party chair for the County. Come-lately doesn't know anything."

"Locals are bad enough. They're going to hassle me for weeks."

"Hey, you knew it was coming. I gave you a heads up. You tried to cut It off. Didn't work. What about coffee? Shirley's waiting to pour it."

"No damn coffee."

"It's good."

"Damn it, Chance. What are we going to do about this?"

Chance shook his head woefully. "Gwen Ellen, I told you I can't stand Brock Henry. Heck, you can't either."

"I back the Party, Chance. You should too."

Chance sighed. "I've backed the Party for forty-some-odd years, Gwen Ellen. Really voted for some sad candidates. Fortunately, the Republicans haven't been any better. Politicians get rammed down our throats, qualified or not. I can't swallow Brock Henry, simple as that."

"Damn, Chance, I told you that you signed a document to support the Party candidate."

"And I told you I haven't voted yet."

"So, the Party can't sue you."

"They have to have something to sue me about. Don't think an elector has ever been sued."

"You want to be the first?"

"Told you, Gwen Ellen, I have to do something that you can sue me about."

"Not me. The Party."

"Yeah, same story."

"So, no one can sue you until after you cast your vote as an elector?"

"I guess. I'm no lawyer."

"This could go to the Supreme Court."

"Ha, as if it would ever get that far. I'll surrender before that."

"So, you'd just be trying to make a point?"

"Sure. It's no big deal. The Party will still have 271 Electoral Votes. That's all they need. Mine is just icing on the cake."

"What if someone else doesn't vote for Henry?"

Chance chuckled. "Then, I guess you've got a problem."

"Not me – the Party. I've already got a problem - you."

"Well, I'm sorry about that. We don't need another Goldin."

"Good Lord, Chance. Brock Henry's no I. Am. Goldin."

"Thank Heaven, no one is, but Henry does his best."

"Maybe that's what we need. Black thunder against lightning."

"So, Henry is lightning?"

"Damn, Chance, you know what I mean."

"You're being rude, Gwen Ellen."

"What?"

"Shirley's still standing in the doorway. Sit down and she'll pour you that coffee. I can add Irish whiskey if it will help." He pointed at Gwen Ellen's copy of the Pierce County Observer lying on the table. You mind? I need to see if it's as bad as you say."

Shirley sniggered. "Just listening, but the coffee is available."

Gwen Ellen looked beseechingly at Shirley. "Shirley, do something. You're going to catch it too."

"I know. I talked to him – warned him. You know Chance. I'll shelter in place, take the phone off. Done it before."

"That was the damn virus."

“Hope it’s not as bad as that.”

Gwen Ellen sighed. “No coffee but thank you. I’ve got to go call Bill Hastings.”

“Who’s that?”

Chance answered, “The state party chairman.”

Shirley turned back to Gwen Ellen. “We feel for you.”

“Chance, too?”

Shirley glanced at Chance, who sighed, and then back at Gwen Ellen. “Yeah, believe it or not, he does.”

Chapter Twenty-Nine

The dereliction of Chance FitzBourne was known at the Headquarters of the Democratic National Committee by ten o’clock Thursday morning. It was public knowledge and addressed widely on the various media platforms by eleven.

Damson received a phone call from Brock Henry shortly before eleven. “Christ, Ed, what’s going on? I thought you had the Party under control, that I was a shoo-in for the Presidency. How many idiots are out there? We only have two Electoral Votes to play with.”

“Stay cool, Brock. We’re working on the guy. The state chairs are working it. We’ll have him straightened out pronto.”

"God, you'd better. Others could follow. Screw up everything."

"Hey, not to worry. We're canvassing all the states. So far your support is solid."

"I hope so. I hope you guys on the Committee know what the hell you're doing. This is a tight schedule. If you screw up, we may not have time to recover."

"Works two ways, Brock. You need to be out there acting Presidential, on the networks, in the papers. We've got you on three Sunday morning shows this weekend. Be confident and Presidential, but don't overdo it."

"Overdo it. What does that mean?"

"Don't be cocky, watch the language, don't be superior. Be sincere. Be honest. Be American."

"Shit, aren't I always."

"Damn, Brock, just behave."

"Always, Ed. No worries about me. You're the one who needs to worry."

***

The calls continued to pour in starting a few minutes after Damson spoke to Henry. Skylar worked hard to screen the calls, but Glore, Gwently, and other senior legislators had precedence. Damson had to handle them, had to assure them that things were under control. He hoped he was convincing.

Early in the afternoon, he called Elwood Smethers and Darlene Meletta to his office. They came with notes in hand, randomly assembled, not in folders or notebooks. Damson studied them dubiously. "Sit down and tell me about the convention. Where does it stand?"

Smethers fingered through his notes. "We've booked part of the Washington Convention Center for six-hundred people, November 28th."

"November 28th? God, three weeks. Why can't we do it next week?"

"There's an auto show."

"Damn, isn't there a big hotel or something?"

"They're booked. This is short notice. We're lucky to have the Convention Center with hotels across the street. We've blocked out three-hundred and fifty rooms, two hundred across the street, and the rest at other hotels within a few blocks."

Meletta interjected, "Ed, we have to give everyone a chance to plan their trips, get their lives organized. The invitations are just going out. This weekend was just too soon and, as Elwood said, there's an auto show next week."

"When do the invitations go out?"

"Er, tomorrow."

"So, it's not too late to change the date?"

"No, but...."

"So, what about the week after the auto show."

"Thanksgiving, Ed. The hotels are booked, and no one will want to travel.

"Shit!"

"Sorry, Ed. It's the best we can do."

"Guys, we need to solidify the votes."

Elwood, remorsefully, said, "What can we do, Ed?"

"Prepare to travel. Everyone on the Committee is going out to the states - gather the electors together and talk to them. You two give everyone a heads up and put together a travel plan, get the states ready, etc."

"Are you traveling, Ed?"

"Yeah, definitely. Everyone travels except our attorney, Sean O'Rourke."

"Glore and Gwently?"

"Uh, see if they're willing. Big guns will help. Put Glore on Virginia."

Chapter Thirty

By the next afternoon, Shirley had taken the phone off the hook, unplugged it from the wall outlet, and removed the SIM card from her cell phone. She had stuffed the cell phone in a bureau drawer, not wanting to see it again.

When Chance came in from working with his stock just before lunch, she was waiting. "You left me all alone with the telephone, Chance. Why aren't they calling you? It's been going on since the paper came out and today it's gotten wild. Yesterday it was locals. Now it's calls from all over, politicians, reporters, and nuts. You know what, Chance, we're being threatened. I never had any idea. People are crazy. Why aren't they calling you?"

"I pulled my SIM card last night."

"Well, thank you. Dumped it on me, did you?"

"Didn't you pull your card?"

"Yeah, after a while. Tried not to answer, but it became a steady ring. Maybe we should put in call waiting and never answer. It would at least make them wait on the phone – get what they deserve."

Chance began to feel guilty. "I'm sorry Shirl. I thought I had a right to say and do what I believe. It doesn't hurt anything. The Party has votes to spare. I didn't think it was national news. Heck, I'm not much of anybody. It seemed simple – my little protest."

"Well, early on I answered some of the calls when I recognized the caller ID. Lizbeth Harlowe called and thought what you had done was fabulous – a real lark. She said you had really stuck it to the Party."

"Yeah, she said that?"

"Thought it was a real joke."

"You know Lisbeth and Johnson are Republicans?"

Shirley drew in her breath. "So, what she said wasn't praise. Maybe a little sarcasm."

"Maybe, but I expect she was having a real laugh. Who else called?"

"Gary Winter."

"From Town?"

"Said he always liked you, but that you've let the elector business go to your head."

"To my head? That's crazy. I just don't care for Brock Henry. What's the big deal?"

"Well, Winter didn't think so. He thought you were looking for publicity, just playing things up."

"So, the Democrats are unhappy with me and the Republicans are happy with me?"

"You think the Republicans are pleased because Lizbeth Harlowe called."

"No, I think so because there are pickets at the gate with signs supporting me."

"Supporting you?"

"Yeah, Billie Joiner and some of his friends."

"Billie Joiner? Who's he?"

"The fellow down on the Valley Road who has the sign by his gate that says, 'Farmers for Goldin'."

"So, that's not good?"

"No, there are photographers there, even a television crew. And Joiner is posing under our sign."

"'Wood Fern Farm' with 'Chance FitzBourne' below it?"

"Right."

"At least your name is in small letters."

"Not small enough."

***

There was a knock on the kitchen door about five-thirty in the evening. The door opened before Chance could rise from the chair in the living room where he was sitting with Shirley. Junior came in through the kitchen and found them.

"Dad, what are you doing?"

"You know what I'm doing. I'm simply saying I don't like Brock Henry."

"But he's the President-elect."

"No, he's not. He's the President-appointed or President-designated or whatever, but no one elected him."

"It doesn't matter. He's going to be President."

"Yeah, looks that way, and we'll live with him, but I still have to make my little protest."

"You're spitting into the wind, Dad. It's a fight you can't win."

"Not planning to win. Just making a little protest. How come you waited a day to come? The news was out yesterday."

"Kids didn't get to Chip and Jen until today in school after they listened to their parents last night."

127

“The kids said bad things to them at school.”

“Generally said you were crazy and senile.”

“Senile, huh. Didn’t know senile people could think for themselves.”

“It’s a word, Dad. A derogatory word. Kids are mimicking their parents. They think you’ve gone off the deep end.”

Chance sighed. “Well, I’m sorry. Don’t mean to hurt Chip and Jen, but they’ll survive. Things like this don’t last. When Henry becomes President, everyone will forget.”

“God, I hope so. I’m staying out of town for a while.”

“You too?”

“Probably until Henry becomes President.”

“That’s silly.”

“Yeah, well I felt silly when those guys at the gate cheered me and pounded on my truck.”

Chapter Thirty-One

Chance responded to the knock Saturday morning. The gate alarm had buzzed, and he was waiting. Gwen Ellen was on the stoop outside the kitchen door with her back to him. She turned and looked sullenly at him. “Get your coat, Chance. We’re going to Richmond.”

“What are you talking about, Gwen Ellen? I haven’t even had my coffee.”

“Fill up your damn Nationals traveling cup and let’s get going.

"What the hell, Gwen Ellen. What's going on?"

"Bill Hastings phoned and told me to get myself down there."

"The state chairman?"

"Yeah, not quite in the polite terms I just used."

"What's that got to do with me?"

"It's for a meeting of the electors."

"You're not an elector."

"Yeah, but you are, and they think I'm responsible for you."

"But it's Saturday."

"Don't I know it, Chance. Get your damn coat."

"But can't you just go and take care of what's bothering them?"

"Chance wake up.   You know what's bothering them and I sure as hell am not going without you."

"Lord, because I said I wouldn't vote for Brock Henry. What's the big deal?"

"The big deal is that you've fractured the party. They're afraid Humpty Dumpty is falling and will never be put back together again."

"Heck, Gwen Ellen, I'm just one vote. We have two to spare."

"Yeah, but you're leading a rebellion. They're afraid you'll have followers."

"Gwen Ellen, I'm not leading anything. I'm just taking care of my cattle, staying out of sight."

Gwen Ellen stomped her foot. "Damn it, Chance, say goodbye to Shirley, get your coffee and coat, and let's go."

"Damn it, Gwen Ellen, ..."

"Damn it, nothing. You created this mess and I'll be damned if I'm going to face it alone."

"Geez, okay. Seems damned stupid to me.

***

They went in the back entrance of the Jefferson Hotel and up the grand staircase to the lobby. Gwen Ellen went to the desk and inquired as to where the meeting was. When they got to the meeting room, Gwen Ellen pushed Chance forward through the door. Inside, she slipped to the side. Suddenly, Chance felt bare. He saw someone notice him and whisper to his neighbor. In a moment, everyone was looking, and a low hissing began.

Bill Hastings rose from a chair in the front of the room. He didn't hush the hissing but effectively did so by beginning to speak.

Chance quickly took a seat, being careful not to look at the woman sitting next to him. *Where the hell is Gwen Ellen?*

Suddenly he realized that Hasting was speaking. "…. a unified party is essential at this moment in history. The continuation of the Goldin Presidency will be a disaster for our Country, for our Democracy, for the survival of the Constitution. The solidarity of the Democratic Party in our fight to restore our County is so essential that the Democratic Leader of the United States Senate, Senator Everett Glore, has journeyed here today from Washington to address us." Hasting held out his hand to someone in the front row. "Welcome, Senator Glore."

A graying, slightly balding, dignified, and obviously self-confident gentleman rose from the front row and turned to face the gathering. He looked around at the various attendees and his eyes finally rested on Chance. "Thank you, Bill."

Why the hell didn't he look at Hastings while he was thanking him?"

Glore looked about the crowd more generally. "Ladies and gentlemen, I very much appreciate your taking time from your busy schedules to join us at this meeting. Today, we are all Democrats, locked in a mortal battle to save our Country. The solidarity you are showing today is a recognition of the imperative that binds us. I commend you for recognizing the place you occupy in the history of this Country - in the history of the World."

While he spoke, he eased down the aisle until he was standing next to Chance, who wouldn't look up. Chance could feel the Senator's eyes boring into the top of his head.

The Senator continued. "You are the posterity of this great nation – men and woman who will always be remembered." He lifted his hands to the crowd as if he were a preacher beseeching his congregation. "We're going to vote as one for Brock Henry. Let's hear it. Brock Henry!"

The crowd shouted, "Brock Henry! Brock Henry!"

Glore shouted, "To the new President, Brock Henry!"

"To the President! To Brock Henry!" the crowd echoed.

"United we stand!" shouted Glore.

"United we stand!" shouted the crowd.

Glore looked down at Chance. "Do you hear us, Mr. FitzBourne? We're Democrats! We're united!"

Chance rose, brushed past Glore, and hurried out the door. Glore shouted after him. "Virginia is depending on you, FitzBourne. The Nation is asking for your loyalty! Loyalty, FitzBourne! Loyalty!

The crowd repeated, "Loyalty! Loyalty!"

***

Gwen Ellen found Chance sitting on a bench inside the back door of the hotel. "You ready to go?"

Chance, his face drawn and tired, looked up at her. "How'd they know who I was?"

Gwen Ellen held up a copy of *USA Today* she had picked up at the hotel reception desk. "Your picture is on the cover. A person sitting next to me at the meeting said *The Richmond Times Dispatch* had a bigger picture."

"You sent the picture to them?"

"Oh, hell no. Jace put out a press release."

"Jace did?"

"National news – he doesn't get many shots."

Chance stood up with a groan. "Did you know this would happen?"

Gwen Ellen sighed deeply. "Thought we'd get a pep talk."

"You threw me into the lion's den."

"I didn't know how bad it would be. But, yeah, I wasn't going to take it alone."

"How'd they know who you are? Your picture's not in the paper."

"Hastings would have pointed me out. They weren't going to have that meeting without someone to target."

"Do they think they won?

"Didn't they?"

"They pissed me off."

Gwen Ellen looked at Chance, her mouth agape.

She shook her head. "Shit, Chance."

Chapter Thirty-Two

Damson pushed himself hard Monday morning. It had been a heck of a weekend. He had hit four states. Some of the DNC was still out, working on the electors, ensuring loyalty. What he had felt was just that – loyalty – a united Party. He thought of Alfred E. Neuman – "what I worry." Yes, he worried. That was his job. *Two Electoral Votes* – it plagued his mind – *only two damn Electoral Votes. Why doesn't everyone realize how narrow that is? Why doesn't this idiot, FitzBourne, know-how narrow that is? Even my* *advisors don't seem that worried. All the votes have been certified by the states. They think that assures victory, damn it. An inauguration and Goldin leaving the White House is what assures victory. I won't be happy until that happens.*

He was in his car on time. Bennie smiled, "Some weekend, huh?"

He had picked up Damson at Reagan National in the middle of the night. "Thought you might sleep in this morning."

Damson climbed into the car. "No, Bennie. I would have let you know if I were going to do that."

"That's why I'm here, boss. But you could have. Been all right with me."

"I had to get going, Bennie. I need to see how everyone did with their pep talks – see how bright the world looks this morning."

"Yeah, I understand."

In the office, Skylar seemed reluctant as she handed him the day's Goldin tweets. Damson looked at her with uncertainty. "They bad?"

She nodded once. "You need to read them."

Damson sighed, sat on the edge of Skylar's desk, and read.

"Dems flood the country looking for loyalty, under rocks, in trash cans. Hard to find." "Dems riot in Richmond. Loyalty rally fractures. Beautiful chaos. How are they going to govern?"

"What the fuck?" Damson said under his breath. He shook his head and thought, *keep your mouth shut. No feelings on your damn sleeve.*

He headed for his office. How the hell did Goldin know about the meetings? Someone's talking. And what the hell happened in Richmond? Is this FitzBourne bastard talking to the press?

He turned back. "Skylar, get Senator Glore on the phone."

He rushed into his office, closing the door behind him. Sitting at his desk, he thought, *God, this is getting old.*

133

The phone buzzed. He didn't bother answering Skylar. He punched the button that was lit. "Senator, good morning."

"Good morning, nothing. Goldin is full of crap."

"You know people believe his crap."

"Yeah, but it's not true. The meeting went well. Lots of cheering for Brock Henry. Got loud, but the Party was together. Shamed the hell out of FitzBourne. He became so embarrassed, he ran out."

"You think he talked to the press?"

"I don't think he'll ever talk to anyone again. He knows that everyone is for Brock. I think he'll hide."

"How loud was the meeting?"

"Like a football rally, Ed. The crowd was really into it."

"Maybe someone just heard the noise and made assumptions."

"Hell, maybe. Everyone was really into it."

"And, in the middle, FitzBourne bolted."

"You think a reporter saw that?"

"Maybe, and maybe FitzBourne talked."

After the call, Damson sat, defeated. Good stuff turns to shit. I'm going to kill that guy, FitzBourne.

There was a knock on his office door.

"Come in."

It was Sean O'Rourke, Senior Counselor to the DNC.

"Yeah, Sean, what's up?"

"I'm sorry to tell you this; The Attorney General is suing the State of Pennsylvania."

"The DOJ?"

"Yeah, in the name of the DOJ, but it's the AG."

"What the hell about?"

"He wants the election thrown out."

"On what grounds?"

"Because of the legislative candidate who cheated getting his signatures."

"That guy lost."

"That's not stopping the AG."

"Let me guess. He filed it in a court where Goldin appointed the judges."

"The majority of them, yeah."

"How many Electoral Votes did we get from Pennsylvania?"

"Twenty."

"Wonderful."

O'Rourke left.

Damson sighed and tried not to cry.

Chapter Thirty-Three

It was already ten in the morning. The sale of Chance's lot of cattle was scheduled for eleven-thirty. A blew out his breath in relief as the last of his heifers entered the pen outside the auction arena. It hadn't been easy.

First, Pete hadn't shown up the day before when they were getting the cattle groomed and ready for the sale. The man was supposed to have been at the farm at nine in the morning. Chance had waited and then had finally phoned his helper.

"Where the hell are you, Pete? We've got to get these animals ready."

"God, I'm sorry, Chance. I'm at the magistrate's office. They came and arrested the wife this morning. I'm talking to Delma about getting my wife free. It may take some money."

Delma Wickens was the magistrate.

Chance had groaned. "What the hell did Mrs. Pete do?"

While he had spoken, Chance had thought, Gosh, it sounds silly, but Pete never uses his wife's name. It's just "the wife," so I refer to her as Mrs. Pete, although not usually to Pete himself. I need to i.d. the woman somehow.

Pete had seemed hesitant to answer. "Last night she shot out the tires on Beau Coon's camping trailer."

"What the hell, Pete? Why'd she do that?"

"Coons had Louise in the trailer."

"Louise? Who the hell's Louise?"

"My daughter."

"I didn't know you had a daughter."

"Three of them."

"So, why the tires?"

"She couldn't shoot Coons."

"No, I would hope not."

"She tried to explain to the magistrate. She was trying to take care of Louise. The wife explained to Delma that her father always told her to shoot varmints, but shooting human varmints was against the law, so she shot the tires. Got Coons' attention – Louise's too. Got them out of the camper. Coons didn't take it kindly, though, and filed a complaint. Delma doesn't seem to completely understand the wife's thinking. She's setting up a court date and asking a thousand- dollar bail."

"Okay, pay the bail and get back here."

"Hey, I would, Chance, but I don't have the money."

"Damn, Pete, where are you?"

"Magistrate's office."

"The little building near the sheriff's office?"

"Yeah."

"Okay, be there in a minute."

That had cut the day in half.

Then in the late afternoon, he had called Junior to remind him to be at the farm early the next morning to help load the cattle and manage the farm end of things.

Junior had grumbled. "You want me early?"

"Seven will do."

"Gosh, Dad. Chip has a game tonight. Last one before the Thanksgiving game. I'll be up late."

"You can sleep tomorrow afternoon."

"Saturday afternoon?"

"Yeah, I only need you in the morning unless I have to bring stock home, and I can't imagine that."

"Pete can't do it?"

"Pete will be riding in the pickup hauling the stock trailer. It's going to take two trips. You and he will handle the second load by yourselves while I'm watching the cattle at the auction site."

Junior moaned and acquiesced. "Okay, I'll be there."

"I only go to auction a couple of times a year, son. I try not to ask you much, but I'm running this place by myself."

"And you know what I think of that."

"Not now, Junior. Let's get the auction done."

There was a sigh and one word was said with a great lack of enthusiasm. "Okay."

"Seven o'clock."

"Is it light then?"

"A little."

"Seven o'clock."

***

Loading and transportation had gone well. Pete said that Junior drove out the farm gate ahead of him on the second trip, hadn't waited at all. "Good it went smooth," Pete had said.

Chance stood with his right foot on the lower rail of the fence. He chewed on a stem of grass. That's what he did when he waited. He mused, *chewing-on-grass – isn't that what all cattlemen do? Isn't that what Marlboro men did between smokes? Hell, all the Marlboro men are dead now – cancer. Chewing-on-grass is all that's left.*

His eyes caught some motion across the pen. He adjusted his sunglasses and looked. There were two guys in suits – suits at a country cattle auction! *What the hell?*

The shorter of the two men spoke to some of the auction personnel by the fence. One of them replied and nodded toward Chance. *Oh, shit.*

The two men started walking around the pen – a short black guy who had asked about Chance and a big white guy. They were cut off by a trailer unloading cattle into the pen, but persevered and walked around the trailer and its truck.

Chance looked around. *No place to hide.*

He took his foot off the bottom rail and leaned on the top rail, closed his eyes, and appeared to wait for the lash of a whip across his back.

"Mr. FitzBourne?"

He opened his eyes. The shorter man in the suit was extending his hand.

Chance looked down at the hand, and back up at the man. "Yeah."

The man's hand wavered. "I'm Emery St. John from the DNC. I'd appreciate a word."

Chance hesitated and studied the man. He was a little heavy. Chance was sure the man never worked out. His cheeks were jowly. His eyebrows and sideburns were beginning to gray. Not only was his suit out of place at the auction, but so was the man. Overalls wouldn't have helped.

Chance looked at the man behind St. John. He appeared to be in his thirties, in excellent shape. What awed Chance was that the man was probably six-five or six-six and was looking down at Chance with no expression.

Chance looked back at St. John. "Are you here about the election?"

"I'd just like to have a little chat, Chance."

Chance, hell. You're not my friend. "Yeah, well the auction of my cattle is about to begin. I'm going up in the grandstand."

"Fine, we'll come with you."

Chance strode off as if hoping to lose the two men.

They stayed with him, although the littler man appeared to have to skip some.

Chance sat on the wooden grandstand.

St. John sat down next to him.

The big man stood on the seat in front of Chance in order to pass. He looked eight-feet tall. When he sat down, he crowded in on Chance.

Chance tried to move over, but St. John was in the way.

Chance drew in his breath. "Okay, get it over with. What do you want?"

"We want you to be loyal to the Party. Simple as that. We know you've been loyal for forty years and don't understand what you're doing now."

Chance turned to St. John and looked him in the eye. "I am loyal to the Party. I'm just not loyal to Brock Henry. He's a self-centered jerk."

"Shh! Someone will hear you."

Chance looked around. There was no one within four rows. "Yeah, Okay. I'll whisper. He's an embarrassment. I can't believe the DNC picked him."

"They picked him because he had the second most delegates. A lot of people liked him."

"And a lot of people didn't. That's why he lost."

Just then one of Chance's heifers was brought into the ring and the auctioneer began. It was hard enough to understand what was going on without dealing with other people. Chance glared at St. John. "Do you mind not talking for a while. That's my heifer in the ring."

St. John jerked his head around, suddenly realizing that an auction was going on. "That little cow yours"

"Six hundred pounds. Yeah. Now shush."

"We just want to ask you not to talk."

"Talk, talk about what? Geez, guys, there's an auction going on."

"About opposing Henry."

"I'm not opposing Henry. I'm not voting for him."

"But you're talking about it. You talked to the press about the rally in Richmond."

"Are you talking about the Goldin tweet.... ah, hell. What did she sell for? I asked you to be quiet."

"Yeah, you talked to the press about what happened, gave Goldin the information."

"You're not even sorry that I don't know what my heifer sold for?"

"No. You'll find out later when you get the money. Let's stick to the subject."

"The subject? You're damn subject – not mine."

"About what's important – your talking to the press."

"I haven't talked to anybody. I talked to the editor of the Pierce County Observer two weeks ago and I haven't talked to anyone since. You think I talked about what Glore did in that chaotic meeting where he tried to embarrass me. No way. That was sad, but I didn't talk about it. Anyone in the hallway, no, anyone in the whole damn hotel could have heard what was going on. Glore's damn rally could be heard all over Richmond. I was angry, enraged, but I didn't talk to anyone. I haven't spoken to anyone. Is that clear? You wasted your trip. You've wasted my time. You've messed up my auction!"

Chance started to rise from his seat. A giant hand clamped down on his shoulder and he sat back down. He glowered at St. John. "You going to have your man beat me up now?"

"Lord, no, Chance. We don't do that kind of thing. Do you really mean you haven't talked to the press, to anyone?"

"That's what I said, and I'm not going to. Creates too much trouble."

"Oh, I agree - way too much trouble. So, you'll vote for Henry?"

Chance wanted them off his back. "I'm thinking about it."

"Good. Think hard. The Party needs you."

"Will do."

St. John and the big man got up. "Have a good day, Chance."

The big man crossed in front of Chance and smiled down at him. There was something malevolent in the smile. Chance waved to them. "Don't break your necks on the grandstand."

If only.

St. John looked back at Chance as if he understood cynicism when he heard it. Suddenly he stumbled awkwardly, but then caught himself. Again, he looked back and grinned.

Chance gave him a thumbs up.

***

As Chance approached his gate to Wood Fern Farm, he saw a car parked by the farm sign. The big man standing next to it.

Chance stopped and rolled down the window. "May I help you?"

"Just checking out where you live."

"It's no secret."

"I know, but I wanted to eye-ball it. Nice place."

Gosh, the man knows how to talk after all. He didn't say anything at the auction. "Yes, it is. The state road's free. Stay if you want. Have a nice day."

"Oh, I am."

Chance rolled up the truck window as he turned into his farm lane. *Geez, the intimidator has come to live on my doorstep.*

Chapter Thirty-Four

St. John was in Damson's office Monday morning. Damson looked at him hopefully. "Did you make any headway with FitzBourne.?"

"God, have you ever been to a cattle auction. I had to run my shoes under the kitchen faucet to get the dirt off. My suit's at the cleaners. Never been stared at so much. You'd think I was an alien."

"Doesn't answer my question."

"He says he'll think about it."

"Think about what?"

"About voting for Henry."

"You think he was being honest or trying to appease you."

"He was honest that he'd think about it."

"So, it doesn't mean shit."

"I did my best. I took Jack Gaines to intimidate him."

"Did it work?"

"Yeah, the guy blanched when Jack gave him 'the look' from up high, but Jack couldn't do much else. Jack did, kind of firmly, clamp the guy back into his seat when he tried to stand up. Unfortunately, when he asked if we were going to beat him up, I said we didn't do that kind of thing. I should have let him think."

"Anything else?"

"I had Gaines meet FitzBourne back at the entrance to his farm. I told him to hang around a while – see if he could make the man nervous."

"So, what you're saying is that we don't know what he's going to do."

"Well, he says he's not going to talk about it anymore, not to the press or anyone. He says the only one he's talked to is the editor of his local paper. He says, adamantly, that he didn't talk to anyone about the meeting with Glore. He claims that the meeting was so loud and raucous that the whole hotel could have heard it and that anyone could have seen him leaving the meeting."

"Yeah, I've heard that elsewhere. I think the Senator got carried away. We're lucky he didn't have a bonfire in the middle of the hotel."

"So, what's next?"

"If this were a movie, we'd send a prostitute to pick him up in a bar, take him to a hotel room and take pictures."

"From what Gaines tells me, there are only five or so bars in the county. In four of them, the prostitute would stand out unless she wore jeans and a plaid shirt. And I'd guess FitzBourne has never been to the other bar."

"Well, it's not a movie, anyway."

"Right, so, as I asked, what's next?"

"I guess the convention after Thanksgiving."

"You think he'll come?"

"Good point. We'll apply pressure to everyone in the state so that it ends up at FitzBourne's front door. Have the convention invitations gone out?"

"I haven't seen them."

"Damn. On your way back to your office, will you tell Meletta and Smethers that I want to see them?"

Meletta and Smethers came into Damson's office together as if they wished to present a united front. They defended not having sent out the invitations because they hadn't wanted to be too early, because they hadn't wanted to do it before Thanksgiving, because they had thought people would be distracted by the holiday and would not respond, etc, etc. Damson told the two that that made no sense - that people had to make travel plans and hotel reservations - that people needed to organize their lives.

At that point, Smethers grumbled sotto voce, "Maybe the convention's at a bad time."

Damson flared. "You set the time!"

Smethers defended himself. "It was the only time available."

Damson rolled his eyes. "So, get the damn invitations out. Get FitzBourne's hand-delivered by his district's chair. If you can't do that, drive it to him yourselves."

"Sure, Ed."

"On it, Ed."

As they left, Damson's phone was buzzing. He snapped it up and answered. "Skylar, don't you know I'm in a meeting?"

"They just left the boss."

"The damn phone started buzzing before they were out the door."

"I felt them leaving."

"You're prescient?"

"Since I was a child."

"Who'd calling?"

"Sean O'Rourke's on two."

Damson punched the flashing button. "Counselor, what's up."

"The court voted two to one in favor of the AG."

"For real. Did Goldin appoint the 'two'?"

"Of course."

"How did they justify it."

"In a very convoluted manner. They didn't have much time. Expedited the whole thing because time was of the essence and so forth."

"So, what's next."

"The Pennsylvania attorneys are furious. They were angry before the court's decision and they're more irate now. They're appealing to the Supreme Court."

"Expedited?"

"Damn right."

Chapter Thirty-Five

The front-doorbell rang. Shirley was startled. She hadn't heard the buzzer from the gate. No one rang the front doorbell - at least not anyone she knew.

She opened the door. Gwen Ellen was standing there with a man she didn't know, a heavy man with jowls and a bulldog face.

Shirley reflexively addressed Gwen Ellen. "Why are you at the front door, lady? You never come in this way. Did someone die?"

Gwen Ellen tried to pretend nothing unusual was happening. She gestured toward the man. "Shirley, this is David Schofield, the Party's district chairman." She turned to the man. "David, this is Shirley FitzBourne."

The man reached out his hand, "David."

Shirley shook the hand. "Gosh, this is formal. It's scary. Please come in."

"Thank you, Shirley. We just need to give something to Chance. Is he here?"

"A summons or something? What's going on?"

"Not a legal summons."

"There's another kind of summons?"

"It's an invitation."

"Okay, I can take that."

Gwen Ellen glanced uncomfortably at the man and back at Shirley. "We'd like to give it to Chance."

"You're kidding. Does he need to sign for it?"

"No, we just have to be able to say we gave it to him."

"And you came with a witness."

"Kind of."

Shirley raised her eyebrows and sighed. "Okay, I'll get him."

She left the two standing on the front porch.

A moment later, Shirley came back followed by Chance, who was a bit bewildered. "Gwen Ellen, what's going on?"

He stuck out his hand to the man. "Chance."

"Mr. FitzBourne."

"I prefer 'Chance'."

Gwen Ellen cut in, "Chance, this isn't a social visit. This is David Scofield. He's our district chairman."

"No kidding, I'm glad to meet you, Mr. Schofield."

"David," the man stated.

Chance grinned and pointed two fingers at the man. "Right. And I'm Chance."

Gwen Ellen continued. "Mr. Schofield has been tasked to bring you an invitation."

"Tasked? That's a strange word."

The man offered Chance an envelope.

Chance took it and turned it over a couple of times. "From the DNC, huh? Looks like it should have a wax seal - fancy paper. Invitation to what?"

"A convention."

Chance turned from the man. "A convention, Gwen Ellen, the convention was last summer."

"A special convention of the electors." Gwen Ellen almost blurted.

David Schofield finally spoke. "The Democratic National Committee very much wishes you would come."

Gwen Ellen said. "They told us to make damn sure you come."

Chance chortled. "And what will they do to you if I don't?"

Gwen Ellen raised her eyebrows and looked wide-eyed in resignation. "I hate to think."

Chapter Thirty-Six

Chance threw the letter onto the hallway table. "Now. they're taskmasters, making people do what they don't want to do."

Shirley followed him into the living room. "Maybe they were asked to do it."

"No, they said they were tasked. Came together as insurance, to make sure they didn't throw the letter in the creek."

"Don't you want to open it?"

Chance looked back at Shirley, who was holding up the letter. "You going to open it?"

"Okay, if you're not curious, I am."

"They're just figuring out new ways to harass me."

Chance sat down in a chair while Shirley ran her finger under the flap of the letter. "Nice ecru-colored paper."

Chance snapped his fingers. "That's what I was trying to think of – ecru."

Shirley chuckled, "Not surprised you couldn't think of it – don't see much of it in this house."

"This house doesn't need it. Ecru's for weddings and such – at least it was before internet invitations."

Shirley scrunched her lips together as she studied the letter. "It's from the DNC."

"I know."

"They're inviting us to a convention at the Washington Convention Center."

"Us?"

"Yeah, both of us. They're bringing the electors and state committee people together to formally endorse Senator Brock Henry to be the Democratic nominee for the Presidency of the United States at a nationally televised event.

"I can't do that."

"Why would you have to? All you'd have to do is stand in the back of the crowd, move your mouth when they ask for a unanimous approval and plop hors d'oeuvres in your mouth if they dare ask for those opposed."

"They're going to come after me some way – try to humiliate or intimidate me, as they've done before."

"On national television?"

"In a back room, or something."

"You think they're going to waterboard you or something?"

Chance groaned, closed his eyes, and leaned back. He opened his eyes and looked at the ceiling. "No, they just harass."

"Not with me around, they're not."

"Are you going to fight them off?"

"If I have to."

"Gosh, Shirl, you sound like you want to go."

"Why not. Unlike what you're going to do next month in Richmond, this is free – two nights at the Marriott Marquis, free meals, free parking, etc, etc. The first night there we could go to the Kennedy Center. Yes, let's go."

"Oh, Shirl. Really?"

Chapter Thirty-Seven

"*C*ourt throws out Pennsylvania election results after massive Democratic cheating scandal – justice prevails."

That was the Goldin tweet that had ruined Damson's Thanksgiving. After she had handed it to him, Skylar had asked if that meant Goldin would say he won the Electoral College - that he had won the election. Damson had nodded and said he was sure that such a tweet was coming. And it did come – the Friday after Thanksgiving. It had further ruined the weekend.

Thanksgiving was bad enough without tweets. Damson was a divorced man. His ex-wife had said he loved the Democratic Party more than he loved her. He had told her that a man had to do his job. She had said she understood, and that she knew she wasn't the first to feel as she did, and that he was not the first to throw himself into a job. She said she understood that life was shit. She left him just the same, took the children, and went to California. The children came to see him now and then and he saw them during election campaigns, but they didn't come to Washington for Thanksgiving. That was something a family did at home.

He had ordered a pizza and opened a bottle of wine. He had been embarrassed when he had opened the door for the delivery man. He had thought he had seen pity in the young man's eyes. *Oh no,* he had thought, *the poor bastard is no better off than me, delivering half warm pizza on a holiday.*

So, he had eaten the pizza, without even reheating it, drunk half the bottle of Chianti, and watched two football games.
He had been glad when Friday came. He had had to drive himself, but he went to work.

Skylar hadn't been there. The whole building had been eerily quiet.

He had gone to his office, turned on his computer, and searched Twitter.

"Great day for the nation. Your President has won the Electoral College vote, 266 to 252. The Country is great again."

Damson had screamed and then had wondered if anyone was in the building to hear him. After bringing himself back under control, he had turned off the computer, driven home through the quiet traffic, and finished the bottle of Chianti.

✳✳✳

Damson was still thinking about Friday when he arrived at work Monday morning.

Skylar handed him the tweets:

"Join my big rally at George Mason University on Thursday. Help affirm my beautiful Presidency as we triumph. It will be really, really big - and beautiful."

"Damn," Damson barked. "That's the day of our convention."

Skylar tried to reassure him. "They don't usually televise the Goldin rallies."

"Yeah, that's true. What time is his rally?"

"Uh, I looked it up on-line – four o'clock."

"To make the news, try to circumvent us – hog the headlines."

"Does that surprise you, boss?"

"No, what surprises me is that he's not doing it at FedEx Field."

"I think the Washington Football Team may have a Thursday night game. Besides, why would Goldin take a chance on having empty seats?"

"Good point, Skylar – two good points."

Chapter Thirty-Eight

Chance pulled his Explorer up to the entrance to the Marriott Marquis. He and Shirley had never been to a big in-town hotel before. He was startled as a man in uniform opened the door for Shirley and two men popped the car's rear door and lifted out their luggage. *Christ, I wonder if the DNC reimburses for the tips. I don't think I've got but a couple of ones, a five and some twenties.*

When Shirley was halfway out of the car, Chance put his hand on her arm to get her attention. "Will you check-in? I don't want to be seen. I'll park the car."

Shirley turned back to him. "Chance, these guys park the car. You'll have to hide behind the luggage rack."

"I think these guys take the luggage rack or cart or whatever it is."

"So, what are you going to do? You can't hide for two days."

"I'll be across the lobby. I'll follow you when you head for the elevator."

Shirley shook her head, got out of the car, and headed for the entrance and then the registration desk."

Chance walked around the car and gave the man in the uniform his two dollars. *Damn, I should have given Shirley a twenty to get change.*

From the other side of the lobby, Chance watched Shirley. He was relieved when no one approached her.

He glanced around the lobby. There were several people milling about, but no one he recognized – no one on the Virginia Democratic Committee – no one from the infamous meeting with Senator Glore. He felt liberated. There were people from fifty states here for the convention – maybe they didn't know him, or, at least, they didn't recognize him. Still, he felt he had a target on his back.

When Chance was in the hotel room, he sat down in the one upholstered chair with relief. Shirley busied herself unpacking.

As she did so, she looked at Chance who was staring blankly straight ahead. "Where are we going for dinner?"

"We're having room service."

"Really, we're staying here?"

"Room service puts the bill on the hotel bill. Makes it simple to file a claim."

"Really, Chance. Two nights in the big city and you never want to leave the hotel room?"

"Maybe tomorrow."

"You are going to the theater with me tonight, aren't you?"

"Yeah, okay. Where are we going?"

"It was too late to get tickets to the Kennedy Center, so we're going to Ford's Theater to see A Christmas Carol."

"Are you kidding me, A Christmas Carol?"

"It's after Thanksgiving. It was that or The Nutcracker."

"Okay, maybe Tiny Tim won't make it this time. Isn't Ford's Theater where Lincoln was shot?"

"Yes."

"We're not in a balcony, are we?"

"No."

"Good, I'll have people all around me."

✳✳✳

The next day at the convention, Chance stood at the edge of the cocktail area behind the seating area. He held a glass of Shiraz in his hand, picking hors oeuvres off trays as waitresses passed him. The caterer wasn't serving Claret. They never did. The other reds all tasted the same to him. He made them do.

The spouses had been separated. They had their own party and their own seats, over to the right of the stage. He tried to spot Shirley but couldn't see her. *Maybe she's hiding, too.*

He suddenly began to feel a chill. He was sensing something. Then he spotted it. A television camera with a big

153

lens was pointed at him. *The damned networks know who I am. How can I hide? I can't turn around, I'll be facing the wall, looking like the bad kid in school, like I'm standing in the corner.*

Chance abruptly perceived someone standing next to him. He stepped forward and turned to face the man. The man tried to shift to the side. Chance moved with him. He looked up. It was "The Intimidator."

"Don't like the attention, Mr. FitzBourne?"

"You're better looking, Mr....?"

"Gaines."

"First name?"

"Jack."

"So, Jack, are we buddies, mates, as the British would say, or are you my keeper, my warden?"

"Just want to make sure you have a pleasant afternoon – that you have whatever you need."

"Are you going to guide me to my seat, make sure I don't get away?"

"I'll point it out if you wish."

"Yeah, is it next to some other elector who's going to rib me the whole time I'm sitting there?"

"No," Gaines responded, shaking his head. "It's next to Bill Hastings, the Virginia state chair."

"Oh, Lord, has he got a message for me?"

"Probably. He was in a conference on Zoom yesterday with Damson and Gwently."

"The Speaker?"

"Right. I'm sure they gave him some guidance, offered some advice. You know, that sort of thing."

"Oh, Lord. Who's sitting on the other side of me?"

"Emery St. John."

"The same guy I met at the auction?"

"Yes."

"Shouldn't he be sitting with the DNC?"

"He thinks you're more important."

"Good Lord, I'm one lousy vote."

"You're THE lousy vote."

Just then Chance felt a presence to his right. He turned to face an attractive woman in carefully tailored blazer and slacks.

His head snapped back to where Gaines had been, but he was gone. *How the hell does a 6 foot five, 250-pound man vanish?*

He turned back to the woman, who reached out to shake his hand while maneuvering so that they were both in profile to the television cameras. "Chance FitzBourne?"

He shook her hand while gaping.

"Close your mouth and smile, Mr. FitzBourne. I'm Jane Meyer Grete."

"I know who you are, Ms. Grete."

"And I know who you are. You're the rogue elector, the defiant one."

"I just don't care for Mr. Henry, Ms. Grete. Are you going to tell me to vote for him, too?"

"I'm for a united Party, Mr. FitzBourne. It would give us strength."

"The Party has already won, Ms. Grete."

"Goodness stop calling me Ms. Grete. Call me what my friends do, Meyer. And may I call you Chance?"

"Yes Ma'am."

"Yes, Meyer."

"Yes, Meyer"

"Good. Now, Chance, may I ask you to think hard about your vote. It's important to the Party."

"I am thinking hard about it. It's Mr. Henry who's the problem."

"Well, if you don't vote for him, who are you going to vote for?"

"I'll vote for you."

Now, it was Jane Meyer Grete's turn to gape.

Chapter Thirty-Nine

The Saturday after the convention, Junior and Bev asked Chance and Shirley over to their house to watch the Army-Navy football game. That was unusual, but the NFL hadn't started playing on Saturday yet and the SEC Championship game was at night and would run late. "Actually," Junior had said, "Bev wants to ask you about your convention."

Junior had the game channel on when Chance and Shirley arrived. The Midshipmen had just marched onto the field. Bev met Junior's parents and led them into the living room. She said, "You guys watch the game. Shirley and I will go to the kitchen."

Junior protested. "Hey, I want to hear, too. I'll turn the television down. We can just watch while we listen."

Bev rebutted Junior's protest, "I need to get snacks and drinks."

"Sounds fine. We'll just wait."

Chance held up his hands in resignation. "Well, there's really not much to say. They endorsed Brock Henry by acclamation."

Junior laughed, "Hell, we all know that. We want to know what happened to you."

Bev smirked. "I bet Shirley can fill us in."

Junior quickly admonished the women, "No talking till you get back here."

Chance settled into a lounge chair. He knew it was Junior's, but he figured seniority had earned his claim. Obviously, Junior had left it for him. "Where are the kids?"

"Wish they were kids. It'd be a whole lot easier. They're in their rooms. They have their own televisions, computers, the whole wired thing."

"Did I ever tell you we didn't live so well when I was young."

"Ten or twelve times."

"Well, we didn't."

"I know. You watched Kukla, Fran, and Ollie in the living room.

"Hey, be gentle. I'm not that old."

"But you know who they were?"

"My Grandfather must have told me. When's the game going to start?"

"As soon as they get the Midshipmen and Cadets off the field."

"The Cadets haven't been on yet?"

"I don't know. I just turned it on. We need to kill time, anyway, until the women come back."

"Doesn't matter. They're not interested in the game."

"Yeah, but if we get involved, they'll be back in the kitchen before we can say anything."

The women returned. Bev had a bowl of chips in one hand and used the other to clear space on the coffee table. Shirley settled a bowl of dip and a platter of sliders in the space. She picked up the dip and carried it to Chance. "You get served once and then you're on your own."

"Don't want to be difficult, but have you got some little plates? I can be more independent with a loaded plate."

"Sure, I'll get them." She swiveled her head around to Junior. "What are you drinking?"

"Beer."

"You, Chance?"

"Early in the day. You have a Mountain Dew?"

"Caffeine"

"Doesn't bother me."

"You drink decaffeinated coffee with dinner."

"Are you looking for logic?"

"I guess not."

The women went back to the kitchen.

Junior glanced at the television. "The game's starting."

"Keep the sound down. Maybe the gals won't notice."

The women returned. Bev handed Chance a plate and a canned soda. "Now you can load up."

Shirley gave a plate and beer to Junior and then settled into a chair. "How come you have the sound turned down?"

Junior sighed. "Because we want to hear about the convention and you guys won't settle down."

Bev looked annoyed. "And you'd be complaining if we didn't get you some food. You know you could have gotten your own beer and I could have been sitting."

"Okay, let me pull my foot out of my mouth and apologize."

"Humbly?"

"Humbly."

"With bowing and scraping."

Junior made a face and mouthed, "The hell you say," while Bev grinned with satisfaction.

Junior turned to Shirley. "Okay, tell us about it."

"You don't want to watch the game?"

"Shirr-leee."

"Okay, Chance can correct me. He expected the worst, but it didn't really happen. Made me check into the hotel while he hid. Made us eat room service so he wouldn't be seen. Then, they separated us at the convention so that I couldn't defend him."

Chance threw his head back, groaned, and protested. "Shirley, cut it out. Get on with it."

Bev interjected, "You know, Chance, we saw you on television. They gave you a lot of attention. They talked about your recalcitrance - called you 'the rogue elector'. Did everyone freeze you out – treat you like a leper?"

Chance scoffed, "I wish they had. No, I got more attention than I wanted. First they sicced this big guy on me."

"Yeah, we saw him towering over you."

"You see his look? The intimidator-look?"

"No, he didn't look bad – just big."

"Well, he's not fun to be around."

"Then we saw the Vice President."

"Jane Meyer Grete, the Vice President-elect."

"She sure knows how to smile for the camera. Bet she practices. Did she say sweet things to you?"

"Just pitched the usual party-unity stuff."

"What did you say to her?"

"Told her I was going to vote for her in the Electoral College."

Bev stared at Chance during a moment of silence. "Yeah, and what did she say?"

"Nothing. She just stopped smiling."

"Have you ever seen her that way before?"

"I don't think so."

"So, what happened after that?"

"I took my seat. Sat between the state Democratic Chairman and a guy from the DNC named St. John."

"They work you over?"

"A little, but they were constrained by having to listen to the speeches."

"Yeah, we heard them. Glore and Gwently – a lot of rah, rah, and hot air being blown through space. Who was the guy who introduced them?"

"That's Edwin Damson, the Chair of the DNC."

"He looked pretty harassed. Did you cause that?"

"I wonder – maybe. But he's got the Pennsylvania thing too."

"The suit?"

"Yeah, it's going to the Supreme Court."

"You think the Court will hear it?"

"They've already agreed to – expediting it."

"I thought they'd laugh it out of the building."

"Not yet."

"They better be careful, or they'll be the ones being laughed at."

159

"Yeah, well, tell the Goldin people."

"The Emperor's court?"

"And his loyal vassals."

"Well, as I see it, the convention was fine until Gwently finished. They should have cut it off then. Letting Brock Henry speak was a mistake."

Shirley laughed. "You really think they could not let the Party-anointed-one not speak, not accept the thunderous recognition?"

Chance sighed. "If he had held it to half an hour, it wouldn't have been too bad. People want their medical bills paid and free college doesn't sound too bad. At least he wants to do something about the climate. It's just that an hour was too much."

Junior laughed, "Well, it didn't bother the networks. At six o'clock, the local news came on as scheduled. They cut Henry off in the middle of a sentence with his arms in the air."

"What happened on the national news?"

"They showed Goldin making fun of all the Democrats. Fortunately, he was talking at the same time as Henry – maybe ten minutes less."

"Did he make fun of me?"

Bev perked up. "Don't tell him."

"He'll hear it on the talk shows or read it in a tweet."

"That's better than the national news."

They were all saved from the further discussion when Jen entered the room. She went to the coffee table without saying anything and filled a plate. "Where are the sodas?"
Bev replied. "Still in the frig."

Jen looked around at the group. "How come everyone looks so serious?"

Junior offered, "We were talking about the convention."

"Convention? Oh yeah some of the guys were talking about that at school Friday. Dullsville."

"Your grandfather was there," Bev offered.

Jen turned to Chance. "Oh, yeah, did they give you a hard time?"

Chance responded cautiously. "No, not too much. I'm not their favorite person now."

"No, you made a splash when you announced you weren't voting for Henry."

"Yes, I'm sorry about that. I understand you and Chip received a flack.

"Yeah, it bothered me at first, but then it seemed kind of cool."

"Oh?"

"Yeah, I had a grandfather taking on the world – Don Quixoteish."

Chapter Forty

"The Dems have let the bat boy into the big leagues and he's already stolen second - sad."

Chance mulled over the tweet as he drank his coffee and watched the talk shows. Some of the pundits laughed about it, acted kind of like he was some-kind-of-celebrity. He finally decided it wasn't so bad. He could live with it. At one time he had thought he was in over his head. Now, he decided, he would just ride with it.

The telephone rang. He turned the television down while Shirley answered. "Good morning, the FitzBourne's ... I'm sorry, who is this? Yes, well I'm sure he'd like to speak to you ...Yes, he probably talked to lots of people at the convention ...Yes, I'm sure he'll remember you."

Shirley lifted and dropped her shoulders, looking for direction from Chance. He extended his hand to take the phone and she gave it to him with obvious relief.

"Hello, Chance FitzBourne."

"Good morning, Chance. Meyer here."

Chance blinked at the thought a second. "Mrs. Vice President? ... Or is it Miss?"

"It's Vice President, Chance – just Vice President. Well, for now, Vice President-elect – non-sexist, non-racial, non-denominational, non-anything-you-can-think-of."

"Yes, Ma'am, of course. What may I do for you?"

"The woman who answered needs to practice on blowing people off."

"Oh, yes. That's my wife Shirley. We get a lot of calls these days. She tries to screen them."

"I should send my admin assistant down to give her lessons. It's a real talent."

"Yes of course."

"Listen, Chance, I was interested in what you said the other day – what you said about voting for me."

"Yes, I think you should be President."

"That was sweet to hear. It makes two of us, although I'll deny it if you quote me."

"Oh, of course not – no, no, no – I would never do that."

"Quit being nervous, Chance. It's just politics - denial, denial, denial. If Goldin has taught us anything the last three-plus years, it's denial – that's so-and-so's responsibility – that's the state's responsibility – I've never met the man – I don't know the guy - I don't know her – I didn't pay her. He's been an expert at it."

"Oh, yes, I agree."

"Nonetheless, I agree with you. Are you still going to vote for me?"

"Absolutely, although it won't do much good."

"Hey, Chance.   Little ants build big mounds – cause irritation too. You never know what's going to happen. Stick with it, Chance, stick with it – and I thank you very much."

"Yes, ma'am – I will."

"You're a good man, Chance. Hope I'll see you again."

She hung up. Chance still held the phone in his hand.

Shirley looked at him incredulously. "That was the Vice President, Jane Meyer Grete?"

Chance put down the phone and smirked. 'Meyer' to me. 'Meyer' to her good friends."

Shirley made a face. "Don't give me garbage, Chance. Why'd she phone you?"

"To test out how good you are at screening calls – she says it's an art. Says she has people who could give you lessons."

Shirley sighed, groaned, picked up a section of the Sunday paper, walked over to Chance, and swatted him. "Damn, Chance, I said no rubbish. What did she call about?"

"What call? I deny there ever being a call. 'Denial'. She taught me you can't be in politics if you don't understand 'denial' – another art."

“So, you’re not going to tell me?”

“Only if you convince me that you understand ‘denial’.”

Shirley hit him again, only harder.

Chance decided that next time he would block her with his hands.

Chapter Forty-One

Damson sat in his office two days before the meetings of the Electoral College. He was in a good mood.

The previous afternoon he had received wonderful news. The Supreme Court had announced that they had voted down the AG's suit over the election results in Pennsylvania. Damson pondered what had happened. He had been amazed that the Court had decided to hear the case. Then, as the hearing had dragged on, he had worried that the lack of a decision would muddy the results of the Electoral College vote. He had held his breath, but the Court had finally come through, albeit with a vote of seven to two. *Two,* he thought, *the Court ought to be embarrassed. They should hide in their offices. They should ostracize the two who voted for the suit. They should be ashamed.*

Still, Damson had gotten the vote he wanted. *There's hope for this thing we call democracy.*

As he mulled these thoughts, there was a knock on his doorframe.

He looked up.

Sean O'Rourke stood hesitantly in the doorway.

"Come in Counselor. Have a seat. I hope you won't do anything to alter my good mood?"

"No, I don't think so. Just want to give you something to think about."

"Good or bad?"

"I don't know. Goldin's doing something weird."

"Something new weird?"

"Yes."

"All right. Give it to me."

"He tried to issue an executive order to make the result of the Electoral College vote secret until the joint session of Congress in early January."

"He can't do that. The states control that process."

"The White House Counsel told him that."

"So, what's he going to do?"

"He's asked the states to keep things secret, and some are going to."

"Some?"

"Minnesota told him they wouldn't do it. They said they'd been through secret ballots before and weren't going to change again. However, some of the states with Republican governors are going to do what he asked."

"Florida?"

"Yeah, Florida's doing it."

"Texas?"

"Doing what the President asks."

"What happens when the results of elector's votes get to Washington?"

"They come by registered mail to the National Archives and the President of the Senate."

"The President of the Senate being the Vice President, Stoney himself."

"Right."

"So, Goldin controls both."

"Right, again."

"So, what's he up to?"

"I've no idea, but you know it's a cabal and it isn't kosher."

"The SOB ought to know he lost the election."

"Do you really think so? You know he only lost because the Democrats cheated. He thinks his followers will storm this the capital and keep him in power. He just needs to give them a little justification and encouragement."

"Will democracy endure?"

"I pray."

167

Damson's phone buzzed.

"Yeah, Skylar."

"Mr. Henry's here to see you."

Damson gave O'Rourke a questioning look.

O'Rourke headed for the door. "I'm out of here."

Damson nodded and returned to Skylar. "Send him in."

A moment later Brock Henry stormed through the door.

"We on track, Ed? You don't contact me enough."

"St. John talks to Dill every day."

"St John isn't you and Dill isn't me. I want to be in the loop."

"Dill doesn't talk to you?"

"Yeah, of course, he does. But I want you talking to me."

"Brock, when you're President, everyone can't talk to you directly."

"When I'm President, I'll be in charge. I don't want any second-hand gibberish. I want to know what's going on. I'm going to be making the decisions, not a damn chief of staff or some other peon."

"Brock, you know that can't be true. There are going to be a million things going on at once. They're going to hit you like a ton of bricks on Inauguration Day. We've talked before about Goldin stiff-arming the transition, refusing to have his people meet with the transition teams that Vickers put together."

"Vickers and you."

"Yeah, part of my job. You can replace anyone you want. I've told you that before."

"No sense. Goldin won't let them in."

"After the Electoral College votes, he'll have to. We'll raise a stink. You'll raise a stink."

"Right - damn right."

"So, have you made any progress on the cabinet or your staff."

"I've talked to a few guys."

"Guys?"

“Yeah.”

“You’re being diverse, aren’t you?”

“Yeah, I’ll do that. Shit, Ed, I’ve got a month.”

“Look, Brock, even Goldin was picking out people by this time. “

“Yeah, well I haven’t got rich buddies.”

“So, you need to find qualified people.”

“Yeah, how are we going to do that?”

“You’ll need a committee. They’ll screen candidates and send the best people to you to interview. Do you want the DNC to help you form the committee?”

“Yeah, that sounds good.”

“Okay, I’m on it.”

“Let me know. That’s you and me – no St. John – no Dill.”

When Henry had left, Damson held his head in his hands and then went to get a cup of coffee. He desperately wished someone would bring it to him. He longed for the day administrative assistants were secretaries. He longed to be politically incorrect.

Shame on you, Edwin Damson. Shame, but don’t confess.

Chapter Forty-Two

Chance didn't know what he would have done if the Virginia Board of Elections hadn't sent him a parking pass. It was a two-hour drive to Richmond. Chance had allowed three-and-half hours, an extra hour-and-a-half for getting a snack, and for getting lost. He ended up using nearly all the time.

He wondered why anyone set up meetings at noon. *When are you supposed to eat?*

That's why he had to plan time for a snack.

He entered the state capitol, asked the guard for directions, and was directed to the Senate Chamber. Fortunately, the legislature was not in session and the building was quiet.

In the chamber, individual desks had been set up in two semicircles, six in the front semicircle, and seven to the rear. Chance asked a clerk at the door where he should go. The Clerk pointed to an easel with an illustration of the chamber's layout, with names next to each desk. He was assigned the end desk in the back row. *I'm as far from the podium as they can put me,* Chance chuckled. *I'm getting used to it.*

He took his seat and looked around. Half the room was looking back at him. He sighed, looked down, and picked up a pen from a commemorative pen and pencil set on his desk. He noted the writing on the pen – "Electoral College of the Commonwealth of Virginia", and the year. *A lot of writing for a small pen.* Chance held the pen out in the palm of his hand to check the weight. *It's definitely not gold.*

Chance set the pen down and looked around. Most people had turned away from him. He looked forward to the front of the gallery. A man was standing high up in the front of the room - up*on the dais – or podium or pulpit or whatever it is.*

The man began to speak. He told the audience that he was Walter Irving, Chairman of the Board of Elections for the Commonwealth. He introduced his Vice Chairwoman who was sitting next to him on the podium, welcomed the electors, apologized for the Governor not being there, and passed the Governor's greetings to the crowd.

Next, he introduced the Secretary of the Commonwealth, thanking her for giving her valuable time.

She made a brief speech about the importance of the Electoral College and its vote.

That was followed by an invocation and the Pledge of Allegiance.

Next, the Chairman announced that the electors would take their oath.

Oh, oh, thought Chance. I hope the oath doesn't mention his pledge.

It didn't. He just had to support the U.S. and Virginia Constitutions and fulfill his duties faithfully and impartially, etc. to the best of his ability. He figured he could do that.

They called the roll of the electors. He was on the list. *So far, so good. I haven't been fired yet.*

Irving returned to the microphone and proceeded to go through the process of electing a president and secretary for the meeting from the electors present. There were nominations and seconds, all previously determined. Chance thought, *no one coordinated with me.*

Next, Irving introduced five pages that would support the proceedings. They were children from seven years in age to fourteen or so. Chance wondered how they had been selected.

The woman from Bristol, who had been selected as president, moved to the microphone. The elected secretary took the seat beside her.

The President announced that the vote for President of the United States would next be conducted. She directed that the secretary would call the roll and that each elector should stand when called and state their vote.

Oh, hell, Chance thought. Here it comes.

Each elector stood when called. Some made short speeches about who they were voting for, then stated who they were voting for, all for Brock Henry.

Chance was the last to be called. He stood with trepidation, feeling everyone staring at him, wondering if he was really going to be faithless.

"Chance FitzBourne of Pierce County. I vote for Jane Meyer Grete of the State of Maryland.'

He quickly sat down, while the room buzzed.

The President tapped her. "Did I hear you correctly, Mr. FitzBourne? Jane Meyer Grete is the Vice-Presidential Candidate."

Chance reluctantly stood again. "You heard me correctly, Madame President. Jane Meyer Grete for President."

The President looked hesitant, but then announced the results. "Twelve votes have been cast for Brock Henry of the State of Nebraska for President. One vote has been cast for Jane Meyer Grete of the State of Maryland for President.

We will next vote for the Vice President."

The same procedure was followed.

Chance again voted for Grete.

There was a discussion on the podium. Eventually, the President addressed Chance. "We are uncertain as to whether you can vote for the same person for President and Vice President."

Chance gave her an innocent look. "Can you show me anything that says I can't."

Again, the President looked at her compatriots on the podium, but they all shook their heads.

The President faced the assembly. "We don't know of anything that negates Mr. FitzBourne's vote. Therefore, let me summarize: thirteen votes have been cast for Jane Meyer Grete of the State of Maryland for Vice President; No other person has received a vote. Next, we will sign the Certificate of Vote."

A stack of papers was handed to the Secretary who looked uncertain. He gave one of the papers to the President amidst a discussion between the two. The President then discussed the paper with the Chair and Vice-Chair of the Board of Elections. Eventually, the Vice-Chair took all the documents and began writing on them. They were passed back and forth with everyone doing some writing. Finally, the President began signing all the documents followed by the Secretary doing the same thing. Chance watched and counted – 6...7...8.

The certificates were next handed to a page who took them to the first desk in the first row where the elector began signing them, each on its second page while being photographed by a professional and by other electors with cell phones. The man finished the eighth certificate with a flourish and passed them to a page. The process was repeated at the desk of each elector.

Finally, a young female page brought the certificates to Chance. She held them out and whispered, "You're the bad guy, aren't you?"

Chance took the documents and whispered back, "Not bad – just different."

He lay the documents on his desk and opened it to the second page. The certificates had been preprinted with thirteen votes of Brock Henry for President. The "thirteen" had been scratched out and twelve written above it. One vote had been added in pen for Jane Meyer Grete. Everyone at the podium had initialed the changes. A mess had been made of a carefully printed document. As Chance signed the eight documents, he

173

sighed. *My legacy for the Archives of the United States is a really screwed up document.*

As Chance looked up from signing, he noted all the electors in the room had their cell phones up further recording him for posterity.

He passed the certificates to the page who was shaking her head slightly.

The page returned the certificates to the Secretary.

The President announced that the Certificates of Vote would be placed in envelopes for the various addressees along with the Certificates of Ascertainment, explaining the latter had been issued by the Governor following the election listing the names of the electors and the votes the candidates had received. Two copies had been forwarded to the Archives of the United States and eight other copies retained to accompany the Certificates of Vote. She further indicated that the envelopes were to be endorsed by the electors.

Oh, Lord, thought Chance. *This is going to last forever.*

While the envelopes were being endorsed, the President had copies of the minutes of the meeting passed out for review. "When the envelopes have all been endorsed and forwarded to the Chairman of the Board of Elections, we will vote on the minutes and have you all sign them."

Goodness, Chance fumed; *they're going to keep us here forever.*

He picked up the minutes and perused them. Just like the Certificates of Vote, the minutes had been corrected in pen and ink. Chance moaned. *I'll be noted as the annotated elector forever.*

When all the activities of the Electoral College were completed, the Chairman of the Board of Elections began thanking all those who had worked to set up the meeting. As soon as he began, Chance bolted for the door. A man guarding the entrance reluctantly stepped aside. Quickly, Chance was across the foyer and down the steps. He was happy he had avoided reporters. He guessed they were still in the balcony.

Soon he was in his car and racing toward Interstate 95/64.

The only guilt he felt was in not pleasing a young page.

Chapter Forty-Three

Chance had a hurried home after the Electoral College meeting. He had hired the fire hall for a press conference at five o'clock. He had thought it would make life easier at home by directing the press away.

As he entered the building, he noted the folding chairs were lined up just as he had left them with one in the front of the room where he planned to sit.

The large room was eerily silent.

He glanced at his watch. It was five minutes to five.

Where the hell is everybody?

He sat in his chair and stared at the empty seats.

At five o'clock, Jace walked in. He walked to the front of the room and eased himself into the front middle seat. He looked at Chance.

Finally, Chance said, "What the hell?"

Jace squeezed his lips together and rolled his tongue in his cheek before he spoke. "Didn't you listen to the radio coming home?"

"Yeah – a country music station."

"No 'breaking news'?"

A bad feeling began creeping up Chance's neck. "No. What happened? A terrorist attack or something?"

"Or something. Two Democratic electors in New York voted for Goldin."

"You're kidding me?"

"Wish I was. All the reporters have gone there. Sorry, Chance. You're not news."

"Two of them? God, that means we don't have the 270 votes we need."

"That's right, and Goldin has 268."

"268 and counting."

"You got it."

"Shit."

Suddenly there was a noise at the door. Gwen Ellen entered the room with Marvin standing nervously behind her.

She stood inside the doorway and glowered at Chance. "You happy, Chance? You cost us the election. This county will never live it down."

Chance protested. "I voted Democratically. I didn't cost us the election. Those guys from New York did. They abandoned the Party."

"They were only two votes. That got us down to 270. You were the killer."

"Hey, you're deciding who came first, the chicken or the egg."

"Doesn't matter. Without your egocentric one-man campaign, we wouldn't have lost."

"Are you saying these two guys abandoned the Party because of me? I never asked anyone to vote for Goldin. There's something screwy here. They must have been bought off."

"Yeah, there are all kinds of theories flying, but you were the catalyst."

"Damn, you don't know that Gwen Ellen. You just want someone to blame."

"As does the world. It's on you."

176

As Gwen Ellen exited, she tried to slam the door behind her and shouted, "Damn," as the door closer caught it and eased it closed.

Chance looked at Jace who hunched his shoulders and made a face as if to say, "So, what did you expect?"

Jace stood up and picked up the briefcase he had never opened. "Wouldn't have made this week's paper anyway." He took one last look at the forlorn Chance FitzBourne. "Go home, Chance. Get a beer or a glass of wine, eat a good dinner, and forget it all. The world goes on."

Chance nodded. "I hope you're right."

Chapter Forty-Four

Wilson "Willie" Grete came home from his office in Baltimore. He parked in his reserved space next to Government House, the brick mansion of the Governor of Maryland in the government complex in Annapolis.

As he entered the house, he shouted "Meyer," but there was no answer. He guessed she was working late, but knew it was only a short walk home. He worried about her. There had been such excitement and hope when Vickers had picked her to be his running mate and she had stood before the convention and pledged herself to the Country. Now, she had been abandoned by the Party and they had selected Henry. It kept going through Willie's mind that if Vickers had died after the ascertainment of the Electoral College vote, his wife would be President.

He shook his head. *Fate has its way.*

Still, she was on her way to becoming Vice President.

He wondered what his life was going to be like.

When Jane Meyer had become Governor of Maryland, Willie had cut back his law practice. He pretty much just handled wills, real estate closings, and the like. He now stayed away from anything that bordered on the political. He wondered what he would do as the husband of the Vice President. He hadn't known the spouses of Presidents to work at a regular job, but Jill Biden had continued teaching when her husband had been the Vice President. Still, he couldn't imagine continuing his law practice. Maybe he could teach. *Georgetown has a law school. George Washington? Howard? Heck, there are lots of schools. Still, I must be non-controversial. I can't cause problems.*

He hung his suit coat in the closet, took two wine glasses from a cabinet, and pulled a bottle of wine from the wine rack. He studied its label, decided it would do, uncorked it, poured wine into the two glasses, set them on opposite sides of the kitchen table, sat by one, and waited for his wife.

The cook was off for the day. They would probably send out. *I should have brought something home.*

He heard Jane Meyer come in the front door and a moment later she entered the kitchen. She sat down at the table as if she knew that he would be waiting.

"Well, I survived to live another day. Maybe I still have a chance at the Presidency."

"I heard it's between Goldin, Henry and you."

"Yeah, the top three. Isn't that a laugh?"

"Well, you still have 272 Electoral Votes for Vice President. Why do you think they did in Henry and not you?"

"Obviously, someone screwed up. They didn't give the two idiot electors sufficient instructions."

"Maybe you'll be Goldin's Vice President?"

"Oh, God. Talk about nightmares. The government thought they solved that problem with the Twelfth Amendment."

"If the things can go wrong..."

"...they will. I know. I know."

"You need to practice your stone-face in the mirror."

"Ha, ha."

"Maybe, if Henry and Goldin don't get enough Electoral Votes, they'll choose you."

"Ha, fat chance."

"It's known as compromise."

"In your dreams."

"You'd be better than either one of them."

Jane Meyer smiled. "It's nice to be loved."

Chapter Forty-Five

Damson had hardly slept. The phone had started ringing in the early afternoon as the result of the Electoral College voting. After the first two calls, he had set up a meeting of the DNC for ten o'clock the next morning. As he arrived for work, he cringed as Skylar handed him the day's tweets from Goldin:

"The tide has turned. The Dems have lost - Heart-warming - Beautiful. It's better by the minute."

"The Goldin wave is rolling in – overwhelming – all-consuming – ubiquitous – pervasive – overwhelming – fantastic!!!."

"The people decided – Goldin! – Goldin! – Goldin! – so beautiful!"

Damson read them while standing by Skylar's desk. Then he balled up the paper and fired it at Skylar's trash can, barely missing her as she ducked. He missed and the paper landed on the floor. Skylar rolled her chair, scooped up the balled paper, and flipped it into the trash with a quick flick of her hand. She then looked back at her boss, but he was gone.

In his office, Damson sat down at his desk. He opened his middle desk drawer and slammed it shut, hoping it would make him feel better. It didn't.

Skylar appeared in the doorway, holding a cup of coffee. She walked softly to the desk, removed Damson's empty cup from a coaster, and replaced it with the cup she had brought. "I'll bring your cup back full in a few minutes."

Damson nodded; his two hands flat on the desk. His facial expression didn't change. "Does everyone know about the meeting?"

Skylar responded with a timid "Yes, boss."

"Is the Zoom set up with the New York Governor and New York DNC Chair?"

"Ten o'clock, boss."

"I hope they're cowering."

"The people I talked to said that they're in bad moods."

"They damn well should be."

***

Damson entered the conference room ten minutes before ten. He looked around at the nearly full conference table. "Where's Senator Glore?"

Allison Gwently responded. "The Senate's in session."

Damson was incredulous. "It's not supposed to be."

"Majority Leader Slocum called for the session."

"Grayson Slocum? Damn him. The man's got too damn much power. The 'do nothing' Senate and Slocum don't do anything unless it's something Goldin pre-approves. So much for legislative independence. Why's he calling the session this time?"

"In order to gloat. He needs an audience for that."

Damson groaned, took a deep breath, and gradually let it out as he looked down at the papers on the table in front of him.

180

"Okay, let's go over where we stand. Our boy, FitzBourne, did what he said weeks ago. He didn't vote for Henry. He voted for Grete." He looked at St. John. "Who did he vote for Vice President?"

"Grete."

Damson frowned. "I guess he hedged his bet. Let's talk about him later. In a couple of minutes, the Governor and Democratic State Chairman from New York, Davis Whitten and Hildi Van Hayden will join us via Zoom. We know that two electors in New York did not only not vote for Brock Henry, they voted for Goldin instead."

Just then Henry entered the room, walked to Glore's seat, threw copies of *The Washington Post* and *The New York Times* on the table, and announced, before taking the Senator's seat, "And that cost me the damn election. What the hell are you going to do about it?"

Damson shook his head. "What are WE going to do about it?"

Henry glared at Damson. "Between this idiot FitzBourne, whom you've let run wild, and these two crooks from New York, we've lost the damned election."

Gwently glowered at Henry. "You didn't lose, Brock. You just didn't win. 269 votes are one short."

Damson slammed his fist on the table. "The trouble is we don't even know if Brock has 269 votes. We've got a bunch of Republican states that have hidden their votes as Goldin directed. I don't know how he did it, but he's turned two Democratic electors already. If he's turned two more among these secret voters, he wins the election."

O'Rourke grunted, "And unless something leaks to the press, we won't know until the beginning of January. Merry Christmas to you all."

"Funny, funny, funny," Damson grumbled. He turned to the television screen on the wall at the end of the room, while the DNC personnel at the end of the table swiveled their chairs around.

Whitten and Van Hayden appeared on a split screen.

Damson addressed the television monitor. "Governor, Chairwoman, do you hear me all right?"

The two responded in unison. "Yes."

"I won't ask how you are today. I imagine you feel about as badly as we do. What happened and what are we going to do about it?"

There was hesitation and then Whitten cleared his throat. "We have two renegades. They both signed a pledge document when they agreed to be electors. They pledged to vote for the nominee of the Democratic Party."

"Okay, they violated their oath."

"Not oath – pledge."

"Okay, but they're in violation. What can we do about it?"

"We can kick them out of the Party."

Henry interrupted. "Whoopee. Big deal. Can we take them to a court or something?"

Van Hayden joined the conversation. "We've been talking to our committee counsel. We've never had a situation like this before and have no precedents. There's a big question as to whether or not Henry fits the bill as a nominee."

Henry exploded. "What the hell. The Party picked me. A convention picked me. I'm the damned nominee."

Van Hayden continued, almost as if she had only barely heard Henry. "I know, and the New York Democratic Committee endorsed you based on what the national committee did, but there's nothing that says that was a valid way to do it. All the other elections in this Country are by a majority of the vote. When an elected official dies, each state has a procedure for replacing them. If a nominee dies well before an election, they get replaced. If they die within a few days of an election, the voting proceeds, and if the deceased wins, he, or she, is replaced by the state's procedure. But, in this case, it's a Presidential Election and all the rules go out the window."

Whitten joined back in. "Rules-going-out-the-window isn't the right term. The fact is that there aren't any rules. Back when Horace Greeley died after the election against Grant, his electors went in multiple directions. It didn't really matter because he lost. Here it matters. What you guys did in picking Senator Henry is to try to hold the Party together, to make sure that the electors didn't go in multiple directions, but, in fact, you didn't have any real power to dictate anything. The Constitution doesn't say anything, and precedent doesn't support us. Maybe we could go to court somewhere, but I don't think we'd win."

Henry protested. "The Supreme Court said that states could require electors to vote for the party's nominee."

Damson sighed. "No, SCOTUS said states could require the electors to vote for the candidate who won the popular vote. As Justice Kagan specifically pointed out, it was a decision limited to cases at hand and specifically noted that it did not address states binding electors to a deceased candidate. As to binding electors to a candidate selected after the election, it didn't address that at all."

Henry groaned. "So, all this shit we've done means nothing."

Damson ignored Henry and tapped the conference table impatiently with his fingers. Finally, he looked back at the television screen. "Okay, where are the elector's voting documents right now?"

"The Secretary of State has them on her desk."

"You sure?"

Whitten nodded. "Yes. I checked with her this morning and told her to hold them."

"Do you think we can do anything to change them?"

"Well, the state rules say we can replace an elector if he or she opposes the party nominee."

"Did they?"

"Not a hint about how they were going to vote."

"So, now we're after the fact."

"Well voting for someone else is clearly opposing the nominee."

Damson sighed. "Clearly, by definition, but would a court agree?"

"Who knows?"

"Okay, let's say they might. Let's say you replace the two electors. What do we have to do?"

Van Hayden groaned. "The envelopes on the Secretary of State's desk contain Certificates of Vote with all the electors' signature and the Governor's Certificate of Ascertainment where all the electors' names are listed. Further, the envelopes have been endorsed by all the electors."

"So, we'd have to get two new certificates and replace all the envelopes."

Van Hayden breathed deeply. "The electors are all over the state, from here along the Hudson to west of Rochester. Besides, the dates would be different, not the dates required by law. We can't ask people to fake it. This is going to be all over the news anyway and the Republicans will throw a fit."

Damson chuckled. "They'll probably sue us in some Federal Court they own. Maybe that would delay the ballot counting and, maybe, even the inauguration."

Henry threw up his hands. "Talk about a cockeyed comedy. We'd never win. The judicial process will be expedited, and we'll look like fools."

Damson sighed. "Yeah, you're right. I'm grabbing at straws. Is there any other way to invalidate these two votes?

O'Rourke said. "Show these guys had their votes bought - prove Goldin bought them off. I'd bet that's the story."

Damson agreed. "There's no doubt in my mind, but he would have worked through a third or fourth party. He'd cover the trail."

St. James offered, "This morning, *Morning Joe* had a picture of one of these crooked electors at a ribbon-cutting ceremony five years ago with Goldin next to him with the big scissors, all of them grinning and happy."

Gwently expounded, "Don't know him – never heard of him – never met him – get photographed with all kinds of people – a hazard of the job. The Goldin twitter is probably out already."

Damson nodded in resignation. "So, when do the letters have to be someplace?"

O'Rourke seemed to wake up. "They have to be sent by registered mail, one to the President of the Senate, Sidney Stone, and two to the Archivist of the United States. Two others go to the New York Secretary of State and one to Chief Justice of the Federal District Court in Albany - have to be there by December Twenty-Three."

Damson twisted his mouth in thought. "So, we have three days."

O'Rourke corrected, "You have to allow time for the registered mail."

"Do you think they'd accept them if they were hand-delivered?"

O'Rourke considered that. "I don't think it's ever been done before."

Gwently laughed. "Do you really think Stone is going to turn down two votes for Goldin?"

Damson chuckled. "Maybe. These guys didn't vote for Stone – only for Goldin."

St. James exclaimed, "Hey, you're right. Jane Meyer is still clean. Somebody screwed up the conspiracy. Either they forgot to tell these two guys to vote for Stone or the two guys said, 'screw you', and voted for Grete."

Damson came back to the subject at hand. "Three days is what we have, guys. What can we do? Is there any way to invalidate these two votes?"

St. James suggested. "Let's get the FBI to investigate. Maybe they can hold up the whole process. What do you think, Allison?"

Gwently raised her eyebrows and sighed. "I think the AG will politely tell us to go screw ourselves. He'll say the Electoral College is state business and he'll say that no crime has been committed. There have been faithless electors before. But be that as it may, Glore and I will request an investigation and hopefully stir things up some."

Damson looked at the television monitor. "Governor, are you still there?"

"Wouldn't miss this for the world."

"Do you think the state can investigate?"

"We can try - maybe get the state police involved. But, again, the votes are not crimes. A conspiracy is. The trouble is that what we think about the conspiracy is just in our minds – hardly justification for an investigation. Still, I'll stir up some things a little bit." He then addressed Van Hayden, who was sitting at her office in Manhattan. "What do you think, Hildi?"

"I think you should do what you can. Push the newspapers, too. Tell them to go win their Pulitzer. I'll do that too. I also know some people who might help. After all, these two guys come from around here. People know people and I'll learn about them. Learning about the conspiracy, unfortunately, is something else. That will be hidden deep."

Damson sullenly admitted, "What I hear is that we can't do anything to stop the letters with the votes from being mailed in and we might as well mail them. Hopefully, what we can do is to make these votes look bad, make them really stink, and pray that Florida, or some other secret Republican domain, doesn't come up with two more votes for Goldin. As of now, I don't feel particularly good."

Chapter Forty-Six

Friday morning, Chance sat deliberating over his coffee.

He had told Shirley that he still wasn't hungry. She put a piece of toast on a plate at the head of his placemat and left him to his brooding. He knew that she was worried about him and had expected her to express her concern, even her distress. She didn't. He knew it was a matter of time.

As he fretted, his mind tried to find a way he could fix what had happened, but he knew anything he could do would be inconsequential. His sole relevance in the world had vanished with his vote earlier in the week and he had again been relegated to an insignificant role in a minor county in an average-sized state. He couldn't get much less important.

He picked up *The Washington Post* and studied the picture of Goldin cutting a ribbon at a Manhattan construction project standing next to Ivan Yaroslavna. He had read the accompanying article twice. Yaroslavna was an electrical contractor who ran I-Y Electrical Ltd in Queens, New York. The other elector who had bolted the party and voted for Goldin was a man named John Botiller of Botiller Plumbing and Drainage in Manhattan. *Both are contractors,* thought Chance. *I bet they've worked for Goldin or some of his buddies – maybe even his son's in-laws. I bet they're all an inbred group.*

Chance picked up his laptop, pushed his coffee and placemat aside, set the laptop on the table, and turned it on. He went to the yellow pages and quickly found the telephone numbers of the two companies. It seemed too easy for bad guys. Chance guessed they had to be visible to get contracts.

He disconnected his cell phone from the charging wire in the kitchen, returned to the table, and dialed his new voting compatriot, Ivan. An answering machine came on. Chance hung up. He didn't want to take a chance on his name being recognized and on not being called back.

Five minutes later he called again with the same results.

Chance got another cup of coffee thinking he might be at this awhile.

On his third call, a Slavic voice answered, sounding wary. Chance asked if he could speak to Mr. Yaroslavna. The voice answered, "Ivan's not taking calls."

"Tell him it's Chance FitzBourne."

"Chance what?"

"Another guy who didn't vote for Brock Henry."

Chance found himself listening to silence. "Hello, hello, you there?"

There was a commotion on the other end of the line. "Yeah, Ivan. Who the hell are you?"

"Another guy with the phone ringing off the hook. I didn't vote the way I was supposed to, either."

"Yeah, the press trying to interview you too?"

"Yeah, driving me nuts. How do you stop them?"

"Don't answer or tell them to go fuck themselves."

"Yeah, how do you defend yourself for not voting the way you were supposed to."

"As I said, tell them to go fuck themselves. Tell them you voted the way you had to."

"Why'd you have to?"

"Hey, who are you?"

"I told your guy. I'm Chance FitzBourne. Check the votes. I didn't vote for Henry."

"Fucking high sounding name. You vote for Goldin?"

"No."

"Then I don't want to talk to you. You're in a different boat."

Suddenly, there was a click and Chance was listening to silence. He wondered what boat Ivan was in. He concluded that it wasn't his boat.

Next, he tried to phone Botiller. He soon lost track of the number of calls. It took well over half-an-hour.

Finally, a voice answered. "Area code 540 huh? Is this Mr. Fitzcrap?"

"FitzBourne. Yes."

"Mind your own business, pal. You comprehend?"

"Uh, yeah, but...."

Chance was holding a dead phone. Well, that accomplished a lot. At least it wasn't the mafia – no *capire*.

He lay the phone on the table and speculated. *Not talking – not talking a bit – won't talk to the press, screening their calls, not talking to anyone. Embarrassed? I don't think so. I think they're scared. What the hell's going on?*

✳✳✳

That night the phone rang five times, four times from area code 718 and once from 212. When Chance answered, there was only breathing on the phone. No calls were from "unknown callers." The callers wanted Chance to know where the calls were coming from.

At 2:00 A. M. Chance and Shirley unplugged all the phones in the house.

The next day, the calls came in every couple of hours.

Again, they unplugged the phones at night and began a routine of unplugging each night and plugging the phones back in each morning. Each day the calls came in at regular intervals. By Friday afternoon, Shirley demanded to know what was going on. Chance reluctantly admitted that he had tried to play detective as an expression of remorse for not voting the Party line. His admission did not go over well. Shirley had fumed that he didn't know what he was doing and had endangered them. He argued that it would all blow over. They just had to ride it out.

On Sunday, some of the calls came from 202 and 571 area codes. Chance didn't tell Shirley, but she checked later herself and immediately erupted. "Damn Chance. These guys are coming closer. You've jeopardized our lives. These people may be killers. What are we going to do?"

"Stay calm, Shirl. People don't kill each other in Pierce County."

"Pierce County? You're being naïve, Chance – burying your head in the sand. These people aren't from Pierce County. They're from New York – from Queens, of all places, and they're coming this way."

"Okay, okay, Shirl. I'll get us an unlisted number tomorrow."

"How early can you do that?"

"I'll get up early and call until I get someone."

"That'll help, but how are we going to keep them from knowing where we live? Shoot, dumb question. We can't. All they have to do is ask someone in town."

"I'll get the Sheriff to patrol."

"Yeah, how many people has the Sheriff got – a dozen including the 911 operators?"

"Maybe she can get help from the state police."

"Lord, Chance, this is a real mess."

"Maybe we should go to stay with Junior?"

"And endanger them? That's crazy."

"Look, Shirl, the chance of these people doing something is really remote. I'm a small cheese in this world. They just want to scare us – put us in our place."

"Yeah, so small that they call us a dozen times a day. Sounds like a lot of effort to me."

"As I said, I'll talk to the Sheriff in the morning."

"Yeah, so she'll have a heads-up on who kills us."

"Shirl be real. That's not going to happen."

"Yeah, well then you won't mind my going to stay with my parents in Rockingham County."

"Shirl?"

"I'm gone, Chance. You need to decide what you're going to do."

Chapter Forty-Seven

Chance had done what he had promised Shirley. Early Monday morning he had phoned the telephone company. By mid-afternoon, the phone had stopped ringing, but he had felt only minor relief. He had known that whoever was phoning was still out there.

As soon as he had finished making arrangements with the telephone company, he had gone to see the Sheriff, Selma Woodley. He had been made to wait to talk to her. She had been on the phone dealing with Richmond about replacing a wrecked patrol car. Her door had been closed and he had barely been able to hear her. However, he had been able to hear the 911 operator in another room. She had dealt with a heart attack. She had called the rescue squads from Danesville and Wainright. Then a call had come in about someone who thought her father had COVID 19. *Lord,* Chance had thought, *it will never go away. We need a vaccine that lasts more than six months and to make everyone get vaccinated. Some people just won't do it – fear all kinds of side-effects even though science has shown there are none. If COVID doesn't get those people, the measles will.*

Finally, he had been ushered into the Sheriff's office. "Sorry, Selma, I thought I needed to see you face-to-face. Otherwise, I thought you might laugh at me. I'm being stalked."

"Stalked?"

"Well, not physically. Just by phone. I get called ten or twelve times a day, mostly from Queens and Manhattan. When Shirl or I answer, we just hear breathing on the phone. It's been going on for nearly a week. Yesterday, a couple of calls came from D.C. and Northern Virginia. It's scared the hell out of Shirley."

"But not you?"

"Worries me too."

"Did you call the phone company?"

"Got myself unlisted today."

Selma looked sternly at Chance. "Why's it happening, Chance? I know you ticked off a lot of people by not voting for Brock Henry."

"We get a lot of calls about that too, but those people aren't quiet – they don't just breath – they fuss and yell - and a few threaten, but I don't take it seriously. It's the breathing that worries me. These people are trying to intimidate and they're succeeding."

"So, if it's not your vote, what is it?"

At that point, Chance told the sheriff about his phone calls to Yaroslavna and Botiller in New York, explaining in the process who the two men were. He had further explained that Yaroslavna had ended the conversation quickly and then had apparently phoned Bottiler before Chance could get his call through to the latter and that Botiller had cut him off instantly.

After Chance's narrative, the Sheriff sighed deeply. "So, these are the same two guys who have been in the paper all week with everyone offering theories about why they voted for Goldin and you think they're threatening you."

"I don't know who's threatening me. Maybe someone thinks I know something or that I'm contributing to the theories and that they want me to be quiet."

"Do you know anything?"

"No. I tried to learn something by calling those two guys but learned nothing."

"Well, it sounds like you tried to play detective and it made someone unhappy."

"But I don't know anything."

"But you're afraid someone thinks you do?"

"Look, Selma, I came to you in person because I was afraid you'd laugh at me if I phoned you."

"Well, it is hard to conceive of mobsters in New York City worrying about a farmer in Pierce County."

"But they are. What can you do?"

"Heck, Chance, you were worried about me laughing at you. What do you think the NYPD is going to do?"

"But you will contact them?"

"Yeah, I'll send an email."

"How about staking out the farm?"

"Staking out? Chance, I've got two patrolmen at night to cover the whole county. I'll have them run by your place some, but you're way up in a hollow. There's only so much I can do."

"Please, do the best you can. I'm worried."

"You really think the mafia is coming to Pierce County?"

"One guy with a big gun would be bad enough."

***

On Christmas morning, Chance was up early and drinking his coffee while watching the morning news on television.

He heard the buzzer go off as someone crossed the cattle gate at the entrance to the farm. He went to the front door, looked out, and saw a Pierce County Sheriff's car coming up the driveway. He felt uncertainty run through his intestines.

A young deputy exited the cruiser. Chance didn't know him and thought, *must be a new guy.*

The young man walked up the sidewalk toward where Chance stood. "Sir, are you the owner of this farm?"

He is a new guy.

"Yes, may I help you?"

"Uh, sir. I just wanted to let you know that there's a skunk hanging from your gate post."

"A skunk?"

"Looks like road-kill someone nailed up there."

Chance closed his eyes and groaned. "Will you tell the Sheriff?"

"Oh, yessir."

"As soon as possible. It's a message."

"A message?"

"A warning – a threat."

"Sir?"

"You'll tell her?"

"Yessir."

Chapter Forty-Eight

Christmas day was the first Chance remembered that he hadn't celebrated the day with Junior or Junior and his family.

He phoned Junior early. Bev answered. He apologized to her and said that he and Shirley would not be coming over for Christmas.

Bev wanted to know if anything was wrong.

"No," he said, "but Shirley has gone to her parents in Rockingham County."

"Oh, that was kind of sudden."

"Yeah, kind of a last-minute decision. Is Junior there?"

"Yeah, he's in with the kids opening presents."

"May I speak to him?"

"Uh, sure."

A moment later Junior came on the phone. "What's up, Dad? You're not coming over? Mom's gone to her parents?"

"Yeah, it's a long story. I didn't want to worry Bev."

"Worry her? What's going on? You and Mom having problems?"

"No, no, nothing like that. You have a minute?"

"Of course."

Chance sat down and told Junior what he had done in calling people in New York and all that had followed and why Shirley had gone to her parents. He finished by telling Junior about the dead skunk.

"Gosh, that's scary Dad. Do you think you're in danger? Do I need to come over?"

Chance assured his son that someone was just trying to intimidate him and that he didn't think it would go any further. "After all," he said, "I don't know anything."

"Yeah, but do these people know that?"

"Well, I haven't said anything to anyone except the Sheriff – not to newspapers or anything. I would think these people would realize, because of my silence, that I'm not going to do them any harm."

"Yeah, maybe, call me if anything more happens."

"Okay, but don't worry and wish everyone a Merry Christmas."

Chapter Forty-Nine

Damson was at his desk the day after Christmas before Skylar had gotten to work. His Christmas day had lasted forever - at least it had seemed that way.

Goldin had been strangely quiet on the internet, but rumor had it that he was raging, the West Wing was in turmoil. Despite the rumor, when Skylar had brought in a single tweet, it was one wishing the Country a fantastic Christmas and a beautiful New Year.

To Damson, the atmosphere in Washington had seemed ominous.

While Goldin was being quiet, Brock Henry was running wild. He had practically covered every talk show the Sunday before Christmas and had been on MSNBC, CNN and the local morning shows every other day. He had been talking about a White House conspiracy, saying that Goldin cohorts were paying bribes and offering contracts to buy off electors.

Goldin reappeared briefly on Monday morning to issue a couple of tweets:

"Brock Henry was seen sneaking into Santa's sleigh and opening empty boxes – a real loser."

"And they accused the GOP of pushing conspiracy theories – be real - Dems are sad and desperate – pushing more fake news."

Damson felt desperate, indeed, but Henry was exacerbating everything. Goldin was using it as best he could.

Still, Goldin wasn't declaring victory.

That was interesting.

If Goldin had more Electoral Votes coming from the secret ballots in the Republican states, why wasn't he bragging – why was the West Wing in turmoil – or was the turmoil fake news issued so that a Goldin victory would come as a magical triumph and Goldin could appear as rising from the ashes to save the Nation?

Or was something wrong?

Damson rubbed his forehead and thought of chaos, turmoil, and utter disaster.

***

Damson's telephone buzzed.

"Yes, Skylar."

"Someone named Van Hayden's on the phone."

"She's the New York State Democratic Chairwoman."

"Oh, now I remember."

"Is it line two?"

"Yes, boss."

“I’ll take it.”

Damson punched the button. “Yes, Hildi. What’s up?”

“Just wanted to let you know what’s happening.”

“I’m waiting with bated breath.”

“Well, you’ve seen the picture of Yaroslavna with Goldin five years ago. He was working on one of the President’s towers then. He hasn’t worked for Goldin since but has worked for the father of the President’s son-in-law. Still is. Has a contract right now.

The other guy, Botiller, has never worked for Goldin, but he has a bid in now to rehab the plumbing in several tenements owned by the uncle of the son-in-law.”

“Have you told the Governor about this?”

“My next call.”

“Have you leaked it to the papers?”

“Already done, but there’s more. I’ve had the two guys being watched, at their offices and their apartments.”

“The NYPD?”

“No. I’d have to go through the mayor to do that and this isn’t official. Just using some guys I know.”

“And?”

“The two electors are pretty well holed up. The press has been after them both. But Yaroslavna did come out of his office the day before Christmas and got a cup of coffee at a restaurant nearby. He sat down at a table that was already occupied by a man named Joe or Joey Griolli. The same man visited a bar where Botiller was having a beer last Saturday.”

“Yeah, so who’s this guy Griolli?”

“A hood. Usually works for a higher up.”

“Do we know the higher up?”

“A friend in the NYPD says it’s Bernie Stein.”

“Doesn’t sound like the mafia.”

Van Hayden chuckled, “Similar, but he’s more society friendly.”

“So, he knows people?”

“Bet there’s a picture of him with Goldin someplace.”

"I'll get a guy I know at *The Post* to check the archives."

"You can do that and hold it in reserve. Right now, however, we're not able to show a direct link to our rogue electors."

"Faithless electors."

"Whatever. All I know is that they have a link to bad guys."

"We already guessed that."

"Yeah, but a guess is just a guess. It doesn't rock the world."

"Well, leak what you can. Let's create uncertainty."

"Trouble is, I've never known Goldin followers to care."

"Yeah, we need a picture of his bare ass in bed with one of his hookers."

"Wouldn't that be beautiful? You think his pompadour would be mussed?"

"I think it's solid lacquer. Probably springs back in place when you hit it."

"You sound jealous, Ed."

"Of the hookers or the hair?"

"Don't be crude, Ed."

"Well, we bald guys can dream."

Chapter Fifty

By ten o'clock on Friday, two days after Christmas, Chance had finished his third cup of coffee.

For more than a day no one had phoned. There had been no skunks hung on the gate posts.

He thought, *Maybe it's over. Maybe Shirl can come home.*

Then the phone rang. Chance picked up and glanced at the screen – "Pierce County Observer."

He answered. "That you, Jace?"

"Yeah, Chance. Happy Holidays."

"You, too, Jace. You sitting there bored? I see you didn't publish yesterday."

"Too soon after Christmas. We're putting out a big edition Tuesday, next week, getting it out before New Year's."

"So, you're working hard?"

"Always."

"What can I do for you Jace?"

"You see *The Post* this morning?"

"No, I haven't been down to the gate to pick it up. Is there something in it I need to know about?"

"Something that might interest you. An article about those two guys in New York, the Democrats who voted for Goldin."

"Oh?"

"Seems that they're both involved in contracts with relatives of Goldin's son in-law, the father-in-law and uncle-in-law."

"Uncle-in-law?"

"Father-in-law's brother."

"Keeping it in the family?"

"Looks that way. The article also points out that the two electors have been getting visits from a guy named Joey Griolli, a New York hood with a long rap sheet."

"Oh, hell!"

"Oh, hell, Chance? What's that mean?"

"Did the paper say where the information came from?

"Anonymous."

"Damn."

"What's going on Chance? Why do you care?"

"Bad guys might think the information came from me."

"Did it?"

"No! Do you really think I stake out businesses in New York?"

"I didn't think so. So, tell me. What's going on?"

"You promise not to put it in the paper?"

"Really, Chance?"

"Really."

"Okay."

Chance hesitated and then told him.

"Gosh, Chance. That's weird. Kind of goes with this story in the paper. Sounds like the mafia or someone like that is involved."

"Yeah, and I don't want the involvement. Scares the hell out of me, and these guys harassing me may think I put that in *The Post*. If something happens to me, you know why."

"Don't joke Chance."

"I'm not."

***

When Chance returned home, he rummaged through the papers on his dining room table and found the phone number for Ivan Yaroslavna. He picked up his cell phone and started to dial but stopped before he put the call through. *Heck, I was about to give them my cell number.*

He picked up the house phone and dialed. On the fourth try, he got through.

The same man answered. "We're not taking any calls."

Chance quickly replied. "That's what you told me last week."

"It's worse now."

"But you put me through."

"You the guy who didn't vote for Henry?"

"Yeah."

"Well, you didn't make Ivan happy."

"Just want to say something."

"I'll ask him."

A moment passed.

"What do you want now?"

201

"That stuff in the paper wasn't from me. I don't know anything.
Did you tell someone about me?"

"You dumb shit. Stay out of this."

The phone banged down.

Chance stared at the phone. I hope the hell he heard me.
I hope he tells the bad guys and they believe me. God, I hope.

Chapter Fifty-One

That night Chance sat reading. He was lonely without
Shirley. He had decided to wait one more day and then
try to get her to come home.

He had watched television until ten o'clock, his normal
bedtime, but hadn't gone to bed because he knew he wouldn't
sleep.

Suddenly, the buzzer from the gate sounded. He glanced at his watch. Seven after eleven. *No one in the county visits this late. It's either a deputy or no good.*

Chance picked up his shotgun. He only had #4 birdshot, but it would have to do.

He headed for the front door. He turned out the hall lights so that he wouldn't be silhouetted and opened the door. He didn't turn on the porch lights or the yard lamp. He stepped out onto the porch and at the top of the steps he stopped and stared into the dark. He didn't see any headlights. *It's not the deputy.*

He moved quickly across the front yard to the head of the driveway and stopped to listen. *Some cars are quiet these days, but the gravel always crushes.* He heard nothing. He again stared into the darkness. He couldn't see a thing. It was overcast and threatening to rain.

He started down the drive but then decided to move off to the side a few feet so that he wouldn't meet someone head-on. He stumbled over tufts of grass and prayed that he wouldn't step in a cow patty.

He still heard nothing. He hadn't seen a car door open, but maybe the guy knew how to turn off the inside lights. Still, he hadn't heard a car door close, but maybe it hadn't been closed. Chance felt for certain that he was not alone.
Suddenly there was a cry a few feet ahead. He recognized the cry of a hurt calf. He flipped on his cell phone, shining it ahead. A man was standing over a calf that was trying to getaway. The man was cutting the calf's neck with a long knife.

Chance shouted. "Stop. I've got a gun on you."

The man froze. Chance held the shotgun with one arm, turned the phone toward himself, and started to dial 911. As he did so, his eyes recognized some motion in the dim light of the reversed phone and raised his gun to fire. Before he could do so, a huge black shadow crossed in front of him knocking the intruder down, as the man fired his weapon, the shot going heaven knows where. The momma heifer had arrived to care for her calf.

Chance hadn't been able to shoot because he knew what was happening and didn't want to shoot the heifer. He could hear the 911 operator answering as he charged forward, his phone again shining its light forward. The man was scrambling, looking for his gun.

Chance kicked it away while shouting directions toward the phone, hoping the operator could hear him. "Sit still, or you're going to get a load of buckshot."

The man stopped moving.

"Lie flat with your arms out. I'd love to fire this thing. You hurt my calf to get at me. You're a low, goddamn bastard."

Chance turned the phone back to his face. "Did you hear me?"

"We're on the way Chance."

Good. *The operator is someone I know.*

Chance sat on the ground, ten feet from the intruder, with his shotgun at the ready. He didn't want to shoot, but there was no doubt in his mind that he would.

He listened to the heifer caring for the calf. He prayed that it wasn't badly hurt. *I'll phone Forjambi as soon as the deputy gets here.*

Five minutes went by. It seemed like long five minutes.

A car with flashing lights came down the road and turned in the driveway, its headlights blinding Chance. He quickly covered his eyes and looked away so that he could still track the intruder.

The door to the deputy's car opened and closed and Chance could see a figure coming toward him.

A second car with flashing lights came down the road and turned in the driveway.

Chance sighed with relief. Thank God, there are two deputies. They can take control. The first deputy to arrive was the young man who had told him about the skunk. Fortunately, he recognized Chance and turned his gun toward the intruder, his hand shaking a little. "What happened?"

"The bastard tried to kill my calf."

"Was he stealing it?"

"No. He was sending me a message."

"Like the skunk?"

"Exactly."

"Damn. That's mean."

"It sure as hell is."

The second deputy arrived. Chance knew him. "Hi, Charley. Good to see you."

"Gosh, Chance. What the hell's going on?"

"Man tried to kill my calf."

"Damn." He turned to the intruder. "Get your ass up fella."

Chance picked up the intruder's pistol and handed it to the young deputy who took it gingerly as Chance told him, "The guy brought this with him. Fired one round into the never, never, so it needs the safety put on." He turned to Charley. "You got this, Charley? I need to phone the vet."

"It's midnight, Chance."

"Yeah. Life of a big animal vet. He better have the phone by his bed."

Chapter Fifty-Two

Chance heard the buzzer from the gate mid-afternoon the next day. He picked up the shotgun and looked out the window. Jason Phelps was driving up the driveway.

He looked at the gun in his hand, shook his head, and set it down next to the door, leaning against the wall – *some way to live.*

He opened the door, stepped out on the front porch, and waited for Jace to exit his car.

As Jace came up the walk, he greeted Chance. "Hey, man, I hear you had a wild night."

"You might say that."

"How's the calf?"

Chance laughed. "I thought that would be the last thing you asked about. She's stitched up. Sorry to say she is stumbling a bit. Some nerve and muscle damage. She'll live to go to market, but she won't be good for much else."

"Sorry to hear that Chance. Hell of a thing."

"So, you heard about everything?"

"Just came from talking to Selma. She'd just come back from taking your culprit to the district jail. Not the kind of guy she wanted to keep locally."

"Did she identify him?"

Jace flipped open a small notebook. "Gus Fromach from Queens."

Chance sighed. "Damn, this whole thing is international."

Jace laughed. "I guess they're all after you. Not a nice guy. Rap sheet in New York long as your arm – armed robbery - assault and battery - two stints in prison. It goes back to when he was twelve years old. Now he's forty-two. Selma called the F.B.I. because of the guy traveling across state lines to commit a crime. They said they'd be out mid-morning to interview the guy, but they didn't show. She called them back, and they said the AG had told them not to come."

"The AG, as in the Department of Justice?"

"Yeah, came down from the top."

"You're kidding me?"

"Cross my heart and hope to die."

"How'd the AG even know what happened?"

"Interesting question. I didn't put it out. Didn't even learn about it until late morning."

"Strange as hell."

"Indeed. Heard you cornered the guy with your shotgun."

"After the calf's momma ran the guy down. Otherwise, I might not be here. The guy had a pistol."

"No shit."

"Ugly thing."

"So, what do you think it's about? I understand you had a skunk hide tacked to your gate a few days ago. Now, this. Do you think someone is getting back at you for not voting for Henry?"

"No."

"No?"

"I think it's got something to do with those guys I phoned in New York. I think someone thinks I know something and is trying to intimidate me."

"What the hell, Chance. All the way down here in Pierce County. That's unreal."

"My conspiracy theory."

"Hmm, that's a hell of a lot to think about."

"And now the AG's involved."

"Direct line from there to the President."

"And a direct line from there to where?"

"You mind if I send this to the AP?"

"No, but you might go easy on the conspiracy theory."

"You think?"

"Yeah, you don't want people to think you're nuts."

"Heck, the President supports them all the time."

"Well, some people think he's nuts."

"And others believe him."

"Everything he says."

"Hell of a world."

Chapter Fifty-Three

Damson arrived at work the next morning with the first section of *The New York Times* under his arm.

Skylar handed him the Goldin tweets:

"Democrats attack their own – kill a calf because Virginia farmer didn't vote as he was told – vicious."

"Democrats, you need to watch your backs – behave yourselves or the long arm of the Party will reach out and punish you."

"Democrats are desperate, attack their own as their election dreams fall apart and the Nation turns to me for salvation."

Damson shook his head, muttered "Me, me, me," looked at Skylar and told her to get Rossi to his office.

Rossi arrived with another copy of *The New York Times* in his hands. He found his boss with the previous day's paper spread out on his desk.

Damson looked up and saw the paper. "Dom, have you got something new today?"

"Yeah, *The Times* sent someone down to Wainright from their Washington Bureau yesterday. The guy talked to the Sheriff at her home, FitzBourne at his home and the local paper's editor while he was standing in the middle of a stream fishing."

"All that in the article?"

"No, but I have a friend at the bureau."

"And?"

"Well, FitzBourne just repeated what was in the paper yesterday about the attack on his cow."

"On his calf."

"Right."

"Killed the calf?"

"No. The calf's hurt but not dead."

"Another Goldin lie."

"Misinformation."

"Right. Intimidation. Was the guy intimidated?"

"Article didn't say."

"And the newspaper editor?"

"Told the story that was in yesterday's paper about FitzBourne involving himself with the New York people. Said FitzBourne called the Russian back and asked the guy to back off or have whoever back off. Told the Russian he didn't know anything and to pass it on."

"Evidently, it didn't work. Did *The Times* make a connection?"

"They suggest a few things, but it's vague."

"Maybe we need to un-vague it."

"Un-vague?"

"Clarify, illuminate. What the hell, Dom. Don't give me a hard time."

"Okay. What do you want me to do?"

"Write tweets. I want you to gather whoever you wish and start producing tweets, implying collusion in the Goldin Administration. We'll get Henry, Glore, Gwently, and legislatures of their choice to flood the world with them. Henry hasn't been doing much anyway. He meets with groups here and there and talks about his socialist ideas. He's not attacking. There are so many stupid and criminal actions coming out of this White House that it should be fodder for his speeches."

"I thought the "s" word isn't allowed in this building."

"Between you and me, Dom. Between you and me. The point is that what Henry's saying gives the Republicans ammunition to use against him. That's crazy, especially when Goldin and his peons are providing ammunition we should be using. We must turn this elector fiasco against him – put it where it belongs. He's selling this as something the Democrats have done. We need to lay it on the President where it belongs."

"But we don't have any facts."

"Stretch what we know. Make them facts. The innuendo is growing. Use it. Goldin somehow turned these electors with offers of contracts, threats, who knows what. Make them real. This is politics, Dom. Do what Goldin does. We have a week left before the Electoral Votes are tallied in a joint session of Congress. We don't know what Goldin is going to pull. Whatever it is, the American public has got to believe that it's bogus, that it's a criminal cabal of the most malevolent kind. Now organize your most obnoxious friends and accomplices and get to work."

✳✳✳

"Chairwoman Van Hayden's on the phone."

Damson had just returned to his office and was settling into his chair". Line three, Skylar?"

"Yes, boss."

"Good, the 'two' button is getting worn out."

He pushed three. "Hey, Hildi, our two boys acting up?"

"No, it's something new."

"Oh"

"The elector from Medford didn't come home Christmas Eve."

"Yeah, where's Medford?"

"Long Island."

"Another local boy, huh?"

"You talking about New York City being the nexus of faithless electors?"

"Yeah, Goldin territory. So, what happened?"

"The guy went out for a six-pack and eggnog about six and never came home."

"The police can't find him?"

"Nah. They've been looking since late Christmas day but weren't fully manned till the next day. They found the store where he bought the stuff, but no one has seen him since."

"Did they find his car."

"No, he walked to the store."

"You think he was supposed to be the 269th elector?"

"We'll never know, but that was my thought."

"You think they'll find a body?"

"Ed, we've got the Long Island Sound on one side of the island and the Atlantic Ocean on the other side."

211

"You really think he might have been killed?"

"Hell, Ed, if big money was paid and someone didn't produce, people might become pissed."

Chapter Fifty-Four

The DNC met the day before the Joint Session of Congress to Tabulate the vote of the Electoral College. Damson called the meeting to order. "Ladies and Gentlemen, I think we've done all we can We've flooded the internet, Twitter, Facebook, Instagram, and half a dozen other social networks with our position relative to a probable conspiracy by the Goldin Administration to circumvent the vote of the Electoral College. We've been on the morning shows and the news networks. We've been on talk radio. Our members of the House and Senate have held town meetings. In summary, we've brought our story to the public in every way we can. With that all said and done, we still are subject to the unknown votes of the electors in some of the states under the control of Republican Governors. Four of those states have had their votes leaked – Texas, Wisconsin, Utah, and Wyoming. They voted Republican and for Goldin anyway, so the leaks really tell us nothing. This year, we Democrats won the popular votes in Florida, Illinois, and New Jersey, states with Republican governors. Therein lie our worries. We don't know the results of the Electoral College votes in those three states. If two voters in those states flip on us, we're dead and Goldin will have four more years as President. Unless someone else has ideas, all we can do is wait."

Elwood Smethers raised his hand.

Damson recognized him.

"Ed, Speaker Gwently is going to be sitting behind Stone while he's serving as President of the Joint Session. When he gets ready to announce the election results, why can't she stick up fingers behind him on each side of his head and give him horns if we lose?"

Damson made a face and shook his head. "I'm sorry, but if that's all we can think to do, maybe we deserve what we get."

Smethers looked chagrined. "Just a joke."

Damson sighed, "Sorry Elwood. I think we're beyond jokes." He hesitated a moment. "Okay, let's consider the best case."

Glore looked up. "Best case?"

"The best case is where we now stand. Goldin has 268 Electoral Votes and, as of now, Henry has 269. If Goldin doesn't flip anymore, we don't lose. The trouble is, if he flips two, we do lose. Flipping votes has never been a problem with Electoral College because the vote hasn't been this close. Besides, the history of the vote has all happened before Goldin. If he flips one more or even none, the House of Representatives will have to decide who will be President per the Twelfth Amendment to the Constitution. That is going to be a challenge. Nonetheless, it's not what we are hoping for."

St. James grinned. "That would be great. We've got a majority in the House."

Damson nodded. "Yes, we do, but the Amendment says each state gets only one vote."

"Oh, Lord, so that means all the Representatives of each state have to get together and decide who they vote for."

Damson squeezed his lips together and raised his eyebrows. "That's what I would surmise, although it hasn't been done in over two hundred years."

"So, the party with the most Representatives in each state gets that state's vote?"

"I would assume so."

"What if a state has the same number of Representatives from each party? Then, how is the vote determined?"

Gwently spoke up. "It would be a draw, wouldn't it?"

Damson said, "I guess it would be up to them whether they abstained or simply didn't vote. I think they'd have to do the former if they wanted to be considered part of the quorum."

St. James asked, "What's a quorum?"

"Two-third of the states."

"Two-thirds of the Representatives of the states?"

"No, two-thirds of the states."

O'Rourke shook his head. "Does that mean the winner is the one getting a majority vote from those present, and if only the two-thirds quorum is present, which I would assume is thirty-four states, then eighteen votes would win."

Damson shook his head. "No, the winner must get a vote of the majority of the states, twenty-six, no matter how many states are present."

Smethers exclaimed, "Oh, Golly, in how many states do we have a majority of the Representatives?"

Damsons smiled weakly. "Twenty-three."

"And the Republicans?"

"Twenty-four."

"Oh, Golly. And the fifty-three Representatives from California and the one Representative from Wyoming each have one vote."

"Correct."

Glore intervened. "I think the term is 'oh, shit', Elwood." He looked at Damson. "Tell us about the other three states." They're divided with an equal number of Democratic and Republican Representatives in each, two Representatives in Rhode Island, two in New Hampshire, and four from Iowa."

"That means eight out of the 435 Representatives control the whole shooting match."

Damson nodded in agreement. "That's right, and I talked to all four Democrats this morning and told them either not to vote or abstain on every damn vote unless they can turn a Republican."

St. James shook his head. "This could go on forever unless someone dies or is absent."

Damson smiled malignantly, turning to Gwently. "Fortunately, the Speaker is the one who convenes the meetings."

St. James smiled. "Move quickly, Allison, if a Republican dies."

Damson confirmed. "Yes, Emery, you're right, it could go on forever because the Twentieth Amendment screwed up everything.   Under the Twelfth Amendment, when the inauguration day was the 15th of March if the House didn't elect a President by the 4th of March, the Vice President-elect became the President.   The Twentieth Amendment says that if the President hasn't been chosen by the Twentieth of January, the Vice President only acts as President until the President becomes 'qualified,' whatever 'qualified' means."

Glore shook his head.   "So, we could have an acting President for two years, until the next House is elected?"

"Or longer, I guess unless I don't understand something."

"That's a hell of a note."

"No, it's no damn way to run a country."

Damson turned to Gwently.   "Allison, you're going to have to be ready.   The Constitution says that if the Electoral College doesn't elect a President, the House will 'immediately' select the President.   I'm not sure what 'immediately' means.   I assume you'll have time to kick the Senate out of your chamber and take a bathroom break, but you don't want to give the Republicans something to complain about."

Gwently looked at him apprehensively.   "What do I do if we can't get a majority of the states to agree to meet?"

"Then it's on your shoulders, lady.   The Constitution only says for you to do it 'immediately'."

"Well, thank the Constitution for all its help."

Chapter Fifty-Five

The day was a big deal. The Joint Meeting of Congress to Tabulate the Vote of the Electoral College had been a PBS presentation in recent years. This year, however, it was on all major networks, each with a team of newscasters to provide a lead-in before the meeting and analysis afterward. As the broadcasts came on, there was extensive discussion of Goldin having been soundly beaten in the popular vote and how incredulous it was that he was still very much in the running to win a second term of his Presidency. There was discussion of the faithless elector from Virginia, who, perhaps, had opened the door for Democratic electors to change their vote, followed by an extensive discussion of why two New York electors had mysteriously and puzzlingly changed their pledged votes from Henry to Goldin. All kinds of unsubstantiated theories were discussed. Depending on the network, Goldin was either inferred to have done something bordering on criminal interference with the election process, or not.

Finally, the discussion turned to three states which had Republican governors but had voted for the Democratic slate. These states had followed the Goldin directive to maintain secrecy in the Electoral Vote and, therefore, if there were to be any more faithless Democratic electors, they would have to come from these states. They were universally known as "the secret states". They were the states that controlled the future of Isaac Ambler Goldin, Florida, Illinois, and New Jersey.

Chance watched from his living room, alone. He cringed to think he might have opened the door to all this chaos. *I had nothing to do with those guys in New York. They're criminals, doing all kinds of illegal stuff. I was voting my conscience. That had nothing to do with what happened in New York. What happened there had nothing to do with conscience. It had to do* with illegal manipulation on the part of Goldin's cohorts, perhaps Goldin himself. *Don't blame it on me.*

At last, the meeting was convened. The Speaker welcomed everyone, including the television audience, which was very unusual, thus acknowledging the importance of the session. She then introduced Vice President Sidney Stone to serve as the President of the meeting. Stone went through formalities, indicating that they were there to ascertain the vote of the Electoral College and asking the tellers to be seated at the clerk's desk. Two members of the Senate and two members of the House had been selected as tellers to present the votes.

Stone said that the tellers would dispense with the reading of the formal part of the certificates and stated that after determining that the certificates were regular in form and authentic, the tellers would announce the vote cast by the electors of each state beginning with the State of Alabama.

Republican Senator Stan Bernecker was handed certificates by Stone and approached the microphone. "Mr. President, the certificates of the Electoral Vote of the State of Alabama seem to be regular in form and authentic and it appears therefrom that Isaac Ambler Goldin of the State of New York received 9 votes for President and Sidney A. Stone of the State of Nebraska received 9 votes for Vice President.

As Representative Aaron Wilson rose to read the votes of the electors of the State of Alaska, Chance bolted for the kitchen to get a drink.

By the time Chance returned to the living room, Senator Bernecker was back at the microphone announcing the Electoral Vote from California. Chance listened carefully, but California was solid blue, casting all its fifty-five votes for Brock Henry of the State of Colorado for President and Jane M. Grete of the State of Maryland for Vice President.

Chance sighed. He had already known the California vote but was still relieved to have it official. That was one Democratic state down, twenty-some-odd to go. Four more Democratic states followed quickly. Colorado, Connecticut, Delaware, and the District of Columbia. All voted Democratic as everyone already knew. They were not secret states.

The next state to vote was the one of "the secret states", Florida, which had voted for the Democratic slate for the first time in several years despite having a Republican governor. Goldin made his winter home in Naples. Chance felt that if a disaster were to strike his Party, it would be in Florida.

Representative Wilson was up again. ".... that Brock Henry of the State of Colorado received twenty-nine votes for President......"

The crowded chamber erupted, cheers coming from the Democrats, and some from the gallery. Stone pounded on his desk with his gavel. "The chamber will come to order!" He pounded again and shouted again.

Chance had been holding his breath and now let it out. Florida was secure.

The voting dragged on and Chance began to dose.

".... Brock Henry of the State of Colorado received nineteen votes for President and Isaac Ambler Goldin of the State of New York received one vote...."

Chance shook himself awake. "What, what the hell?"

"...for President, Jane M. Grete of the State of Maryland received nineteen votes for Vice President and Sidney A. Stone of the State of Nebraska received one vote for Vice President."

"Damn, what state was that?" Chance had lost track and hadn't heard the name of the state. He thought *that was Wilson again. He would be number 2, 6, 10, 14. State fourteen.* Chance went down the list of states. *Fourteen. That's Illinois. I should have known. I should have been awake. The bastards screwed us. No wonder Wilson smirked. Damn Republican. What's Goldin building in Illinois? Bet the guy, the elector, is a contractor. That gives Goldin 269 votes. New Jersey can kill us. Where's Tony Soprano when you need him?*

Chance counted down the states. New Jersey was number 31. *At least it's not that damn Wilson again. Should be the Democrat, what's her name, Sylvia Prossner, Representative Prossner.*

Chance looked back at the television screen. They were in Iowa. *What the hell happened to Indiana? I'm thinking too much – missing things.*

Chance drained his soda and went to get another.

Must stay awake.

He started to sit back in his club chair but decided on a straight chair instead.

They were now in Louisiana.

Lord, will they never get there?

Chance's hands were clenched. He felt like his blood pressure was going through roof. He felt blood pumping in his temples. The sound on the television seemed to be going in and out, up and down.

New Hampshire went fine. All the votes were for Henry – all four of them.

New Jersey was up.

"Do it right, Prosser! It's all on you!"

Don't I wish.

"Mr. President, the certificates of the Electoral Vote of the State of New Jersey...."

Chance was bouncing in his chair. "Come on! Come on!"

"...seem to be regular in form and authentic. It appears therefrom..."

"Hurry!!!"

"...that Brock Henry of the State of Colorado received fourteen votes for President...,"

Chance came out of his chair, throwing his arm into the air and spilling his drink. "Yeah, we did it."

He set his drink on the coffee table and plopped into his club chair, pounding his fists on the arms. "Damn, we survived!"

Finally, he settled into the chair and realization came over him. "Damn, I'm cheering because we didn't lose."

His mind turned back to the television and the proceedings. Stone was still hammering his gavel.

Suddenly, Chance's telephone rang.

220

He looked at the telephone screen – Gwen Ellen Dunbardy.

He turned down the television and answered. "You haven't talked to me in nearly two months."

"Yeah, well you're off the hook, kind of. Those three votes for Goldin would have cost us the election anyway."

"Wonder where his fourth vote went? You think he screwed up?"

"I think somebody screwed up and is going to catch it if he or she hasn't already."

"How do you think he turned those three."

"I can conjecture. I can hope someday we'll know, but I'm certain of one thing, something's not right – something's far from Kosher."

"You think we'll be reading conspiracy theories?"

"Reams of them - fodder for talking heads for weeks to come."

"Goldin loves conspiracy theories."

"Not these."

Chapter Fifty-Six

In the House Chamber an undercurrent of voices continued through the balance of the tabulation of the votes despite Stone's periodic pounding of his gavel and demand for order.

Finally, the vote was summarized - 269 for Goldin, 268 for Henry, and one for Grete.

Stone announced that the meeting was complete and then looked confused. He turned to Gwently who was sitting behind him. They talked for a moment. Then Stone returned to the microphone. "The members of the House will please stay in place. For the members of the Senate, this meeting is adjourned. Please promptly leave the chamber so that the House can proceed with its duties."

As the Senators filed out of the chamber, Gwently took up the President's gavel and pounded a couple of times. "The House will take a break and reconvene here in twenty minutes."

Mild chaos commenced as the Congressmen and Congresswomen joined the Senators in exiting the room. It took only a few minutes for the bathrooms to be jammed. Several Congressmen were verbal in complaining that Senators were using their bathrooms – after all, the Senators had all the time in the world, while the Congressmen only had twenty minutes.

As the Members of House returned to the chamber, a few sat, but most stood in small groups talking.

Gwently tried to judge when all were back. She had to stretch up to see over the podium to make the determination. She hated that she was short and that she was known as the Kathy Bates of Congress. That didn't reflect the power she had.

Finally, she tapped the gavel a couple of times and asked the House to come to order.

The members took their seats, a few rushing in from the lobby.

She turned to the Clerk of the House. "Please take the roll."

Voices came from the chamber in mild protest but finally silenced as the roll was called. It was a long and painful process.

When the roll call was over, the Clerk announced that all Representatives were present except Representative Neale of the State of California.

Gently frowned. "Will the Sergeant at Arms please go and find Representative Neale and bring him to the chamber?"

At that, there was a great deal of grousing. Gwently tapped the desk and silence returned. "This House is about to commence the conduct of an important Constitutional process, that is, the election of the President of the United States. It is important that all members of the House participate in meeting this important Constitutional requirement. We all have a role to fill. All of us must participate."

Gwently sat back in her chair while the chamber of Representatives waited for Neale. She was determined to make a point, establish a precedent for future meetings. In reality, Neale's absence made little difference. He was from California, one of the fifty-three Representatives. But Gwently knew that if one Representative from a smaller state, especially a state with equal numbers of Democratic and Republican Representatives, were absent, it might be disastrous.

The chamber waited and waited. The Representatives became more and more verbal, more and more disgruntled.

Finally, Neale came into the room, looking guilty, and carrying a little girl.

Gwently rose and went to the microphone. "Late for the nursery, Rep. Neale?"

Neale apologized as she hurried to his seat. "My apologies, Madame Speaker."

"Plan your time better next time, Rep. Neale."

"Yes, Ma'am.

Gwently looked around the chamber. "Did anyone escape while we were playing hide and seek?"

There were some chuckles, but the members quickly settled down under the Speaker's glare.

She tapped her gavel again. "The Constitution, in the event no candidate for the Presidency receives at least a majority of the Electoral Votes, requires that the House meet immediately and pick a President from the top three vote-getters in the election. That would be President Goldin, Senator Henry, and Governor Grete. I think, considering our physical needs, this is about as immediate as we can hold this meeting."

A voice came from the chamber. "Objection, Madame Speaker."

Gwently looked out into the Chamber. "The Speaker recognizes Representative DeWitt."

"Madame Speaker, it would appear unnecessary to include Governor Grete. From the vote, it appears that she is not a real player in this election, having garnered only one vote."

"As you note, Governor Grete is a minor player. Nonetheless, the Twelfth Amendment to the Constitution says, 'not exceeding three' and I see no harm in including the Governor. We shouldn't question the Constitution. It gives no guidance as to how to exclude one of the three. So, we'll consider all three."

She looked around and continued, "And speaking of the Constitution, it says we must have a quorum of two-thirds of the House. The roll call indicates we do indeed have a quorum.
Now, the tough part. In voting for the President, each state has only one vote."

There was murmuring in the chamber.

Gwently waited until it settled down. She tapped the gavel. "So, here's what you need to do. The seating in this chamber isn't designed to address this issue. What you all must do, for each state, is meeting in the middle, Republicans, Democrats, Independents, whatever. Form a state mini caucus. If you haven't met, shake hands. I'd like California to meet in the back left of the room, Texas in the back right, Florida in the front left, and New York in the front right. The rest of you meet

where you can find a space. Here's your job. For each state, you will select a foreman to speak on the state's behalf. Then you will pick the person you will vote for to become President. When the smoke settles, I will have the Clerk request each state's foreman to state his or her name to state the vote for President. Any questions?"
She looked around. "All right, have at it."

Representatives of the four states that had been assigned specific locations to meet moved quickly. Others moved with hesitation and uncertainty. For the larger states, each party's Representatives stayed in a group as if for security, and only reluctantly moved to the center to join the other party. Representatives of the smaller states came together relatively quickly.

As the groups came together, the noise in the room grew to a crescendo. A few Representatives stormed out of the group meetings and returned to their seats. Two of these sat with their arms crossed and glared ahead.

After ten minutes, Gwently rose and pounded her gavel. "All right. Face it. Each state is going to vote along Party lines, so pick a foreman and get on with it. You have two minutes."

The state groups returned to talking, but at a lower volume.

At the end of two minutes, the Speaker tapped her gavel and asked the House Members to return to their seats.

After everyone was settled, Gwently directed the Clerk to call the roll of states, record the name of the foreman and then record the state's vote." She turned to the chamber, "When each state is called, the foreman will stand and clearly state his or her name and then will say who that state is voting for."

She turned back to the Clerk and nodded.

The Clerk began reading. The vote went along party lines until they got to Iowa. When the Clerk said "Iowa', no one answered. She said "Iowa:" again. A man and a woman stood, one on each side of the aisle. "We can't agree."

Gwently leaned forward. "Who's the foreman?"

"We don't have one."

It was from the Democratic side of the aisle.

Gwently turned to the Republican side. "Is that correct?"

"Yes."

Gwently glared and then addressed the two standing Representatives. "May I surmise that you haven't selected who Iowa wishes to vote to be President?"

The Democrat spoke, "That's correct."

Gwently looked at the Republican. "Do you concur."

The woman nodded.

"Okay," Gwently continued. "Let's start on the Republican side this time." She looked at the woman. "Do you want Iowa to abstain or simply not cast a vote?"

"Not to vote."

Gwently looked at the Democrat.

"Abstain."

Gwently rolled her eyes. She looked back at the Republican. "If you abstain, you get credit for being here."

"The woman held out her hands in defeat. "Okay, abstain."

Gwently quickly looked at the Clerk. "No foreman. They choose as a group to abstain. Please continue."

When the voting was complete, the result was as Damson had predicted – 24 votes for Goldin, 23 for Henry, and three abstentions.

After the tally was announced, Gwently sighed deeply. "All right, the meeting is not adjourned. We will continue it at ten o'clock Monday morning to try again. All will be present."

She pounded the gavel again and walked away from the podium.

226

Chapter Fifty-Seven

When Gwently arrived at the DNC Headquarters, Damson and Glore were sitting by themselves in the conference room.

She hesitated and asked, "Where is everyone?"

Damson looked down and moved the pad of paper in front of him. "Disinvited."

"So, you had second thoughts?"

"Right, I think the fewer people, the better."

"Sounds sinister."

"No, just a need to strategize in private."

"Okay. Let's hear it."

Glore looked up. "You know the Constitution says the House of Representatives, in the case that no candidate receives a majority of the Electoral Votes, is to select the President."

Gwently gave him a "yeah, so" look.

Glore continued. "The thing is, the Constitution doesn't say how. You've been giving all the states a vote based on the majority vote of the Representatives of each state and getting nowhere."

Damson interjected, "And the problem is that it's a very vulnerable position. People can die or get sick, and one Party or the other becomes vulnerable."

"Yeah, so I have to make sure everyone stays well."

"Easier said than done."

"So, what do we do about it?"

"We change what you're doing."

"I'll catch hell If I do that. I'm afraid I've set a precedent."

Glore jumped in quickly. "We're not blaming it on you. What's happening is what we talked about in the last DNC meeting."

"Yeah, so, what do we do?"

“Set up motion from the floor and a second.”

“Okay.”

“The motion should be based on the ‘will of the people’. That is the single vote for each state should be based on the votes each Presidential Candidate got in each state in the Presidential election.”

“But Henry wasn’t the candidate.”

“Okay, based on the votes each Party received in the election.”

“Did we win the three tied states?”

“We won all of them. That gives us twenty-six state votes to twenty-four for Goldin.”

“God, the Republicans will scream.”

“So, what. You have the majority. It’s a House-wide vote.”

“I’m likely to break the handle on the gavel before an order is restored.”

“Yeah, sounds like a good use of the gavel.”

“You know the Republicans will take it to court. Maybe even succeed in blocking Henry from being sworn in.”

“Yes, you’re right. It will probably go round and round in the courts.”

“Goldin owns the Supreme Court.”

Glore returned to the conversation. “Yes, and if they decide to interfere in legislative procedures, we may lose. But the Constitution says that the legislatures make their own rules. So, maybe the Court can’t interfere.”

Damson summarized. “So, Allison, if you’re willing to go along with it, you need to set it up. You’ll have to be hardnosed and deal with the screaming, but it will buy us some time while we try to figure things out.”

***

Meanwhile, the story of the missing elector had been leaked to the press along with the theory that he had been the failed 270th vote for President Goldin.

Goldin had laughed it off as just another conspiracy theory released by the liberal newspapers.

His reply didn't fit the stories that had whirled out of the West Wing of fury and rage in the Oval Office in the days before and following the joint session of Congress meeting on the ascertainment of the vote of the Electoral College.

Conjecture ran wild. Lies and distractions were one thing, but the possibility of the White House being involved in a missing person and a possible murder was the stuff of newscaster's dreams.

Chapter Fifty-Eight

Gwently called the session to order on Monday morning.

She asked for the roll to be read.

Representative Sheila Berg from New Hampshire was absent.

Gwently looked around for the Sergeant-at-Arms and was about to address him when there was a call from the assembly. "Madame Speaker."

Gwently turned her head to a woman standing in the rear of the room. She glanced at the chart of the seating that sat on the table next to her podium and then looked back up. "The Speaker recognizes the Congresswoman from Massachusetts.

Congresswoman Jean McCormick addressed the Speaker. "Madame Speaker, Congresswoman Berg was in an automobile accident last night. She was driving and went off the George Washington Memorial Parkway into a tree. She's currently in the Georgetown Hospital."

Gwently tried not to show her shock. "Do you know her status?"

"WTOP this morning said she was in stable condition."

"I guess that's a relief. It could be something worse. Thank you, Congresswoman."

The Congresswoman wasn't ready to be dismissed. "The radio said she was sideswiped by another car. Left white paint down the side of Sheila's car."

Suddenly the Speaker was almost without words. "That's horrible. Do the police think it was hit intentionally?"

"They're investigating."

Gwently felt awkward having the discussion in front of the entire house, but it was obvious others were craning their necks to listen. "Did the other car stop?"

"No, it was a-hit-and-run."

"Witnesses?"

"A couple, but they were concentrating on controlling their own cars and couldn't say much."

"Okay, I'll follow up after this meeting is adjourned."

Gwently looked down while trying to bring her mind to order.

"Madame Speaker."

Gwently's mind suddenly came back to the business at hand. "The Speaker recognizes the Gentleman from California."

"Madame Speaker, I move that President Goldin be removed from the list of those being considered by the House for election to the Presidency of the United States on the grounds that he has been involved in criminal activities in regard to the vanishing and possible murder of an elector from the State of New York."

Several Republicans were immediately on their feet. "There are no grounds!" - "This is absurd! -- Show me the body!" – "Conspiracy theory! Not a shred of proof!" Gwently pounded her gavel. "The House will come to order. Everyone, sit down."

When the noise settled down and everyone returned to their seats, Gwently said, "We have a motion before us. Is there a second?"

Again, murmuring began among the Republicans. Gwently pounded the gavel again. "Order!" She looked around. "Again, is there a second?"

No one replied. "There being no second, the motion will not be considered further."

The Speaker's thoughts reeled. *I don't know whether I'm relieved or not. Hearing the motion sure would have put off a lot of other things.*

Gwently pounded her gavel again. "All right. Let's get on with the business at hand. We're trying to elect a President. In a moment we'll go through the vote again. Does anyone need to hold a state caucus to see if anything has changed?"

No one replied.

"All right. Let's proceed."

She turned to the Clerk. "Please take the roll of states."

When the Clerk got to New Hampshire, Republican Representative Solomon Cranston rose, "I would like to express my sympathy and concern for my fellow Representative Sheila Berg. Sheila and I are from the opposite sides of the aisle and we disagree on many things, but we are friends. We travel back and forth from our home state together. We've known each other for many years. Even the possibility of someone intentionally trying to harm her is appalling to me. Sheila and I had an agreement to abstain from the voting. Today, I intend to honor that agreement. The State of New Hampshire abstains."

There was murmuring among the Republicans and some epithets were thrown out.

Again, Gwently tapped her gavel.

When the voting finished, the results were the same as they had been the week before.

Gwently had withheld the strategy that had been planned with Glore and Damson the Friday before. It was intentional. It was her House and she was in control. She had decided to push the strategy implementation closer to Inauguration Day. She wanted as much confusion as possible.

She continued the session to Wednesday, a week before Inauguration Day.

Chapter Fifty-Nine

The next morning, Damson was irritated. He sat in his office, fiddling with a pen between his fingers. He thought he had a deal with Gwently. At least the accusation of Goldin's involvement in the disappearance of the elector had been made. It was always good to stir the pot.

And Goldin had reacted with a full blast of exclamations of fake news and conspiracy theories.

And then there had been the grandstanding by the Congressman from New Hampshire – such nobility – offered with nothing to lose. After all, even if he had voted for Goldin, the incumbent would still have been short of the twenty-six votes he needed.

Damson sighed. Maybe I'm just being cynical. Maybe the guy really is noble. It's obvious that many of his compatriots were not happy with him.

Damson had been to Georgetown Hospital to see Sheila Berg early in the morning. She had been angry. "I was changing the radio station – only had one hand on the wheel, when the car hit me. It really hit me hard. The whole side of the guy's car must be caved in. The police ought to be able to find it."

Damson had patted her hand. "Yes, they did find it. It was abandoned in Southeast Washington. A witness saw a guy with a hood leave it and jump into a white Camry. She couldn't see any faces and didn't get the plate number, although it was

D.C. The car that hit you was stolen. Maybe the Camry was too.”

Berg had leaned back against the pillow and grimaced and then jerked as if even grimacing hurt her. She had a bandage on her nose between two black eyes.

Damson had observed what seemed obvious. “I think it’s clear that whoever hit you was doing it intentionally – that the whole thing was planned. They were trying to keep you from voting.”

“Well, I feel like hell. I’m bruised all over, but the airbag worked. I’ll be out of here this afternoon and back at work tomorrow. What I don’t understand is what they thought they were doing only hurting one person. It wouldn’t have been sufficient to change anything.”

“Well, it turns out Mark Neidich from Rhode Island didn’t go home last night. He stayed with a friend in town.”

“Do you think they were planning to do something to him too?”

“We’ll never know, but I wouldn’t be surprised.”

“Gosh, hurting the two of us at the same time would have been reckless.”

“A tragic coincidence.”

“Who would believe that?”

“You’d be surprised.”

“No – I guess I wouldn’t.”

“Will you be in the House tomorrow?”

“Creaky, but yes – bright and early.”

Chapter Sixty

Gwently called the House to order.

Today, it's all going to hit the fan.

"Madame Speaker."

"The Chair recognizes the Congressman from California."

"Madame Speaker, in as much as this august body is making little headway in electing a President and the accomplishment of that task has urgency, I would like to move that we base the election on the popular vote for the Democratic and Republican Parties in the Presidential Election of last year, the one vote from each state based on the popular vote in that state."

With that, the house erupted, the members from the Republican side of the chamber, standing and shouting.

Gwently pounded with her gavel. "The House will come to order!"

She was ignored. She pounded again as hard as he could. The gavel broke and the head went flying, hitting a Republican in the front row.

She turned to the Clerk. "Get me another damn gavel."

The Clerk hurried off.

The Republican Congressman was rubbing his arm.

Gwently apologized to him, but no one could hear.

She continued to shout for the order.

Finally, the chamber began to quiet, although several Republicans continued to ask for the floor.

The Clerk returned with a gavel and handed it to the speaker, who immediately pounded again.

"The chamber will come to order. We have a motion before the House. If it is seconded, the floor will be open for debate. Until then, the House will maintain its decorum."

She pounded the gavel again.

"The motion has been made that the votes of the states for the President of the United States be based on the popular vote received by each Party in the state in last November's Presidential Election. Do I have a second?"

A preselected Congresswoman from New York rose and seconded the motion."

Again, there was grousing and some shouting.

Gwently pounded the gavel again. "The House will come to order!"

She glared at the front row of the chamber. "I'm going to keep pounding until we have order in the chamber, or I break another gavel and wipe you all out."

When the House quieted, the Speaker noted, "Now, doesn't that sound nice?"

She looked over the chamber. "We have a motion and a second on the floor. I would like to open the House for an appropriate discussion. I have noted that there are several members who would like to speak. I would also note the possibility of over four hundred speakers. I would, therefore, ask that all speakers limit themselves to two minutes. That will hopefully allow us to finish by midnight."

She turned to the Clerk. "Please time the speakers."

She turned to the Republican side of the House. "I will start with the first row. Does anyone in the first row wish to speak?"

The discussion went on for nearly six hours. The Republicans argued that the vote was a setup by the Democrats to ensure they won based on the known results of the election and was unfair to the individual rights of the members of the House, that the popular vote was not representative of the people's will because Brock Henry had not been the Democratic candidate, and that the precedent for the election had been established by the previous sessions of the House and should not be changed. The Democrats argued that the Constitution gave the House the right to make its own rules and in doing so recognized that the majority would rule. They iterated over and over that the Democrats had won the popular election by over two million votes and that it was completely appropriate that their candidate should be President. The Republicans argued that, under the Constitution, the Presidential election was not determined, by popular vote, but by Electoral Vote, and that Goldin led the Electoral Vote by one vote. The Democrats argued that the Electoral Votes for Goldin didn't meet the requirement for a 270 majority and, besides, their validity was suspect.

When the last Congressman had spoken, Gwently asked for a vote. It went along Party lines, among much complaining and moaning from the Republican side of the aisle. When finished, she announced that Henry had won. During the shouting that followed the announcement, she ended the meeting and dismissed the House, although most of the members didn't hear her.

Before most of the members knew what was happening, she had walked away from the podium and out of the chamber.

Chapter Sixty-One

Willie Grete didn't want to go home. He knew his wife would be crushed. She had had little hope, but still, she had had hope.

He found her in the living room. The cook was in the kitchen. It was their only personal space beside the bedroom.

"Well, you won't be Goldin's VP. All that practiced stone-face is gone to waste."

"It's still not set. The Republicans will take it to court."

"They only have six days."

"The courts will expedite things. They don't want the Country to have no government."

"If they don't qualify a President, you'll serve. You will be President."

"Yeah, I'll really be a power. Can you call it a lame-duck Presidency if it's at the beginning of a term? Will anyone pay attention to me?"

"You're damned right they will. For goodness sake, don't act shy. Take charge."

"You think they'll pay attention?"

"You do it right, and they'll be grateful. The Nation will be grateful."

"It's a hell of a situation, Willie."

"Yes, it is."

Chapter Sixty-Two

Before the courts closed Wednesday afternoon, the Republican Party had filed papers with the courts challenging the ruling of the House that Henry was elected President. The lower courts had ruled that the challenge was not under their jurisdiction. By Friday, the Republican National Committee had taken the case to the Supreme Court which was not in session. The Chief Justice then gave the Justices until Monday to assemble for a special session.

It was a busy weekend for the best New York and Washington attorneys who assembled in Washington to prepare their cases.

On Monday, the Court entered in special session. No cameras were permitted within the chamber and the audible broadcasts that had been implemented during the Covid-19 Pandemic were no longer being implemented.

The Nation waited in silence, except for the myriad of reporters and cameramen who stood at the foot of the steps before the neo-classical Supreme Court Building with its many steps and columns towering above them. A few smart ones had brought folding chairs. Others had to stand, shifting their tired feet from time to time. A few sat on the bottom step.

The early morning had brought some excitement as lawyers arrived. There were other ways to enter the building, but an arrival before the grand steps with an opportunity to be filmed and to make brief comments was too much for some lawyers to overlook.

Here and there newscasters periodically went live filling moments on the national news networks with words that were endlessly repetitive, trying to lend meaning to what was happening, questioning whether Goldin's Court would throw out the work of the House of Representatives in an unprecedented action that would challenge the very wording of the United States Constitution. In their minds, the newscasters wondered if the American public had any idea what that meant.

A little afternoon, a delegation of half-a-dozen Court staff exited the door. One carried a microphone which he set between the columns at the top of the steps. Others carried speakers that were set next to the columns adjacent to the microphone. It all seemed amateurishly ad hoc for the Twenty-First Century.

While this was happening, the reporters and newscasters stirred and cameramen jockeyed for position, small lights on many of the cameras coming alive.

A woman approached the microphone. "I'm Jean Simpson, spokesperson for the Court. Chief Justice Munson has asked me to inform you on the status of the Court's proceedings. Today's formal session has ended. After an hour for lunch, the Justices will reconvene and give the matters before the Court a formal deliberation and will reach their conclusion. The Court's decision will be presented in a Majority Opinion, and if needed, a Minority Opinion. These will be released at noon tomorrow.

All this occurred live on television throughout the world and was received with grumbling throughout the crowds who were watching.

Jean Simpson promptly turned and reentered the building followed by men carrying the microphone and speakers.

The television cameras turned to their associated newscasters who tried to give upbeat summaries of where the suit stood.

In Pierce County, Virginia, Chance FitzBourne lifted his control and turned off the television. He knew the networks would talk for hours about the significance of what had happened – sound and fury about nothing. *Of course, the Court must deliberate. Even I know that. Tomorrow, we'll have a decision, and the networks will talk all day about that.*

Chapter Sixty-Three

The court released its decision at noon the day before Inauguration Day.

They invalidated Brock Henry's selection for the Presidency.

The Court did not say that the House of Representatives could not establish rules. They said that the task of selecting the President was the duty of the members of the House and that the rights of the members had been usurped by using the popular vote to elect the President. It was the responsibility of the members themselves to select the President.

Gwently screamed, "It's words, damned words. They've twisted things. Hell, the members are the ones who decided to use the popular vote. The members did vote. What the hell are they talking about?"

She charged out of her office and told her administrative assistant, Linda Agnew, "Get Rodgers in here."

"Raymond Rodgers."

"Yes, the goddamn House Majority Leader."

Gwently's chief of staff, Ben Dailey, stuck his head out of his office. She looked at him. "You, too. In my office."

Dailey hurried across the room, grabbing a notebook off Agnew's desk as she protested. "Hey, I have my notes in there."

"I'll give it back."

Dailey entered the Speaker's office and found her standing at the window, saying to the world, "Shit, shit, shit."

Dailey stood in the doorway, afraid to sit or say anything."

She turned to him. "For God's sake, Ben, sit down."

A moment later, Raymond Rodgers entered the room.

Gwently glared at him. "Have you heard?"

"About the Court decision?"

"Yes, damn it! The Court thinks it can take over the legislative process. They're ignoring the Constitution. What are we going to do?"

Daily offered, "Appeal the decision?"

"Damn it, Ben, appeal it to whom? There is no higher Court. They think they're God. They're not balancing anything. They're trying to run the Government."

Rodgers hung his head in deep thought. "Well, we can tell the Court to go to hell. What are they going to do – sic the Capitol Police on us?"

"Yeah, we can tell them to go to hell, but that doesn't make Brock Henry President. Somebody must swear him in. Do you think the Chief Justice is going to do that after ruling against us? Do you think Henry can put together a government while living under a cloud of indecision? Let's face it, the Country is up shit creek."

"Well, we can't admit that the Court has a right to do this. We need to shout, violation of the Constitution all over the place."

"Yeah, that's your job. Get started."

Daily noted, quietly, "Well, Grete will be Vice President."

Gwently studied him. "An 'acting' President. What a damned title. Like asking the White House chef to run the country. What power does an 'acting' President have knowing she's going to be replaced at any moment? Do you think foreign powers will listen to anything she says? She'll be a damn non-President."

Rodgers concluded, "Allison, it's all we've got."

Gwently thought a moment. "Damn. You're right, and we haven't got her yet."

***

243

Mid-afternoon, Gwently pulled her car to the gate at the government complex in Annapolis and lowered her window to speak to the guard.

"Yes, ma'am, may I help you?"

"Yes, tell me where the Governor's office is?"

The guard leaned down to the window. "Uh, and who are you?"

"The Speaker of the United States House of Representatives."

He backed two steps from the car. "Oh, yeah, I've seen you on television."

"Yeah, I'm famous and am about to make you the bad guy."

"Oh, no ma'am. Do you want me to park your car?"

"No, I'm capable of doing that. Tell me where to park and where the offices are."

"Uh, you can park over there where it says 'VISITORS'. Her office is in the State House, that big building with tower, dome, whatever it is."

"Oh, God. That's a walk. I'm going to park in front of it on that circle."

"Ma'am....?" The guard protested as Gwently drove away.

Moments later the Speaker walked to and past in information desk and into the Governor's Reception Room where numerous people, startled by Gwently's charging figure, rose from their desks and prepared to stop the terrifying woman.

"Where is she?"

"Who?" came from four directions.

"The Governor. Who the hell else?"

"Grete appeared in the office door. "Allison?"

Gwently whirled toward her. "There you are. Get yourself packed."

"Packed? What for?"

"You're spending your night with me."

She whirled to the others in the room. "In case you don't know, I'm the Speaker of the House of Representatives and I was never here, and you don't know where the Governor has gone. Who's in charge here, besides Meyer?"

A man spoke from an office door. "I'm the chief of staff."

"You come with us. We're going to the Governor's Mansion so she can pack. We'll use my car, out front, if the state police haven't impounded it." She wheeled back to the room. "This is not a kidnapping. Your boss is safe. We're headed for D.C."

Gwently put her hand on Grete's back and hurried her to the door, looking back at the Chief of Staff. "What's your name?"

"Packer."

"You have a first name?"

"Billy."

"Not Bill"

They rushed through the lobby.

"Okay, Billy, your job is to wait in the Mansion and tell Governor's Grete's husband where she is when he comes home. Tell him he's welcome to come, too, but he'll have to do it on his own. I'm not waiting for him. U. S. 50's already a mess this afternoon, and I'd like to get home before midnight."

Chapter Sixty-Four

That night, much of Washington was strangely quiet. The completed inaugural platform stood lonely at the Capitol, as did the President's grandstand near the White House, guarded by lonely Capitol Police to prevent vandalism. Shortly, the structures would be deconstructed and many of them returned to storage to wait four more years.

At various medium-priced hotels about town, teenagers walked around the lobbies, and some braved the streets of the city despite the warnings of their chaperones that the streets might be unsafe. In various hotel rooms, as people passed down the hallways, tubas and clarinets could be heard, sounding the beats of marching bands. They were the members of high school bands that, through events, auctions, and raffles, had earned the money to come to the Nation's capital to march in the Inauguration Parade.

In New York, West Point Cadets were marching down to rail cars. In Colorado Springs C-130s were lined up at the airport to await the arrival of Air Force Cadets. In Annapolis, buses were being assembled for the Midshipmen.

Everyone was getting ready for a parade they knew in their souls was not going to happen. Many had dates and blind dates they knew they were going to cancel.

In hotels around Washington, large ballrooms remained dark. The people who were to set the rooms up had been told to stay home. The Democratic inauguration committee had never really jelled and remained an operation of only two people who had canceled the inaugural balls two weeks before.

The extra television equipment that had been sent to the city to cover the parade had never been unpacked, the associated trucks left parked next to local stations.

The Metro schedule which had been expanded for Inauguration Day had been returned to its regular schedule.

People in appointed Government positions throughout the capital sat uncertainly and nervously in their homes wondering what tomorrow would bring.

Civil servants sat in their homes, knowing they would go on, either continuing their work as is or adapting to new and changing Presidential proclamations and directions. Life would go on.

Both appointees and civil servants knew of two possibilities. Goldin would continue as President, things would continue as they had been and the appointees would feel they were living a tenuous life, or there wouldn't be any continuity. Life was going to be chaos. If Russia were going to strike, it would be time. Goldin had barred meetings with any transition teams, and even the existence of transition teams was questionable. Henry had tentatively identified some people to serve in the Cabinet, but the Supreme Court had thrown out his brief status as the presumptive President.

Life was uncertain. Tonight, there was no President-elect. There was no one to inaugurate.

Some people were frightened. Some were only vaguely aware.

Isaac Ambler Goldin sat in the dining room of the White House Presidential Suite where he was served a Porterhouse steak and a glass of fine red wine.

He sipped the wine and thought, *let them get me out of here. They're all losers. Every one of them. I'm not going anywhere.*

Chapter Sixty-Five

The next morning Damson rolled out of bed and stretched while looking out the window. The day was gray and dismal. *Probably cold as hell, too. Maybe it will snow and make the day miserably perfect.*

Downstairs in the kitchen, he banged the old grounds out of the coffee filter, rinsed it, set up the coffee maker, and turned it on to brew. He put a frozen sausage and egg biscuit in the microwave. He knew the biscuit would come out soggy, but he wanted it ready when the coffee was ready. The coffee was the thing that was important.

As always, he was on his own. The cook didn't come in till late afternoon. Half the time he ate dinner out anyway. After all, he was a politician in Washington, D.C., and a bachelor besides.

As he poured his coffee into a blue mug with "READ THE DAMN CONSITUTION" printed on the side, the phone rang. It was Bennie. "Boss, you still going to work today?"

"Yes, there's not much else to do."

"I don't know, boss."

"What do you mean you 'don't know'?"

"You hear the sirens, boss?"

"Yeah, is there a fire someplace."

"I don't know. All I know is that the police have the street blocked. I can't get the car out."

"M Street's blocked?"

"Parking lot from Canal Street as far as you can see."

"The fire's in Georgetown?"

"Don't know anything about a fire, boss. Just police. I hear sirens everywhere."

"Okay, Bennie. Sit tight. I'll try to find out what's going on."

Just then a helicopter flew over, low enough to shake the house.

"What the hell?"

Damson hurried to the television, thinking, *I wish I had a radio in here.*

He grabbed the remote and hit the 'on' button. The screen blinked a couple of times and then came alive, but without a picture. The sound was bleating, and words were spread across the screen, "EMERGENCY, EMERGENCY, WASHINGTON UNDER THREAT."

The screen turned to a picture of the White House. It next showed the White House grounds. Damson recognized where Marine One usually landed. It was covered with olive drab helicopters. He counted them – five - Chinooks. Soldiers were pouring out of them.

Another helicopter whirled past over them – an attack helicopter – an Apache? *Is that what they called them?*

The soldiers spread out heading for the fence line.

The picture returned to the White House. There were men with weapons at every corner of the roof.

The picture panned to the gate. It was closed and men crouched with weapons behind concrete barricades. Police cars were all over the streets.

The newscasters were talking, "Threat to the White House – threat to blow it up – all government buildings in lockdown – jets scrambled and protecting overhead – told to shoot down any aircraft approaching the city – Reagan National closed – all planes diverted – bridges over the Potomac closed - roads in and out of the city are blocked – citizens of Washington told to shelter in place – all pedestrians within a half-mile to the White House to be constrained."

Damson shook his head. *Blow up the White House on Inauguration Day when there's no inauguration? Hell, do terrorists think that small? If I were going to do it, I'd do it when the parade was on, when everyone was distracted. I sure as hell wouldn't tell people I'm coming. But who knows? They're called crazy for a reason.*

He heard a Fire Engine. It sounded like it was getting nowhere,

Damson went to his front door and out on the stoop. He lived on a side street off Wisconsin Avenue. Cars were parked on his street bumper to bumper, some drivers honking aimlessly while others had apparently given up and were standing by their vehicles looking back to the avenue from which they had come. Damson guessed the police had turned them away from the main thoroughfare.

He looked back at Wisconsin Avenue and saw the fire engine and an ambulance trying to maneuver through the vehicles that still plugged the street.

Damson guessed that fire engines must be coming from all over. He wondered if they would make it to the White House and, if they did, where they were going to park. *Maybe they'll park them on the South Lawn – give the television cameras a show.*

He knew the cameras weren't handheld. They were mounted on rooftops, but they could be swiveled. They could still provide a show.

He looked up and down at the frustrated drivers and their passengers. He felt sorry for them, but they weren't his problem. His coffee pot only made ten cups and he wasn't about to share with anyone.

He went back into the house and closed the door.

The television was showing two fighter jets roaring overhead. *Hell, we're just a blur to them. I hope they can see incoming aircraft.* Then he laughed. *Stupid. It's all electronics. Damn planes fly on their own, maybe controlled from the ground or from some C-130 electronic platform three or four miles above them.*

The picture turned back to the White House and panned as much as it could with its swivel to show the defenses that had been set up. It was being described as an armed camp.

Damson wondered how they felt in 1812 when the British were coming. *Barebones then – maybe a few muskets.* He could picture Dolly Madison running out the back door.

The newscasters suddenly announced that President Goldin would address the nation at nine o'clock.

"Damn," Damson muttered. "The bastard is supposed to be out of there by noon." *What the hell does he think he's doing?*

The newscasters were now in a tumult of conjecture; "Goldin is going to say he is still in charge. Alexander Haig-ing the situation – he is going to say he is in command and that as long as he is, the Nation is safe – he is going to say he's not going anywhere - after all, they noted, no one has seen any moving vans at the White House, no one has moved any of that gilded furniture – no moving van has been seen at the Vice President's house either. The newscasters wondered who was going to operate the cameras for the address. They guessed there were servants that stay overnight, maybe some staff. They noted that cameras are set up permanently in some rooms anyway. They believed that a camera setup can probably be wheeled into the Oval Office. They convinced themselves that there was no doubt it could be done. "

Suddenly, the picture of the President in the Oval Office appeared on the screen. There was a moment of uncertainty as if Goldin wasn't sure he was alive. Finally, he looked squarely at the camera. "My fellow citizens. I am speaking to you today as your President from the Oval Office. As you all are no doubt aware, this nation is under attack. Your White House is under attack. Your President is under attack. Threats were received this morning saying that the White House would be blown up – erased from the face of the earth. The threats sought to sew confusion by declaring the attack would be by air, and then a few minutes later, saying it would be by truck, and then by drone. It doesn't matter. I have taken action to circumvent whatever is thrown at us. Our Army and our Air Force have been deployed. The Government has been shut down and secured. The City of Washington has been shut down. The nation is under alert. I, as President, have put in place an impenetrable defense. I am in control. The citizens of the United States are safe. I do not run from threats. On this Inauguration Day of uncertainty, you are not alone. You are not being left flattering in the wind with no leadership. You have an elected President, the only one there is. You elected me four years ago and I will not let you down in this time of uncertainty and doubt. Be assured and have no doubt. I will lead you. I have the strength.   America will remain great. God bless you all and be strong."

Damson turned off the television. *It's all a bunch of crap.*

Damson's cell phone rang. Not many people knew the number. He glanced at the screen – Allison Gwently.

He answered and said, "You hear the damn speech?"

"And hello, Allison. How are you today?"

"Yeah, and that too."

"Yes, I heard the speech. Do you want to hear the expletives?"

"Heard them before."

"And if we don't get the bastard out of there, you'll hear them again."

"So, do you have a plan?"

"Be at my house at noon – no, ten minutes."

"Good thing I can walk."

"Hope you can make it four blocks."

"I'll bring my walker and allow for extra time."

"Don't get shanghaied."

"How would they manage that in this traffic jam?"

"Just make sure you get here. Bring a camera if you have one."

"Are we going to make history?"

"Damn right. And on your way here, stop and get my neighbor, Edgar Warren."

"He's a damn Republican."

"This machination needs a witness."

Chapter Sixty-Six

Grete was up early and downstairs in the Gwentlys' kitchen wondering where the coffee was. She had phoned her husband the previous night. He had been late coming home from his office and said he'd drive into the District in the morning. She gave him the Gwentlys' address so that he could enter it into his GPS. He said he would be at the house by nine-thirty. Grete had been anxious. She didn't know what was going to happen. She wanted her husband by her side. She knew he would support her. *Probably a funny thought for a woman who has been elected Vice President of the United States. Darn, it's been thirty years. We're not quitting each other now.*

"Good morning."

Grete turned to the door. It was George Gwently – *another man who hasn't quit.*

He walked past her. "It's in the wine refrigerator."

"What's that?"

"The coffee. It's right under the pot. Seemed like a good place to keep it."

"Of course. Everyone does that."

"Well, we only have a half dozen bottles of wine. Seemed like a good use of the space."

"You don't separate the whites from the reds?"

As he took the coffee out of the little refrigerator, he looked at Grete. "Are you some kind of connoisseur?"

Grete laughed. "I do take *Gourmet* - use my wine for cooking. Willie says I waste it."

"You cook?"

"Vice Presidents don't cook?"

"Stone-face? I don't think so."

Soon the coffee pot was perking.

Grete sat in silence, waiting on the coffee and brooding.

George Gwently let her.

"George, what's going to happen today."

"Allison's going to swear you in as Vice President at noon."

"She can really do that?"

"The Speaker's done it four times. Hastert did Cheney for his second term."

"It doesn't have to be at the Capitol?"

"It's been done a lot of places. Allie looked up the oath last night. Wrote it down. She's set."

"What happens after that?"

"We'll put it on YouTube, send it out to all the news outlets. We'll try to have some reporters here for the ceremony. We'll make sure the world knows."

George got up to pour the coffee. Grete walked over and stood beside him. He pushed the cream and sugar toward her, and then a full cup.

Gratefully, she took the cup. "Just black. Thank you."

Just then they started hearing sirens.

George, holding his cup, looked around. "Police cars – several of them. Sounds like there's been a shooting or something."

"It's not a fire?"

"No, that's different sound."

Allison Gwently burst into the kitchen, tying the belt around her robe. "What's going on?"

George passed his wife the cup of coffee he was holding. "Here. Take this and have a seat. Must be a shooting, bank robbery, or something. It will settle down eventually."

But it didn't.

Gwently frowned. "Something big's going on. Turn on the television."

George turned it on, and they were quickly immersed in newscasters almost arguing with each other as they tried to learn what was going on and passed on the information being briefed out of the White House. They all seemed frustrated as their sources bore no fruit."

Gwently hadn't sat down. She stomped her foot. "I'm going to the den and make some phone calls."

Grete picked up her phone from where she had left it charging on the kitchen counter. "And I'm going to call Willie."

Willie picked up. "Meyer, I'm stuck. I was coming to U. S. 50 and had just gone over the Anacostia River when the police made me exit. Ended up on South Dakota Avenue and they forced me into a Lowes parking lot. The damned lot is almost full. Don't know where they're going to put more cars."

"How long are you going to be there?

"I have no idea. They won't tell me anything. They just told me to park until we're told differently."

"Gosh, I want you here."

"I don't know what to do, honey. The radio says the White House is being attacked, but everyone seems confused."

"Let me ask George what he thinks we should do."

"George?"

"Allison's husband."

255

“Oh, okay.”

Grete turned to George, holding her hand over the phone. “He’s been stopped by the police just after he crossed the Anacostia River. They have him parked at a Lowes.”

“Out where 50 becomes New York Avenue?”

“I don’t know.”

“Let me have a phone.”

She passed it to him. “Willie, this is George.”

“Glad to meet you, George.”

“You, too. Did you make it to where 50 becomes New York Avenue?”

“Not quite.”

“Okay, leave your car. Ask around. Find out how you get to *The Washington Times* building. Go there, tell them who you are, and tell them they’ll have an exclusive at noon. We’ll phone you then. Keep your phone with you.”

“Can I walk there from here?”

“It’s near, but straight lines can fool you. Ask questions.”

“Okay. I’ll talk to you later.”

Gwently came back into the room. “The damned world has closed. We’ve got a national emergency, and Homeland Security is closed. No one even answers at the Command Center. And the Goddamn Hoover Building has one woman answering and saying no one else is there. Can you believe this shit? A national emergency and the agencies protecting us are closed. I called the FBI offices in Manhattan and they don’t know what the hell is going on.”

George looked on. “Who would have the power to close everything down?”

“The President. Who the hell else?”

“Do you think he’s locked in the Oval Office with the football on his desk?”

“I wouldn’t be surprised.”

Finally, with multiple sighs, the three settled with cups of coffee to watch Goldin address the Nation.

When he had finished, Gwently cynically observed. "The bastard is faking the whole thing. A multi-million dollar lie. He's going out with a big one – the biggest ever."

Grete looked at her. "I bet you're right."

"How long do you think it will take the press to figure it out?"

"By the morning at the latest."

George looked at the women in amazement. "Do you really think he'd do that?"

They both looked back at him. "Absolutely."

Gwently stood up. "Okay, let's get this organized. I'm going to phone the Damson."

Chapter Sixty-Seven

A few minutes before noon, Damson knocked on the Gwentlys' door. Senator Edgar Warren stood on the step behind him looking uncertain.

George Gwently opened the door. Damson swung open the storm door, took Warren by the elbow, and led him in. "George, this is Senator Warren. I told him he was invited for lunch – that you and Allison wanted to get to know the neighbors. His wife will be along in a minute."

George looked hesitant. "Lunch? Yes, we'll all have lunch." He shook Warren's hand. "Always good to meet the neighbors."

Warren was still a little uncertain. "Yes, that's very kind of you."

As he entered the house, he glanced back out the door.

Damson closed it and grinned. "No one saw you. It's okay."

Warren sighed apprehensively as he was led into the Gwentlys' living room. The Speaker and Grete rose to greet him. Gwently stepped forward to shake his hand and then introduced Grete.

"It's a pleasure, Senator. You know the Governor, don't you?"

"Uh, no, I haven't had the pleasure."

Grete stepped forward to shake his hand. "I understand we'll have the pleasure of meeting your wife in a moment."

"Ah, yes. She'll be here in a minute. The invitation was a bit of a surprise."

"Yes, things are happening fast today, as I'm sure you are aware. Do you think the President is in danger?"

"Uh, he said he's not. Says he has everything under control."

"Well, we can depend on him."

"Uh, I hope."

"Hope, Senator? Gosh, Senator, let's have more faith than that."

"Yes, of course."

"Have a seat, Senator. Governor Grete needs to phone her husband to find out where he is. He had some trouble driving over from Annapolis this morning."

"Oh, I sympathize with him. It's been a wild morning."

Grete dialed her husband. "Willie?.... Darling?...Are you doing all right – Have you gotten to where you need to be?.... Great....Yes, I've got noon too."

She clicked a couple of buttons, looked back at the phone, and then passed it to George who stood back and held it up for live streaming. Gwently and Grete faced each other. Gwently said, "Please raise your right hand. I, Jane Meyer Grete, do solemnly swear..."

"I, Jane Meyer Grete, do solemnly swear..."

"...that I will support and defend..."

258

"...that I will support and defend,,,"

Warren rose from his seat. "What's going on?"

The women continued, as George Gwently clapped Warren on the shoulder and whispered, "The Vice President is being sworn in."

"...so help me God."

Gwently shook Grete's hand.

Damson stepped forward to shake her hand.

Grete walked over to Warren and put out her hand. With uncertainty, Warren shook it.

Grete smiled. "Thank you for serving as a witness, Senator."

George Gwently filmed the whole thing. He clicked a button on the phone and put it to his ear. "Did you get that?"

The voice on the speakerphone said, "Loud and clear."

There was a knock at the door. Allison Gwently went to the door, opened it, and smiled broadly. "Hi, you must be Mrs. Warren. Sally? Sally, right? I'm Allison. Please come in."

As they entered the living room, Gwently said, "Sally Warren, you know the Senator of course. The skinny gentleman here is my husband, George. The other fellow is Edwin Damson."

"The Chairman of the DNC?"

"Right, do you know him?"

"No, but my husband mentions him now and then."

Sally Warren frowned and did not move to shake anyone's hand. "And, who's the lady?" It sounded as if the "lady" were not actually standing in the room.

Gwently glanced at Grete, turned back to Sally Warren, and said with a smile, "Oh, she's Jane Meyer Grete. She's the Vice President of the United States."

Chapter Sixty-Eight

Willie Grete finally arrived at the Gwentlys' a little after five in the afternoon. "Thank God the traffic was going the other way. Fire engines, ambulances, police armored vehicles, all kinds of vehicles mixed in with frustrated citizens. A real mess."

George Gwently shook Willie's hand. "Willie, it's a pleasure. Is the crisis over?"

"You haven't been listening to the radio. WTOP is wild. There were so many vehicles around the ellipse, no one could move. They were being parked on the grass on the Mall. The police have been trying to sort it out for hours - trying to figure out what's excessive and what to get rid of. But, no, apparently the crisis is not over. The White House is still saying the threat is active. They still have the grounds as an armed camp, soldiers all over the place. Besides the White House, only the Pentagon is talking, and they don't seem to know what's going on. No one can get through to Homeland Security, or the FBI, or the Secret Service Headquarters. The Capitol and Metro Police are in a tizzy, trying to close down everything and running out of manpower."

He walked over and gave his wife a peck on the cheek. "Congratulations."

Grete grinned. "Oh, yeah. I hope I'm not an asterisk on this day."

"You haven't been listening to the radio?"

"No. There have been reporters here all afternoon. We had to let them in a few at a time. It was too cold to greet them on the front porch and the cameras take a lot of room. They have to have a little room to work."

"Well, I bet those pictures will be all over the news tonight."

George inquired, "If the world is still on alert, why are the emergency vehicles leaving."

"As I told you, there were so many around the White House, they couldn't have responded to anything. They had to be thinned down to what was needed. Besides, you should have heard the Mayor. She's really ticked. 911 hasn't had any ambulances. A woman had a baby where I was in the Lowes parking lot with the world watching and helping. The Mayor says there are other people in the world besides the President."

"Did she ask Goldin about that?"

"She can't get through to Goldin."

Grete asked, "What are the reporters saying?"

"They're starting to question the whole emergency, the lack of response by the agencies that are supposed to respond, the vacuum of information, and, oh yes, they're wondering what you are going to do."

"Yeah, reporters have been asking me that all afternoon."

"And what did you say?"

The Speaker spoke up. "I told them that she's the acting President. She's going to throw out the entire evil empire."

"How are you going to do that? Goldin is claiming he's the de facto President."

Gwently shook her head. "That's not what the Constitution says."

"You know Goldin doesn't absorb the Constitution. He interprets it."

Grete sighed, "Well, the head of the Secret Service is coming here tonight. I'm hoping he's a good man. He came up through the ranks, so there's hope."

Chapter Sixty-Nine

Brigadier General Sal Meranda stood outside the Rose Garden talking to the President's military aide, Major General Hank Davies, as they watched a Chinook helicopter land where Marine One usually stood. Meranda explained, "Chow coming in for the troops. We'll set up tables down just past there.

Davies smiled. "A million-dollar meal. Nothing's too good for the troops."

"Well, the White House couldn't feed them. They only keep one cook on overnight and he must feed the President, some soldiers, Marine guards, some nighttime civil servants, communications guys, the secret service, and any other hangers-on around this place. The White House never sleeps."

"The telephone operator too. Didn't the operator take the threatening calls?"

"I guess. I haven't talked to her."

Meranda chuckled. "Don't you talk to everyone? Don't you have to know everything, general?"

"Don't give me a hard time. Did you ever think you would command a battalion of troops again? Weren't you a division deputy commander?"

"Yeah, we do what's best for the Country. So here I am again, walking the fence line, making sure the soldiers are alert, ready to fight, and looking good for the camera, all at the same time."

"Soldiers in the middle of the city of Washington with bullets that will travel forever."

"Hey, don't scare me. I'm worried enough as it is. If we must shoot, we're going to wipe out a bunch of fire engines."

"I heard the Mayor of this great city is already making out a reimbursement bill for today. You don't want to add to it."

"Not personally, that's for sure."

Meranda thought for a moment. "Sir, do you think this is for real?"

"Damned if I know. I've called everyone on the list in the SOP and only the Pentagon answers and they don't know anything."

"Do you think if I packed up and went home, anyone would care?"

"The President might call it treason."

"Meranda sighed. "Do they still shoot people for that?"

Davies chuckled. "In this town, I'm sure they could find a derelict wall where the bullet damage wouldn't matter."

Chapter Seventy

Shortly after Willie Grete arrived at the Gwentlys', there was a knock on the front door – a firm knock.

Gwently opened the door expecting more reporters.

Two men in dark suits stood there. They held up badges. "We're Agents Gormley and Shedd of the Secret Service, Ma'am. Is Vice President Grete here?"

"She is. She's staying with us. I'm Allison Gwently. Do you need to speak to her?"

The agents' eyes bugged slightly when Gwently mentioned her name. "Uh, we just want to make contact with her - want to let her know we're here to provide her security."

"Oh, okay." Gwently turned and called toward the living room, "Meyer, your guards are here."

She turned back to the agents. "Come in, come in. It's cold out there."

Grete came to the front hallway. "May I help you?"

The men held up their badges, looking embarrassed. "Secret Service Agents Gormley and Shedd. We're not guards. We're here to provide your security."

"Boy, you came quickly."

"Not really. We had to find out where you were."

"Well, I'm yours."

"Yes, Ma'am. We're going to set up a couple of cars in front of the house and if that gate to the right goes into the back yard, we'll send a couple of agents back there."

Grete turned to Gwently. "Is there any shelter back there?"

Gwently shook her head. "Just a glass-topped table and four chairs. They'll freeze to death."

"No, Ma'am. They'll be fine."

Gwently blew out a puff of air with a look of uncertainty. "Tell them to knock on the door and get coffee when they need it."

"They'll be fine, Ma'am."

"Better yet, tell them to sit in the kitchen."

The agent smiled. "They'd appreciate that, but one will have to stay outside. They can switch off."

"Okay, but they can come through the house. They don't have to go through the gate."

"Thank you, Ma'am. I'll send them through in a minute. Do you know who owns the gray Camry out front?"

"Yes, I do. My husband drove it here."

"Oh, is your husband here?"

"Yes. Come to the living room and meet him. I don't want you shooting him because you don't know who he is."

The agents followed her. "This is my husband, Wilson. And the other gentleman is the Speaker's husband, George. And what are your first names?"

The agents looked awkward. One stepped forward. "I'm Shelton Gormley and this is Rail Shedd."

"Willie stepped forward to shake hands. "I'm Willie. Rail? Really?"

"Dad works for the Virginia Railway Express. He thinks it's funny."

"Hey, it's not hilarious. I think it's all right." He pointed at George Gwently. "George and I are both married to a powerful woman. When things settle down, we're going to find a pub and commiserate with each other."

Grete punched him in the shoulder. "You're going to have to learn to behave yourself, Willie."

The agents both looked embarrassed. They addressed Gwently. "We're going to have to ask your neighbors to move their cars and we'll put some saw-horses across the sidewalk."

Gwently groaned. "I'll have to take them cookies tomorrow."

Now the agents were thoroughly chagrined, and they backed toward the hallway. "We'll try to stay out of your hair."

Grete caught them before they could leave. "Your boss is coming here at 7:30."

"Director Carnahan?"

"Yes. Try not to shoot him."

Gormley had had enough. "It's an old joke, Ma'am."

Grete acknowledged it. "Not funny, huh, and not a good start to our working together. I'll do better."

"Yes, Ma'am."

Gwently quickly interrupted. "And pizza is being delivered in half-an-hour."

Gormley smiled. "We won't shoot him either."

"Good to know."

Chapter Seventy-One

Director John Ross Carnahan arrived exactly at seven-thirty. Gwently felt that the road must have been cleared for his black Suburban. He was sixty-two or -three, with graying crewcut and rock jaw. He fit the image. She decided not to mess around – *no joking tonight*.

"Is Vice President Grete here?"

Gwently thought *you have guards front and back. How the heck could she go anywhere?*

"Yes, Director, she's right this way."

He followed her and approached Grete. "Madame Vice President."

There was a small inflection of his head, not quite a bow. Grete thought, *Gosh, is that my title? No, I don't like it.* "Just 'Vice President', Director. All right?"

“Yes, Ma’am.”

“So, where do we stand, Director. Do I have a home? Do I have an office?”

“Vice President Stone will be leaving Observatory Circle tomorrow.”

“He’s still there?”

“Yes.”

“Doesn’t he know he wasn’t reelected?”

“He says the President told him to stay there.”

“Goldin?”

“Yes, Ma’am.”

“Doesn’t President Goldin know his Presidency ended at noon today?”

“He doesn’t seem to believe so.”

“Director, you might show him the Constitution – read him the Twentieth Amendment.”

“Ma’am, he claims no one has been elected to replace him.”

“As I said, read him the Twentieth. I’m the acting President as of noon today. He’s out.”

“Yes, Ma’am. Have you been sworn in?”

“I don’t think the Constitution has an oath for ‘acting President’. It just says that’s what I am until a President is ‘qualified’.”

“Yes, Ma’am.”

“Director, stop saying ‘yes ma’am’ and work with me on how we’re going to do this. So, Stone will be out of his house tomorrow? Does he have a place to go?”

“It’s not your problem, Ma....”

Grete glared at Carnahan. “His things will be stored - right? We’ll pay for a hotel room until he and his wife are settled?”

“If you wish?”

“I wish. I need to get out of the Governor’s Mansion in Annapolis.”

"Does the Government coordinate directly with you on that?"

Grete turned to her husband. "Willie, may they coordinate with you on that? I think I'm going to be busy."

Willie stepped forward and shook the Director's hand. "Director, it's a pleasure. I'm the lady's husband, Willie Grete, chief coordinator."

Grete shook her head. "Willie, no joking here. I need your help."

Willie became serious. "No problem, sweetheart. We'll get through this."

Grete turned her attention back to Carnahan. "And how about my office?"

"Vice President Stone's staff is working to clean it out now."

Gwently broke into the conversation. "That's great, but that's not what she's talking about."

Grete looked at Gwently in surprise as the woman continued. "The President of the United States doesn't work out of an office down the hall.   She works out of the Oval Office. Whoever heard of a President talking to the world from a broom closet?"

"Ma'am, it's not a broom closet."

"But it's not the damn Oval Office."

"Does an acting President work out of the Oval Office? Is that defined somewhere?"

"The answer to your first question is, yes, as of noon today. The answer to the second question is that it's being defined as of noon today."

"Well, President Goldin is still in the Oval Office."

"So, get him out."

"Ma'am, I'm responsible for his security, whether he's a President or an ex-President."

"Well, paint a big X on his back and get him out of there. He's not going to be homeless. He and his buddies own half of New York. He can tweet from anywhere in the world."

Grete sought back Carnahan's attention. "Director, I'll give you until the end of the day tomorrow to get President Goldin out of the White House. I will move into Number One Observatory Circle as soon as it is available. I don't want to move again if a President becomes 'qualified'. I'm flexible on the move, but I'm not flexible on the Oval Office. I will address the nation from there the day after tomorrow. Do you have any questions?"

The big man looked beaten. "No Ma'am."

Grete gave him another glare.

The Director quickly excused himself and left.

Grete plopped herself in a club chair and leaned back. "Whew."

Chapter Seventy-Two

Early the next morning, the Gretes returned to Annapolis. They were led by and followed by black Suburbans. Gormley had wanted to drive them in an official vehicle, but they had declined. They said they needed to get their car back to Annapolis. Gormley had told them to sell it. They had to think about that.

Willie went to the mansion and began making phone calls about moving vans. He wasn't sure who to call at the White House. He tried the Travel Office, but no one answered. He shook his head. *Of course, the White House is in lockdown.* He opened his laptop, looked up moving companies, and made personal arrangements for the move. *Good thing we have a little money in the bank account. I wonder how long it takes the Vice President to get reimbursed. I wonder who fills out the paperwork.*

He spent the balance of the day putting tape on the Grete's personal items. Much of what was in the Mansion belonged to the State of Maryland. He wondered how much of what was in Number One Observatory Circle belongs to the United States. *It would have been nice to have seen the place, but I guess the Stones had their own problems. So much for transitions.*

Grete returned to her Governor's office. She quickly called together her staff and told them she would like them to move to Washington with her. She told them that she understood that some would not want to move from their homes and that the commute might be too difficult, but she asked them to stick with her for at least a month. She would need them.

This was not news to any of them. She had been talking to them individually since the election. But now, she told them they should be in Washington the next day.

She next called in Lt. Governor Cyrus Brent. She had also been working with him since the Presidential Election. They had made plans for their transition. There had been a brief bump during the uncertainty of the ascertainment of the Electoral Vote, but they had weathered that.

After a discussion with Brent, Grete had the legislatures, which were in session, schedule a break at eleven o'clock and had everyone in the building move to the House of Delegates Chamber, along the reporters from the Capital Gazette and the Bay Weekly. She made a brief introduction, called Brent forward, and had him sworn in as Governor of Maryland by the Chief Judge of the Court of Appeals. Brent made a brief speech, apologizing for not being fully prepared on short notice and swore to maintain the high standards established by his predecessor.

While this was going on, some of Grete's staff were working in her offices, preparing lists of telephone members of the staff of George W. Bush and Barack Obama. After Brent's inauguration, Grete spent the afternoon phoning many of the people identified, trying to establish a cabinet, identify some

White House staff, and fill several ambassadorial positions. There would be no transition. Goldin hadn't allowed it and now it was too late. She needed individuals who already knew the jobs.

She had a hard sell. Most of the individuals she phoned held senior positions in industry, academia, or think tanks. They held lucrative positions. She could not offer them permanent jobs. After all, she was only the acting President. She had no idea how long she would hold her position. Some questioned whether she really held the power of the President. She appealed to their patriotism. Most said they were sorry, but she finally put together a skeleton of a government.

Chapter Seventy-Three

Director Carnahan spent the morning coordinating with other agencies of the government. He hated being in his position alone. After all, who was he to depose a President of the United States. Still, somehow, it had fallen on his shoulders. The acting President had put it there. He couldn't help but wonder if she had the right – had the power.

But time was running out. Men were already picketing the White House. They were Goldin supporters. They were carrying weapons. They said it was their Constitutional right. The Metropolitan Police disagreed. Confrontations and scuffles were ensuing. Tear gas grenades were being distributed among the police. The Secret Service and the U. S. Army were in position to defend the White House.

The FBI, whose agents were back in their offices, was reporting that armed Goldin supporters were coming from around the Nation. Roadblocks were being established on all borders between Maryland and Virginia and their bordering states. Cars, trucks, and motorcycles were being searched for weapons. Traffic was backing up for miles. Many motorists were being defiant and being arrested, but many of the small nearby towns couldn't accommodate the prisoners.

Carnahan was frankly frightened. He couldn't fight off an army of people carrying hunting rifles much less the automatic weapons that had proliferated throughout the Country.

Inside the periphery fence of the White House grounds, adrenaline was flowing through the veins of all the soldiers who had been assigned to guard the White House against "a national emergency" that had never transpired. Last night there had been rumors that they were going back to Fort Bragg today – that buses would come this morning, but a rabble had come instead – a rabble carrying weapons as deadly as the soldiers' own.

General Meranda had his junior officers scurrying around the perimeter telling the soldiers to keep their calm – not to load their weapons. Some loaded them anyway. They were damned if anyone was going to shoot at them without their firing back.

Soon Meranda joined those hurrying between groups of troops. He was far too uneasy not to be in action.

Carnahan had gathered all the Secret Service personnel he could find, excluding those manning the gates. He had pulled them from the roof. He had a spotter at the back of the White House to come in and tell him when Marine One had landed. His agents were jammed in the hallway. He thinned them. He felt he only needed a half dozen. The excess vanished along with almost everyone in the building. He couldn't imagine where they had gone.

The Marine guards stood stoically. They told themselves they weren't part of this, but they wouldn't abandon their positions. Damned if they were going to be crazy.

When his spotter reported the helicopter had landed, Carnahan thanked him and led his agents toward the Oval Office, weapons are drawn, like a SWAT team without helmets.

The President's administrative staff was huddled to the side of the room outside the Oval Office.

The President's Chief of Staff rushed out of an office. "You can't"

"We have to."

"This is crazy."

"I agree with that."

The President's secretary tried to intervene.

Carnahan glared at her. "Move aside."

She moved.

He turned the handle of the office door and pushed.

It didn't open.

The secretary said, "He blocked it with something."

Carnahan waved two burly agents toward the door.

They hit it with their shoulders.

The door moved a foot open.

Something crashed.

The agents pushed again, and the door swung open.

Carnahan and his agents charged in.

A credenza was turned over on the other side of the door. The things that had been on it were strewn across the Presidential seal of the Oval Office carpeting.

The President was standing behind his huge desk shouting about a coup, about treason, about having the agents arrested.

Carnahan looked at the man. "Sir, you are no longer President. Please come with us."

"Blasphemy. You're talking blasphemy."

"Blasphemy is a religious thing, sir. Please come with us."

"You're all damn traitors. I'll have you taken to a firing squad."

"Sir, they don't do that anymore."

"Electrocuted."

"Sir come with us. Marine One is waiting."

"Marine One, be damned. I'm the elected President. I'm not going anywhere."

"Sir, your term ended yesterday. There's an acting President."

"Acting? What the hell is 'acting'? A fake? A pseudo-President? Hell, I'm the real President."

"Sir, you're not."

"Who the hell says I'm not? You? You're too big for your britches"

"No sir, not me. The Constitution."

"Ha, the Constitution. A poorly written document if there ever was one."

"Sir, are you coming with us?"

"Don't be ridiculous."

Carnahan drew a deep breath and turned to his men, the two who had pushed the door in. For a moment they looked uncertain. Carnahan nodded and the men moved around the desk and took the President by his arms. He shook himself loose. "You two are going to jail first."

The two men looked at Carnahan for guidance.

Again, he nodded.

The men took the President's arms more forcibly.

He again tried to shake them loose, but the men held on.

Carnahan signaled for two more men to help.

They clamped the President more firmly.

Carnahan waved the other men toward a patio door.

They hurried over and opened it.

The other men manhandled the President out the door while he screamed.

Carnahan implored. "Please, Mr. President, just walk. Try to be dignified."

The man stopped, shook himself. The agents hung on.

Carnahan said, "Release him."

The agents did.

Goldin shook himself, stood tall, checked his tie, smoothed out his suit coat, and began to walk toward the helicopter.

Two agents entered the machine first, then Goldin. On the steps, he turned his back to the helicopter door. Carnahan wondered for a moment if Goldin would raise his hands in two victory signs *a la* Richard Nixon, but he only glared, his mouth moving, his voice silenced by the roar of Marine One's turbines.

Lip readers would later say he was saying, "I'm going to get you, bastards."

Carnahan could have guessed that.

A moment later, the helicopter lifted off and Goldin was gone. Secret Service agents would meet him at Joint Base Andrews and put him on Air Force One. In New York, the ex-President's new security team would meet him and escort Goldin to his apartment in the Goldin Tower where the ex-First Lady had been encamped for over a week.

Carnahan sighed. I'm going to have to keep paying bills to Goldin-owned resorts until the man dies.

***

Meranda stood next to Davies. "Do you think they could have carried him?"

Davies thought a minute. "I don't know. I bet he weighs 250."

"What do you think his medical records say?"

"It's redacted if it says anything."

"Well, the Supreme Court won't let the records become public, anyway."

"You don't think they have more important things to do?"

"Don't seem to. The President's suits keep them busy."

"Do you think we can pull the troops now?"

"Let Goldin's shotgun army leave first. Maybe they'll move to New York. Let the Mayor of the big city take care of them. Now that the pandemic has eased, he needs something to do."

Chapter Seventy-Four

At seven the next morning the Gretes exited the back door of Maryland's Government House to get into their car.

Agent Shedd was standing in the drive. "Your limousine's out-front Ma'am."

Willie looked at his wife who looked startled. Gosh, they address only her now. I'm Mr. First Husband, First Gentleman, or whatever. How am I going to match Michelle Obama?

The couple walked back through the house. Gormley was waiting for them on the front stoop. A huge Cadillac stood at the end of the walk. Men in suits were standing on both sides of the yard and across the street. A chauffeur stood by the car holding the door open. Black Suburbans were parked in front of and behind the Cadillac. Two police cars, with flashing lights, stood a block away ready to roll.

Grete thought, Damn, how life changes.

She climbed into the back seat of the Cadillac while Willie walked around to the other side. An agent had to open the door for him. It was locked from the world.

The convoy rolled. It roared down the U.S. 50 with no one on the road. Police cars or motorcycles were at every intersection with lights flashing.

Willie scrunched down in the seat. Boy, are people going to be pissed at us.

When they got to the White House, they simply roared through the gate, catching a glimpse of Director Carnahan supervising the entrance.

They were met by an army of people at the door to the White House. A butler-looking individual said, "We're sorry, Madame President, we're still moving President Goldin's things out of the Presidential Suite.   It won't be available until tomorrow. We're arranging for you to stay in the Blair House tonight."

Grete reached out her hand. "The Blair House sounds great. And you are?

"The Head Butler, Davis Longley."

"May I call you 'Davis'?"

"I'd be honored, Madame President."

"Davis, I'd prefer to be formally called President Grete – not Madame President. Can we do that?"

"Yes Ma'am"

"And Davis, my husband and I will not be staying in the Presidential Suite.   We'll be staying at the Vice President's place. If the House of Representatives qualifies someone else to be   President, I don't want to have to move again.

Longley looked disappointed. "So, the Presidential Suite will be empty?"

"For now, yes."

She turned to the group and noticed Willie standing behind them. She tried to avoid his eyes. They were twinkling and she was afraid she would break out laughing.

"Now, how do I get to the Oval Office?"

Longley and at least three others said, "Right this way or follow me, please."

The crowd moved down hallways. Grete wondered if she would remember the way. *It would be awkward if the President had to stop and ask directions.*

In the West Wing, they found men hauling large, apparently full, plastic bags out of the hallways. The men quickly moved out of the way. Other bags sat on the floor outside of the offices.

Grete wasn't sure who to ask, so she addressed the group.

"What's in the bags."

A man offered. "Shreddings."

"Shreddings?"

"Yes, Ma'am. President Goldin's staff was here all-night shredding papers and cleaning out their offices. They didn't leave until six o'clock this morning."

"In the President's office too."

"Yes, Ma'am."

"How did they know what to shred in there?"

"President Goldin was on the phone."

"The White-House phone?"

"Cell phone, Ma'am"

Grete gave a quiet chortle and asked with a tired mordacious grin. "Burners?"

She received a serious answer, "I don't know Ma'am."

As they entered the area outside the oval office, Grete was relieved to see her staff from the Maryland Governor's office. She hugged her administrative assistant, Jeanette Bearing, then stood back and looked her in the eye. "God, what time did you get up this morning?"

"Early."

Grete's Chief of Staff, said, "Very early."

"Did you have trouble getting in?"

One of the secretaries said, "It was greased – like riding a magic carpet. They took pictures, finger-printed, and swabbed us yesterday. Badges were ready this morning. They had to shuffle us from the main gate and tell us where to park, but we got here."

Grete smiled happily. "Well, I'm thrilled to see you all."

Bearing said, "Do you want to see your office?"

Grete grinned at her. "You've checked it out?"

"To quote a former Vice-Presidential wannabe, 'you betcha.'"

Bearing held the door as Grete walked in and looked around, trying not to show her awe. "Goodness, Michael Jordan could almost put his home basketball court in here."

"You think the ceiling is high enough?"

"Almost."

She considered the room. "I see the television camera is set up and the mic is on the desk. Did you do that?"

Bearing laughed. "Are you kidding? There are experts for everything here. An army lieutenant colonel came in early with a bunch of soldiers and set that up. Rex was awed."

"Rex is here?"

"Would your publicist be anywhere else?"

"I think they call them Press Secretaries here."

"We'll figure it out."

Grete looked to the side of the desk. "What's in the boxes?"

"Your stuff from your office in Annapolis."

"Looks paltry."

"It's a lot of space to fill."

"The White House must have some stuff we can add."

"There's a guy for that too."

"Well, get him. We need some stuff on the desk, something more than a lamp and a blotter."

"Already contacted him. He's on his way. Eleven o'clock, right? That's what you asked for?"

"Right, is there someplace I can hide and think about what I'm going to say."

"You want your personal bathroom or personal coffee room?"

Grete laughed. "Both."

Chapter Seventy-Five

"My fellow citizens."

Grete hesitated a moment, looking down. Then she looked back up, squarely at the camera.

"You've heard those words before. They have been spoken by many Presidents. By saying them, the President reminds us all that he or she is the President of all the citizens of the United States. I intend to fill that role. The Constitution says that if there is no qualified President on Inauguration Day, the Vice President shall serve as acting President until such time as a President is qualified. The Constitution does not define 'acting'. I believe that the framers of the Twentieth Amendment to the Constitution did not intend 'acting' to mean that the Vice President is intended to be a place holder until the real President comes along. They did not intend there to be a vacuum in the leadership of this country. Such a vacuum could bring us disaster. I believe the Twentieth Amendment meant for the 'acting' President to act as President with all the powers inherent to that role. I intend to be your President, fully and in every sense.

In that role, I intend to be honest with you. I will pull no punches. I will tell you how it is.

I will not lead you without help. I do not believe I am all-knowing. I do not believe I am infallible.

I will ask for your help. Our Nation will continue. Our Nation will persevere.

We are fortunate as a Nation to have a civil service that provides continuity during administrative transfers. They are not and should not be beholden to any Party. We are privileged to have them.

We have a military, unlike those of other nations where the military is controlled by elitists. Our military is nonpolitical. That is a blessing to us all and part of our continuity.

Today is my first day in the White House. Members of the last administration's appointed staff are merely ghosts in the hallway, but the White House continues to function. The permanent staff here is loyal to the Nation and to the traditions of the building in which they work. As all Presidents before me, I am privileged to have them.

Over the last several months there has been uncertainty in our government, but the uncertainty has been at the top. The foundation is solid.

This is not the moment to criticize. It is not the moment to belittle. It is time to move on.

As I said I will not do this job without help. I will fill the appointed positions in my government with professionals. It will not be enough to be my relative. It will not be enough to be my friend, my pal. It will not be enough to be a contributor to my campaign. I have contacted professionals. They are men and women who have worked in Government roles before, mostly at the national level, some at the state level. They are patriots. They are men and women who have agreed to give up their current employment, employment which is often lucrative and exciting. I have published the list of the people I will nominate. Many will have to be approved by Congress, but they all plan to be at work today or tomorrow. Many will walk into the offices they have occupied before.

My fellow citizens, I address you with sincerity. I will give you a government of honesty, a government of experience, a government of strength. As citizens, you will know where you stand.

I ask for your support and your help, and I ask that God bless us all."

***

After the crowd had departed the Oval Office, Willie stepped forward and took a seat in the seating arrangement in front of his wife's desk. "I'm disappointed."

Grete looked at him with mild concern. She knew his nature. "Oh?"

"You didn't say the evil empire is dead. You didn't shout long live democracy. You didn't say the Presidency is not a game, that it's not an ego trip. You didn't tell the country you are going to kick butt."

Grete chuckled. "No, I didn't. I want to change the tone."

"Well, there are a lot of tone-deaf people out there."

"It's my job to bring them around."

"God bless you, sweetheart."

"I need your help, Willie."

"I know. I won't talk to any reporters."

"In time, babe, in time. I need to bring you around too."

Chapter Seventy-Six

The following Monday, Gwently convened a session of the House. She felt she owed it to the Country to try one more time to settle on a President. She expected no different results, but she felt the vote might help solidify Grete's position.

She was also curious. The Republicans had held a caucus in Williamsburg over the weekend, a very secret caucus. No one knew what it was about. She felt uncertainty about it and was nervous as he convened the session.

She brought the session to order.

"Madame Speaker."

Oh, oh, she thought.

The Minority Leader of the House, David Kawalski, was standing.

"The Speaker recognizes Congressman Kawalski."

There was a moment's hesitation as Kawalski seemed to swallow. "Madame Speaker, as you probably know, the Republican members of this House held a caucus in Williamsburg this past weekend. We would like to propose a compromise."

"The House will be happy to entertain your compromise."

"The Republican Party believes that it is in the best interests of the Country to try to settle on the selection of a new President to ensure that the President is firmly recognized as speaking for our Nation. In that interest, I propose that this body vote for Jane Meyer Grete to be selected and qualified to be the President of the United States." He sat down.

Gwently caught her breath. "The Speaker thanks the Minority Leader for his interest in the well-being of this Country. You recognize, of course, that Vice President Grete only received one vote from the Electoral Congress."

Kawalski stood up. "Madame Speaker, you, in your position, recognized that the Constitution allowed for three top vote-getters to be considered by the House of Representatives for the Presidency and you included Vice President Grete in that list. The Constitution does not list a requirement as to the number of Electoral Votes someone needs to receive to be considered one of the three. This is a proposal for compromise. You put Vice President Grete on that list following the joint session of Congress to ascertain the Electoral Vote."

The reaction of Brock Henry ran through Gwently's mind. "Yes, I did."

Kawalski returned to his seat, with a nod.

"Thank you, Congressman Kawalski. Your proposal is received for consideration.

The Majority Leader was racing across the room to the Majority Whip.

"Congressman, you have not been recognized."

The Majority Leader, Raymond Rodgers, turned to the Speaker, his face flushed. "Madame Speaker, I apologize. I believe that the House needs to briefly adjourn so that the Democratic Members may caucus."

Gwently decided to gamble. "I appreciate your request, Congressman, but I believe we have a proposal, or, I might say, a 'compromise', before this chamber. It needs a second. Would you be willing to second it, Congressman, as an act of good faith for the compromise?

Rodgers' face flushed as he felt the world looking at him.

"Uh, yes, Madame Speaker."

"Is that a second Congressman?"

"Er, yes, I second the motion – Congressman Kawalski's motion."

Gwently pounded her gavel, although it was unnecessary. There was stunned silence in the chamber.

She moved quickly. "A motion has been moved and seconded, that Jane Meyer Grete be selected and qualified to be President of the United States of American. In recognition of the needs of our Country, please indicate your vote on the motion by raising your hand."

A smattering of hands was raised. Gwently's face and mind registered frustration.

"Alright, with consideration of Congressman's Kawalski's motion, let us again take a survey of the entire ballot for the Presidency, considering all three nominees, President Goldin, Senator Henry, and Governor, now acting President, Grete." She turned to the Clerk. "Please call the role of states to determine their votes.

Twenty-eight states voted for Grete, twelve for Goldin, and ten for Henry.

Gwently felt like her blood pressure had suddenly returned to normal. She pounded her gavel. "Jane Meyer Grete has been selected and qualified to be the President of the United States of America."

"Madame Speaker."
The Speaker looked around. People were talking. "The chamber will come to order." She spotted a young Congresswoman standing. "The speaker recognizes Elizabeth Downey."

"Madame Speaker, I would like to move that the selection of Jane Meyer Grete be made unanimous."

Gwently didn't wait for a second to the motion. She knew the Goldin people were not going to change their votes. "Thank you, Congresswoman, but the House has voted. This session is adjourned."

She stood and watched the members of the House, amid the noise of many conversations, wind their ways out of the chamber.

Boy, Kawalski has guts. He didn't have a majority of his party behind him. He did it for the Country. God bless him.

Kawalski turned slowly to leave the chamber, trailing behind his colleagues.

Gwently watched him sadly. *The walking dead.*

Chapter Seventy-Seven

Grete had just arrived at Number One Observatory Circle. For much of the morning, she had met with her new cabinet. While doing so, she worried that her husband was at the new house alone with the moving van. She thought she'd grab lunch with him, give some directions as to where things were to go, and then run back for a few more hours work in the West Wing.

Halfway home she decided she was being crazy. Half of Washington is stopping so that I can go to lunch. I can't do this.

When she arrived at the house, she noted the moving men standing around their truck, some leaning against the side.

She hurried into the house.

Willie was not alone. The staff of Number One Observatory Circle was standing with him. They were all doing nothing. "What's going on?"

Willie said, "We're trying to decide what to do about the move."

"What, you don't know where to put things?"

"No, we're going to put things back on the truck."

"What?"

Willie looked at his wife. "You haven't heard?"

"Heard what?"

"The House just voted for you to be President."

"What?"

"The real President."

"You're kidding?"

"No, Ma'am. Your chief coordinator is figuring out how to get all our treasures to the White House."

"For real?"

"The Chief Justice is on his way out here now."

"God, I'm going to be sworn in?"

"Where do you want to do it? It's cold as hell on the porch."

"But there are boxes all over the living room."

"No problem. Your coordinator is here." Willie turned to the staff. "Grab a box. Let's get this stuff to the back of the house."

By the time the Chief Justice arrived, Grete had only heard part of the story of the vote in the House. Life was coming fast and furious. It had been for several days. Grete was quickly becoming convinced that life would be a roller coaster from now on.

They assembled in the living room. A few reporters were allowed in. Grete insisted that the staff of the house be witnesses. The White House photographer was there. He had been at her cabinet meeting that morning. She wondered if he had been given an escort to make it out to where she now stood.

She felt frazzled. No one had given her time to check her makeup. *God, what do I look like?* The Chief Justice is in his robes. I'm rumpled from riding in a car. Damn, damn, damn.

They stood in front of the mantle. Later she would barely remember raising her right hand.

She had promised the reporters outside that she would say a few words, or Willie had promised. Somebody had promised.

She looked for her coat. *God, I need a new coat.* She threw the coat on the hallway bench and went out the front door in her suit. The cold hit her. She wanted to wrap her arms around herself to stay warm but decided it wasn't appropriate.

She addressed the reporters. "Thank you all for coming today. I'm sorry everyone couldn't come inside. This whole thing has happened quickly."

She looked around. "I expect you're all frozen and hungry.   I'll make this brief.

I have been deeply honored today by the vote of the House of Representatives. You may know more about what happened than I do. From what I understand, I am grateful to

Minority Leader Kawalski and the Republican Party. They have put Country ahead of politics. It is amazing to know that. I want the Republican Party to know that I intend to work with them, not against them. Government is a National thing and I intend to make it National.

Nonetheless, I must make it clear that I believe history will note that four years of the aberration of the soul of America has ended. Democracy has survived. The honor and dignity of our Government will be restored from this day on.

I will gather you all together in a warmer room soon. I have plans. I have an agenda. I want to talk to you about them. I want to share them.

In the meantime, I need to figure out where I'm living.

I'm grateful to you all and thank you for participating at this moment."

Chapter Seventy-Eight

Chance was stunned. Shirley was panicked. A woman named Jeanette had called from the White House and said the President would like to come down on Saturday and visit. She would come by helicopter, the land around eleven, and spend a couple of hours.

Shirley had answered the phone. It took her a moment to get her mind together. "Will the President stay for lunch?"

"She'd be delighted to."

"Oh, Lord, thought Shirley after she had hung up, the dining room table only sits six. How many did the woman say were coming. The President and her husband and a couple of others. How about the helicopter pilot, the secret service, and who knows whom else? They won't come in, I hope. Maybe we'll put a couple of extra picnic tables outside.

"Chance, do you think we can borrow some picnic tables from the County Park? You may have to invite the Chairman of the Board of Supervisors if we do that. And how about the supervisors' conference table and the chairs? Do you think they'll fit in the dining room? And how about the barbecue smoker from the Dansville Store? We're going to need to feed a lot of people. Get the Store to make potato salad, coleslaw, and a bunch of pies. Junior and Bev are going to have to come help, maybe the kids too. Who do you want to invite – Gwen Ellen and Charley, maybe, Jace and June?   Sixteen or eighteen around the table. How the hell are we going to do that?"

Chance's head was whirling. "We can't leave Marvin and Bet out."

"Goodness, Chance, how are we going to do this?"

"We'll have to split it up. Put our dining room table in the living room and the supervisor' table in the dining room."

"How do we decide who goes where?"

"The kids are going to have to suffer. Maybe Marvin and Bet, too. It's the way it goes."

"We'll never hear the end of it."

"We'll get them in a picture. They can frame it."

"And what about the President's retinue? It's cold outside."

"We'll pray for a warm day. They've got to be accustomed to it."

"Does anyone ever get accustomed to freezing to death?"

"You want to set them up in the barn – borrow some heaters from a local builder."

"Then we'd have to invite the builder too."

"Well, that's out. They'll have to freeze or sit in cars. Do helicopters have heating when the engine's turned off?"

"How would I know?"

"Okay, the pilots are on their own."

"Where is the chopper going to land?"

"It'll have to be in the lower field. I'll get the cattle up in the lea of the mountain. Don't want them scared to death."

"How are you going to get the field ready?"

"What do you mean?"

"Cow patties."

"Oh, shit."

"Exactly."

"I'll borrow a tractor rake from Titus Moore."

"You can't invite him to the party."

"He owes me."

"Do it quickly. You'll want any residue to dry."

"Okay. I'm on it."

***

Black Suburbans arrived at seven Saturday morning. The agents introduced themselves, asked where the helicopter was going to land, and went off to lay panels. They came back and said the field was a little rough, that Suburbans would meet the helicopter and bring the party to the house. Chance thought that was great – the less walking across the field, the better. He asked if he could ride down to welcome his guests. That was fine.

The agents said they would man the gate. They asked for a list of people who would be coming. Shirley made out the list.

Agents said an ambulance would be coming from the University of Virginia Medical Center.

Chance worried that the local rescue squad would be upset.

The agents said they could come too but would have to park outside the gate.

All but two agents left to set up at the gate. The two agents who stayed behind walked around the house as if they were looking for bombs.

Shirley explained to them the eating plans.

The men seemed to take it in stride.

Shirley thought, Damn, you're welcome.

She pointed out the barbecue smoker in the back yard.

They said it looked black and ugly.

Shirley told them it added to the taste.

The men went out to look at it.

Boog Taylor was doing the cooking. He had set the whole thing up the day before and smoked the barbecue overnight. He looked rustic, to say the least. He wore a red and white checkered apron over his ample girth.

The men introduced themselves. Boog began holding forth about the barbecue while waving a fork and a spatula.

The agents seemed fascinated.

Shirley went back to setting up the tables. She had borrowed white tablecloths from the Town Hall and stainless-steel cutlery from the fire hall. She hadn't found anybody who had cloth napkins and had bought the best paper napkins Walmart offered. She had wished she could get some linen napkins from the Lodge but didn't have the nerve to ask.

She had pitchers of cider and water on the sideboard for the glasses on the table.

She stood back in the dining room and studied the situation. *Not exactly the Ritz, but it will have to do.*

Chance sat on a wicker chair on the front porch. He had been told to stay out of the way. He wore corduroy trousers, a tie, and a tweed coat he normally saved for the church.

He began to hear the clapping of the President's helicopter in the distance. He headed for the drive. A Suburban came from behind him. It stopped and he climbed in.

The gate to the pasture was open. Two more Suburbans and the UVA ambulance were parked inside next to the fence. His Suburban parked on the other side of the gate.

He looked down at his loafers and wondered what the pasture had done to the agents' shiny shoes. *At least it's not raining.*

The helicopter came in for its landing, kicking up a hurricane to grass and other debris. Chance held his hand to his forehead. *Flying shit.*

Chance suddenly realized his Suburban was moving. He looked at the helicopter. The noise of the turbines was decreasing. The blades were slowly coming to a stop.

Agents were approaching the helicopter. The door was opening. Chance saw the President slipping her feet into some loafers. There were short-heeled shoes lying on the floor – beige shoes.

Steps were folded down, a rail in place. Grete rose and descended the steps. The agents stood back. No one offered to help. Chance guessed they had been told not to.

He rushed over to stand ten feet away from the President. Her back was to him. She was watching a man about her age descending the steps   He took her hand and stood by her. Another woman and then a man descended after him.

She turned and looked surprised to see Chance. She quickly stepped forward with her hand extended. "Chance FitzBourne?"

Chance shook the hand. "Yes, I am."

"I'm Meyer."

"Yes, Ma'am. We met at the Convention."

Grete smiled. "Yes, we did, and you promised to vote for me."

"Indeed, I did."

Grete held her hand out toward her husband. "And this is my husband, Willie Grete."

Willie shook Chance's hand. "Wilson Douglas Grete on the White House stationery. Willie to my friends." Then he pointed to the two behind him. "Billy Parker, Meyer's Chief of Staff and Jeanette Bearing, her Administrative Assistant, respectively."

Everyone shook hands.

Chance suddenly noticed a man taking photographs. *Where did he come from?"*

Grete noticed. "Dag's pervasive. I'll tell him to put the camera away later."

Grete climbed into a Suburban and slid over. She patted the seat next to her, looking Chance in the eye.

Chance hesitated and then climbed in.

Willie got into the passenger's seat.

Grete looked around. "This place is beautiful. I love the way it backs up to the mountains. How many acres do you have?"

"Forty-seven acres, fifteen in woods."

"You're not tempted to clear the woods?"

"I love the woods. They make me feel I'm away from the world. You should see the redbud in the spring. The woods are gorgeous."

Grete smiled. "I can imagine."

A moment later, they arrived at the house.

Grete chuckled. "We could have walked this."

Chance held his end out toward the driver. "Would these guys let you?"

"They would if I claimed it was a workout."

Inside the front hallway, Shirley, Gwen Ellen, her husband, Charley, Junior, Bev, Jace, and Marvin were standing as if in a reception line. Grete and Willie went down the line shaking hands while introductions were being made. It was too much for Chance to handle and he lagged behind.

He noticed Shirley had taken off her apron. He whispered to her, "You're looking good."

She beamed.

Gwen Ellen followed Grete down the hall, talking about her local position in the Party. Chance hurried and maneuvered her away toward the kitchen. "Would you mind helping Shirley?"

"Oh, Shirley. Oh sure."

Willie caught up to Chance. "Did I see barbecue cooking in the backyard? I love barbecue. Do you mind if I go out there?"

Suddenly Chance had found purpose. "I'll take you." Chance turned to Parker and Bearing. "Do you want to come too."

Bearing excused herself from the men. "I think I'll look around with Meyer."

She found Meyer in the living room where a dining room table set for six people had been located in the middle of the room. Two teenagers stood from where they had been sitting at the table. Grete smiled and walked over to shake their hands. "Hi, I'm Meyer Grete." She turned toward her Administrative Assistant, and this is Jeanette Bearing."

Chip and Jen tried to recover from suddenly being alone with the President of the United States. They thrust their hands forward to shake the Presidents. Chip finally said, "Er, I'm Chip and this is my sister, J...Jennifer."

Jen pointed at her brother. "His name is Charles."

Grete smiled. "Chip sounds fine to me. Are you both named FitzBourne?"

The children answered in unison. "Yes, ma'am."

"And you're Chance's grandchildren?"

“Yes, ma’am.”

Grete kept smiling. “I just met your parents in the hallway.”

Jen recovered her nerve. “Chance Junior and Beverly.” Then she blurted. “You’re in charge, now? You’re the President?”

“What? Oh, yes, I am.”

“Are you going to kick butt?”

“What? Goodness, you sound like my husband. I’ll do what I have to do.”

“You’ll be assertive?”

“When I have to be.”

“A woman can do it.”

Grete studied the young girl for a moment. “Yes, a woman can.”

Chip interrupted. “I apologize for my sister. She’s into this woman-thing.”

Grete chuckled. “Well, I am too.”

“But you’re not sixteen.”

“That’s for sure.” She smiled at Jen. “But Jennifer is as much a woman.” She looked at Jeanette. “Don’t you think so?”

“Absolutely.”

Jen beamed.

Chip looked at his sister. “Oh, God.”

Grete and Jeanette laughed.

Chip wanted to turn the attention of his sister. “Is it true what they say, that you owe your election to my Grandfather?”

“Yes – absolutely true.”

“But he only had one vote.”

“One vote made the difference. I wouldn’t have been considered for the Presidency if he hadn’t cast that one vote.”

“That’s really cool.”

Grete laughed. “The coolest thing that ever happened to me.”